Emerging from Poverty

EMERGING FROM POVERTY

The Economics That Really Matters

GERALD M. MEIER

Stanford University

New York   Oxford
OXFORD UNIVERSITY PRESS

Oxford University Press

Oxford   New York   Toronto
Delhi   Bombay   Calcutta   Madras   Karachi
Kuala Lumpur   Singapore   Hong Kong   Tokyo
Nairobi   Dar es Salaam   Cape Town
Melbourne   Auckland

and associated companies in
Beirut   Berlin   Ibadan   Mexico City   Nicosia

Library of Congress Cataloging in Publication Data
Meier, Gerald M.
Emerging from poverty.
Bibliography: p.   Includes index.
1. Economic development.   2. Developing countries.
3. Economic assistance.   I. Title.
HD75.M44   1984   338.9'009172'4   84-441
ISBN 0-19-503374-4

69093

Printing (last digit): 9 8 7 6 5 4 3

Printed in the United States of America

To the next generation
of development economists

To the Reader

This book appraises the efforts by economists to understand the economics of being poor as well as the policy measures they have proposed that will allow the countries of Asia, Africa, and Latin America to emerge from poverty. I have wanted to distinguish it from other development books by writing in readily understandable language for the nonspecialist. Also, instead of concentrating only on current problems, I have tried to place these problems in a more meaningful context by adopting a retrospective view—in other words, how have poor countries fared over the past four decades? And, instead of doing this with numbers and graphs, I have related the development record to the changing views and policy advice of economists.

Part I focuses on activities by the international community and evaluates the achievements and failures in the development record—what has gone right and what has gone wrong. Part II traces the evolution of thinking by economists on development problems and policies—first, by summarizing the "Old Growth Economics" and then by explaining the "Early Development Economics" that took shape in the 1950s, which was later to be revised during the next two decades and was then subjected to a radical critique. Part III assesses how economists must now extend their concerns and contend with new questions if they are to show how the disappointments in the development record can be overcome.

I hope that the general reader who desires more understanding about development problems, the student who is beginning a study of the subject, and even development practitioners who want a wider perspective will all gain greater insight into what for many is the economics that really matters.

To the extent that this book has been able to synthesize some of the development literature, I am indebted to the entire development profession for providing a significant number of studies on the development record, development thought, and development policy.

I am also grateful for having been able to clarify some special points through the kind assistance of Robert E. Asher, Edward M. Bernstein, Sterie T. Beza, A. Y. Bobe, Shahid Javed Burki, Ramesh Chander, Bogomir Chokel, Robert E. Christiansen, Anthony A. Churchill, Graham Donaldson, John H. Duloy, Peter Hall, David Kimble, Fred M. King, Mark W. Leiserson, Jack Ling, Robert A. Packenham, Felipe Pazos, W. W. Rostow, Paul A. Samuelson, Paul P. Streeten, Victor L. Urquidi, and Mervyn L. Weiner.

The World Bank provided generous access to its staff members and resources. So too were librarians at the IMF and World Bank most helpful. Neither the World Bank nor the IMF, however, is responsible for any statement. All errors of commission—and omission—are mine alone.

The Rockefeller Foundation supported a productive writing period as a Scholar in Residence at the Foundation's Bellagio Center. For the support of these institutions, I am most grateful.

I am also indebted to Famah Andrew, Pat Sharp, and Srikant Datar for their skills in processing the manuscript.

March 1984   G.M.M.
Shaw Island, San Juans
Stanford, California

Contents

Emerging from Poverty

Mr. President, we have reached this evening a decisive point. But it is only a beginning. We have to go from here as missionaries, inspired by zeal and faith. We have sold all this to ourselves. But the world at large still needs to be persuaded.

John Maynard Keynes, on moving the acceptance of the Final Act at the Bretton Woods Conference, 1944

Most of the people in the world are poor, so if we knew the economics of being poor we would know much of the economics that really matters.

Theodore W. Schultz, on accepting the Nobel Prize in Economics, 1979

Introduction

We worry in this book about what can realistically be done to lessen the pain of poverty still suffered daily by two-thirds of humanity. Two centuries after the industrial revolution, only a few countries have become rich, while more than 100 nations are poor. In 1776, on the threshold of Britain's industrial expansion, Adam Smith offered an optimistic analysis of the *Wealth of Nations;* now in Latin America, Africa, and Asia, policymakers must still overcome the pessimism that envelops the *poverty* of nations.

Since World War II, however, the international community has devoted unprecedented efforts to accelerate the development of poor countries, from Afghanistan to Zimbabwe. This book audits the record of that unique period—its achievements, its disappointments, its lessons. But more than that, I hope to recreate the stimulating intellectual adventure that is a part of the development experience. Beneath the colorless statistics of the development record lie vigorous controversies in ideas and absorbing efforts to translate the thinking of development economists into policy action.

We examine the interplay between economic thought and development policy and relate the lessons of the development experience to the evolution of thought on economic development. We will discover that, much as contemporary economic thought has illuminated some development problems, necessary improvements in development policy still await more attention by economists to an analysis of the causes of the disappointments in the development record. The underdevelopment of economics itself must be overcome if the disappointments are to be overcome. To do this, the economist must generate more knowledge about the forces that contribute to development, design more appropriate policies to support these forces, and become concerned with the effective implementation of these policies.

Economists are now the development professionals, but in an earlier age they could have been called the "trustees for the poor." For the business of economics was from the outset social betterment. The economist's primary goal must be the elimination of poverty. Adam Smith entitled his great work *An Inquiry into the Nature and Causes of the Wealth of Nations* because he believed that "No society can surely be flourishing and happy, of which the far greater part of the members are poor and miserable." Economics began with growth as its grand theme, and economists were to search for the way to the "progressive state" in which the condition of the laboring poor would steadily improve.

In the mid-nineteenth century, however, the subject narrowed. Instead of being growth-minded, economists adopted a static state of mind that focused merely on the conditions of efficiency in allocating a given amount of scarce resources among alternative uses. Static resource allocation became the subject matter of neoclassical economics—the economics taught in Britain and America, in Austria, in Sweden, and at Lausanne between 1870 and 1930. The economist therefore became, in the words of Nobel laureate Kenneth Arrow, "the guardian of rationality." In a world of scarcity, the primary responsibility of the economist is to instruct in the husbanding of resources and in the exercise of choice in allocating resources among alternative objectives. In searching for the best use of scarce resources, the economist specifies rational conduct as the most advantageous conduct: "The economist by training thinks of himself as the guardian of rationality, the ascriber of rationality to others, and the prescriber of rationality to the social world."[1]

This concern for growth did not revive until after World War II.

What was then emphasized as "growth" for the adva[n]
dustrial nations was called "development" for the new[ly] [inde]
pendent and aspirant nations of Asia, Africa, and Latin America. Economists responded to the revolution of rising expectations
with the beginning of a new development economics—an explanation of growth plus change, the structural transformation that
an economy undergoes in the course of its development.

To judge the economist's contribution, we must consider the
extent to which the economist has been able to reconcile the two
roles of "trustee for the poor" and "guardian of rationality" in
advising nations how to develop.

The responsibility for being a trustee for the poor weighs heavily
when the economist realizes that the vast majority of the world's
population in poor countries receives less than 20 percent of the
world's income; that over 2 billion people in the low-income
economies have a per capita income of only about 250 dollars a
year; that almost 60 percent of the population in these countries
are malnourished; that life expectancy of the average person in
the less developed countries is still 20 years shorter than in the
more developed countries; that safe water and adequate waste
disposal facilities are unavailable to 80 percent of the developing
world's population; that the number of illiterates is predicted to
double from 1 billion in 1970 to over 2 billion by the year 2000;
and that every five days, 1 million people are added to the ranks
of the impoverished. The statistics of misery are voluminous, but
even this short list must evoke empathy and compassion.

At the same time, however, the responsibility of the economist as guardian of rationality weighs equally heavily when the
economist realizes that the fundamental fact of scarcity of resources is inescapable; that the forces of the marketplace cannot
be ignored; that the transfer of resources from rich to poor countries must be productively utilized; and that the leading international development agency, the World Bank, is in the words
of its President "not the Robin Hood of the international financial set, nor a giant global welfare agency," but "a development
bank using the most sophisticated techniques available to facilitate development while providing unmatched protection and
strength for creditors and shareholders." The logic of the economic calculus does not succumb to sentiment.

As trustee for the poor, the economist respects the values of altruism and economic justice. As guardian of rationality, the economist respects self-interest and efficiency—in economic jargon, "rational choice models" and "maximization under constraints."

But does not the future course of development depend in large part on the capacity to combine these seemingly incompatible values of the trustee and the guardian? Can the professional developer combine a warm heart with a cool head?

An answer to this question depends on a wider consideration of how moral conviction, technical economic analysis, and policy action can shape the course of development. This book's auditing of development experience thus becomes an inquiry into the possibility of change—through vision in ideas and persuasion in policy guidance—so that ultimately there might be change in the lives of people in more than 100 developing countries.

I
ONLY A BEGINNING

Nyasaland, 1962

Twenty-three economists have been invited to bring their subject of development economics from the university lecture halls of Western Europe and the United States to the tea and tobacco fields of Nyasaland. The British protectorate of Nyasaland in Africa is about to become the independent nation of Malawi. The new Chief Minister, Ngwazi Dr. H. Kamuzu Banda, is "delighted to give his consent and blessing" for a symposium of economists discussing the problems of African economic development.

The plane, bearing the economists, must land at the small Blantyre airport before sunset because the airfield is unlit. Banners of greeting and welcoming committees demonstrate that this conference is to be a national event. Signs at key points indicate the route "To the Economic Symposium."

Waving a fly whisk above his head to signify change, Dr. Banda addresses the visiting economists:

> I wanted economists to come here and tell us of their knowledge and experience gained in other countries, and, if possible, advise us what to do and what not to do.

> So far as I know, this is the first time that experts on the economic development of underdeveloped countries have held a meeting, conference or symposium in the setting of a typically underdeveloped country. I make no bones about it; this is a typically underdeveloped country, a poor country.

The visiting economists present their papers, outline their requirements for development, and present their proposals for the removal of obstacles to accelerated development.

The new government formulates its first Three-Year Plan, designed as "an attempt by the government to translate the desires and needs of the people into development projects." But the country is among the poorest of the poor—a traditional subsistence economy with low income per head, a scant resource base, limited stock of human capital and physical infrastructure, only two primary product exports, no industry, and high death rates from malaria, small pox, and dysentery. A national survey of professional persons listed in the Three-Year Plan shows only six people with "some training in commerce, accounting, or economics," and no statisticians. Yet, progress is to come.

Malawi, 1984

Air Malawi lands at the new Kamuzu International Airport in Lilongwe—a prestige airport as modern as any. In about 15 years, from independence in 1964 until the recession at the end of the 1970s, Malawi has undergone a striking transformation. It has experienced average growth rates in national output of 7 percent; real per capita income has doubled; export volume has grown over 7 percent annually; the country has become self-sufficient in food; nearly 30 percent of national income was being invested in 1979; domestic savings have risen from nothing to 18 percent of national income.

In spite of this progress, one-third of the children die before reaching their fifth year of life, life expectancy is only 44 years, the adult literacy rate is only 25 percent, the secondary school enrollment ratio is only 4 percent, only one-third of the population has access to safe water, and per capita income is only about $200. Malawi is still among the poorest of the poor countries. It is only a beginning.

1

Expectations

Bretton Woods

Known for being the largest wooden building in New England, the Mount Washington Hotel in Bretton Woods, New Hampshire, gained new distinction in 1944 as the site of the Bretton Woods Conference. To smooth the transition from war to peace, President Roosevelt invited delegates from 44 member countries of the United Nations to this "quiet meeting place." At the preinflationary room rate of $11 per day, the delegates were to spend three weeks establishing what would become the most significant international economic institutions of the postwar period—the International Monetary Fund (IMF) and the International Bank for Reconstruction and Development (World Bank). The Fund was designed to mitigate balance-of-payments problems and provide stability in international monetary affairs. The World Bank was to support investment in productive projects in countries recovering from the war and in need of development support.

President Roosevelt had during the war proclaimed what he called the Four Freedoms, which included "freedom from want . . . everywhere in the world," as postwar objectives of the Western allies. The Atlantic Charter had also promised access to trade and raw materials for all countries with the "assurance that all the men in all the lands might live out their lives in freedom

from fear and want." The U.N. charter was to include among its
objectives the promotion of "higher standards of living, full employment, and conditions of economic and social progress and
development." By 1944, the acceleration of economic development in underdeveloped or backward areas (as they were then
called) was becoming a more widely avowed policy objective of
developed countries.

Ironically, however, during its deliberations, the Bretton Woods
Conference remained largely immune from these aspirations—
even though the IMF and World Bank were later to assume ever
increasing importance in the international development effort. The
World Bank itself was a distinctly secondary issue at Bretton
Woods. Roosevelt's invitation referred to a conference "for the
purpose of formulating proposals of a definite character for an
international monetary fund and possibly a bank for reconstruction and development." The possibility of a World Bank actually
reaching the agenda was not resolved until the eleventh hour.

It seems clear from the membership that the conference was
called primarily to establish the IMF. Some less developed countries (LDCs) were invited, but the political power lay with the
United States and Britain. And the intellectual power lay with
John Maynard Keynes of the British delegation and Harry Dex-
ter White, Assistant Secretary of the Treasury of the United States.

From the outset, it was apparent that issues of development
were not to be on the Bretton Woods agenda. In a dispatch to
the British Treasury discussing the countries invited, Lord Keynes
would write:

> Twenty-one countries have been invited which clearly have
> nothing to contribute and will merely encumber the ground,
> namely, Colombia, Costa Rica, Dominica, Ecuador, Salvador,
> Guatemala, Haiti, Honduras, Liberia, Nicaragua, Panama, Par-
> aguay, Philippines, Venezuela, Peru, Uruguay, Ethiopia, Ice-
> land, Iran, Iraq, and Luxemburg—the most monstrous mon-
> key-house assembled for years. To these might perhaps be
> added: Egypt, Chile and (in present circumstances) Yugo-
> slavia.[1]

Although there had been Anglo-American discussions of the
Fund proposal for more than two years before Bretton Woods,
the concept of a World Bank had received relatively little atten-

tion, and then only shortly before the conference. At Bretton Woods, Keynes was Chairman of the Commission on the Bank, but his major concern had been with negotiations about the Fund. The establishment of the Fund was more complex and its provisions raised more intellectually stimulating problems for Keynes' mind, but it was also considered more important than the Bank. Only after he saw that his proposal for an International Clearing Union was not going to be adopted did Keynes give consideration to the Bank.

White's original draft for the U.S. Treasury used the term Bank for Reconstruction. While it was still in draft form within the Treasury, E. M. Bernstein suggested to White that reconstruction would be over in a few years and that the Bank needed a more permanent function, which should be development. Bernstein recalls that he "used this term without being aware that it would become of importance in the future."[2] The draft of the plan distributed to other governments finally carried the name, the Bank for Reconstruction and Development.

In its original form, the Bank was almost entirely directed at the problem of reconstruction. The first draft of the plan stated that the Bank was "designed chiefly to supply the huge volume of capital to the United and Associated Nations that will be needed for reconstruction, for relief, and for economic recovery. . . ."

At Bretton Woods, however, in opening the discussion of the Bank, Keynes did say:

> It is likely in my judgment that the field of reconstruction from the consequences of war will mainly occupy the proposed Bank in its early days. But as soon as possible, and with increasing emphasis as time goes on, there is a second primary duty laid upon it, namely, to develop the resources and productive capacity of the world, with special attention to the less developed countries, to raising the standard of life and the conditions of labour everywhere, to make the resources of the world more fully available to all mankind, and so to order its operations as to promote and maintain equilibrium in the international balances of payments of all member countries.[3]

For the most part, the Bank was considered an American proposal because the United States was the major country with the ability to engage in postwar investment overseas. In a preliminary draft outline of the Bank, Secretary of the Treasury Henry Morgenthau, Jr., stressed national self-interest and benefits for the developed countries:

> It is imperative that we recognize that the investment of productive capital in the undeveloped and in capital-needy countries means not only that those countries will be able to supply at lower costs more of the goods the world needs, but that they will at the same time become better markets for the world's goods. By investing in countries in need of capital, the lending countries, therefore, help themselves as well as the borrowing countries. . . . Foreign trade everywhere will be increased; the real cost of producing the goods the world consumes will be lowered; and the economic well-being of the borrowing and lending countries will be raised.[4]

According to the Secretary of the Commission on the Bank, however, the conference paid almost no attention to development. The U.S. and U.K. delegations were not directly interested in the subject, and even most of the representatives of the LDCs seemed unconcerned. The lending power of the Bank was carefully restricted to financing specific projects rather than broader development programs or the balance of payments of a developing country. The emphasis was on reconstruction.

Only the Mexican delegation advocated strong emphasis on the Bank as a development organization. The President of El Colegio de Mexico, Victor L. Urquidi, now recalls that he was the youngest delegate to Bretton Woods, and that at the first meeting of the Bank Commission, on instructions from the Mexican Minister of Finance, he introduced a draft amendment to one of the early articles of the Bank charter, to specify that resources of the Bank should be used equally for both reconstruction and development. Urquidi's statement contended that

> In the very short run, perhaps reconstruction will be more urgent for the world as a whole, but in the long run, Mr. Chairman—before we are all *too* dead, if I may say so—development must prevail if we are to sustain and increase real income everywhere. Without denying the initial importance of reconstruction, we ask you not to relegate or postpone development. . . . If we tackle our own wide domestic problems—and for that we require sums of capital we do not dispose of at

home—we will undoubtedly benefit not only ourselves but the
world as a whole, and particularly the industrial nations, in that
we shall provide better markets for them and better customers.
We submit, therefore, that capital for development purposes in
our countries is as important for the world as is capital for reconstruction purposes.[5]

Cuba and Colombia supported the Mexican amendment. Urquidi recalls, however, that "Keynes, who had on his desk a
number of amendments submitted in writing, leafed through them
quickly, peered characteristically over his spectacles, and said: 'We
cannot accept that resources should be divided *equally* between
reconstruction and development, but I am sure the word *equitably* would do.' " The result was the insertion of the phrase in an
Article of the Bank's charter that there should be "equitable consideration to projects for development and to projects for reconstruction." But even this was contradicted by the next paragraph
of the same section that directs the Bank to "pay special regard
to lightening the financing burden" for countries that have suffered "great devastation from enemy occupation or hostilities."
For those providing the major contributions to the Bank, the im-
mediacy and urgency of the reconstruction effort clearly dominated the more distant vision of development.

At the closing session, Secretary of the Treasury Morgenthau
stated that "the chief purpose of the Bank for Reconstruction and
Development is to guarantee private loans made through the usual
investment channels. It would make loans only when these could
not be floated through the normal channels at reasonable rates."
Limited as his view of the Bank was, Morgenthau still had expectations based on a wider vision: "The result will be of vital
importance to everyone in every country. In the last analysis, it
will help determine whether or not people have jobs. . . . More
important still, it concerns the kind of world in which our children are to grow to maturity. . . ."[6]

The report to the final session also notes the novelty of the Bank
and its potential for serving the interests of lending as well as
borrowing countries:

The creation of the Bank was an entirely new venture. Never,
during the numerous international meetings which over a period of 25 years have studied all sorts of economic problems,

was any thought given to an organization so considerable in its scope and so novel in its conception. So novel was it, that no adequate name could be found for it. Insofar as we can talk of capital subscriptions, loans, guarantees, issues of bonds, the new financial institution may have some apparent claim to the name of Bank. But the type of shareholders, the nature of subscriptions, the exclusion of all deposits and of short-term loans, the nonprofit basis, are quite foreign to the accepted nature of a Bank. However, it was accidentally born with the name Bank, and Bank it remains, mainly because no satisfactory name could be found in the dictionary for this unprecedented institution.[7]

By the end of the Bretton Woods Conference, Keynes could tell the British public on the BBC evening news:

There has never been such a far-reaching proposal [as that of the Bank] on so great a scale to provide employment in the present and increase productivity in the future. We have been working quietly away in the cool woods and mountains of New Hampshire and I doubt if the world yet understands how big a thing we are bringing to birth.[8]

The Bank was to begin operation with capital subscribed by its member countries, subsequently financing its lending operations primarily from its own borrowings in the world capital markets. The Bank's charter stated that it must lend only for productive purposes and must stimulate economic growth in the developing countries where it lends. It must pay due regard to the prospects of repayment. Each loan is to be made to a government or must be guaranteed by the government concerned. The use of loans cannot be tied to purchases in any particular member country. And the Bank's decisions to lend must be based on only economic considerations.

International Monetary Fund

To stabilize international monetary conditions, the articles of the IMF provided that member states are subject to a code of obligations that the Fund administers with respect to foreign exchange rates and currency arrangements. The Fund was also to receive subscriptions of members in their own currencies and gold, and these resources were to be made available to other members to assist them to meet short-term, balance-of-payments difficulties while observing the code of obligations. But the promotion of development was not a direct purpose of the Fund.

In formulating the Fund's articles, India was the only vocal representative of the LDCs, pushing hard for some "specific reference to the needs of economically backward countries." The Indian delegate stated:

> Our experience in the past has shown that international organizations have tended to approach all problems from the point of view of the advanced countries of the West. We want to insure that the new organization which we are trying to create will avoid this narrow outlook and give due consideration to the economic problems of countries like India.[9]

The Indian delegation proposed an amendment to the Fund's articles that would have required the Fund "to assist in the fuller utilization of the resources of economically underdeveloped countries." The proposal was supported by Ecuador, but was opposed by the United Kingdom and the United States on the grounds that the development of underdeveloped countries was a matter for the Bank rather than for the Fund. Only one of the Fund's articles reflected a compromise, with an italicized clause inserted into the article:

> to facilitate the expansion and balanced growth of international trade, and to contribute thereby to the promotion and maintenance of high levels of employment and real income and *to the development of the productive resources of all members as primary objectives of economic policy.*

No special reference was made to "economically underdeveloped countries" or "economically backward countries" as the Indian delegation had sought. Indeed, the principle of uniformity was emphasized—the rights and obligations are the same for all countries, regardless of stage of development. No provision in the Fund's articles distinguished between developing and developed members. Only later did the Fund find it possible to adopt decisions, such as compensatory financing for fluctuations in export receipts, that were intended to be of special benefit to de-

veloping members without confining the benefit of the decisions
to them.

Other Proposals

In spite of the public statements of Morgenthau and Keynes, the
Bretton Woods arrangements did not fulfill a number of other
requirements that many considered essential for postwar international economic collaboration. Earlier discussions in the American government and among economists envisaged international
organizations that would deal with not only the problems of international currency arrangements and international investment,
but also the problems of international trade in primary products,
trade policies, and development. Moreover, it was hoped that
these agencies would be sufficiently complementary to handle
international problems in an integrated fashion. Although not yet
differentiating between North and South, elements of what would
now be called a "New International Economic Order" were proposed by some economists who were examining the structure of
the postwar world.

In the original Preface to his proposals, for instance, Keynes
had argued that international economic cooperation should proceed along four main lines: (1) the mechanism of currency and
exchange; (2) commercial policy; (3) production, distribution, and
pricing of primary products; and (4) international investment. But
Keynes never related Bretton Woods to his own plan for primary
products, and he left it to the Americans to devise an international investment organization.

Similarly, White's original draft proposals in 1942 were far more
ambitious than what emerged from Bretton Woods. White initially proposed an International Bank that would be a genuine
Central Bank, with a right to issue its own International Bank
notes, backed by a minimum of 50 percent gold, and a right to
hold the deposits of other Central Banks. Keynes was later to say
that "the Bank should be called the Fund and the Fund the Bank."
But the origin of the Bretton Woods terminology is found in
White's original plan.

In White's proposal, the Bank's primary objectives would be to provide or otherwise stimulate long-term, low-interest rate loans for relief and reconstruction and to raise standards of living throughout the world. White believed that

> Asia, Europe, Africa and South America can for many years profitably use for the creation of capital goods $5 to $10 billion of foreign capital each year provided they can get it on reasonable terms. . . .

> Only an international governmental agency equipped with broad lending powers and large resources can both effectively encourage or induce private capital to flow abroad in large amounts and provide a substantial part of the necessary capital not otherwise available.

Beyond reconstruction and development objectives—or in support of these objectives—White's original plan also contemplated that the Bank would arrange its lending so that it could combat international business fluctuations and eliminate the danger of worldwide crises that are financial in origin. The Bank was also to "organize and finance an International Essential Raw Material Development Corporation for the purpose of increasing the world supply of essential raw materials and assuring member countries an adequate supply at fair prices." Besides reconstruction and development loans, the Bank could also make loans for the purpose of providing nations with metallic reserves that would have longer terms of repayment than loans for other purposes.

Ironically, the Bank plan was originally far more imaginative than the Fund plan. But the Fund plan dominated. By the time the conference at Bretton Woods was held, the boldness of White's original plans had been lost in the course of two years' discussion among government departments that removed the more far-reaching provisions. But some of these provisions addressed questions and issues that were to surface time and again since Bretton Woods.

Keynes' original proposal for an International Clearing Union was also more ambitious than what eventually emerged from Bretton Woods. The Clearing Union was to have some characteristics of an international central bank, using a medium of exchange (Bancor) provided by itself, just as a national central bank provides its bank notes. Nations with favorable balances of foreign payments would acquire Bancor deposits, and those with unfavorable balances would be overdrawn in terms of Bancor. The Clearing Union might "be linked up with a Board for International Investment." It could also make what advances it wished to any of its members. Some of these advances might be

> in favor of international bodies charged with the management of a Commodity Control, and might finance stocks of commodities held by such bodies, allowing them overdraft facilities on their accounts up to an agreed maximum. By this means the financial problems of buffer stocks and "ever-normal granaries" could be effectively attacked.

Primary Producing Countries

Problems of future access to raw materials and the stabilization of primary product prices were topics prominent in postwar discussions. Several schemes were proposed to prevent a recurrence of the interwar experience of fluctuations in primary product prices. In the early 1940s, Keynes had circulated a proposal for the establishment of international buffer stock arrangements to stabilize the prices of raw materials (coffee, sugar, rubber, tin). Concerned about excessive price fluctuations for primary products, Keynes looked to a commodity regulation scheme "to maintain more adequate standards of living for primary producers." An international body of Commodity Control would buy and sell stocks of raw materials to "stabilize the price of that part of world output which enters into international trade, and to maintain stocks adequate to cover fluctuations of supply and demand in the world market." The scheme would also be "a means, and perhaps the only means, of implementing the often-repeated undertaking of free and equal access for all countries alike to the sources of supply of raw materials."

Keynes recognized the practical difficulties in securing any international agreement that would avoid excessive price fluctuations and reduce cyclical surpluses and scarcities in the quantity of stocks. But he warned against a defeatist attitude that found it too difficult "to improve this awkward world." The British government, however, did not support the proposals of Keynes. Nor did the American government exercise any leadership in meeting the problems of primary producing countries.

At Bretton Woods the LDCs tended to view themselves more as "new raw material producing nations" and less as countries with general development problems. Comprehensive strategies of development and policies to accelerate national development were yet to be identified. The Brazilian delegation introduced a draft proposal for an international conference to promote stability in the prices of primary international commodities, claiming that "fluctuations in the prices of primary products during the interwar period were as much of a curse as recurring large-scale unemployment." For the successful attainment of the objectives pursued by the IMF and the Bank, some delegates thought it necessary to promote stability in prices of raw materials and agricultural products. Cuba endorsed a conference to promote the "orderly marketing of staple commodities." The delegation from Colombia urged that future agreements on commercial policy consider the "need for enlarging the consuming markets for foodstuffs and raw materials, the prices of which before the war were notoriously far out of proportion to the prices of manufactured articles" that primary producing countries "were obliged to buy from the great industrial nations." Bolivia was concerned about "cooperation in the organization and implementation of International Commodity Agreements designed to maintain fair and stable prices, and provision for the orderly distribution of raw materials throughout the world." But these proposals came to naught, as did a consolidated resolution for "orderly marketing of staple commodities at prices fair to the producer and consumer alike" proposed by Peru, Brazil, Chile, Bolivia, and Cuba.

The vision of a larger design had been in President Roosevelt's mind when he sent his message to the Congress requesting action on the Bretton Woods Agreements:

> Nor do I want to leave with you the impression that the Fund and the Bank are all that we will need to solve the economic problems which will face the United Nations when the war is

over. There are other problems which we will be called upon to solve. It is my expectation that other proposals will shortly be ready to submit to you for your consideration. These will include . . . broadening and strengthening of the Trade Agreements Act of 1934, international agreement for the reduction of trade barriers, the control of cartels, and the orderly marketing of world surpluses of certain commodities. . . .

In this message I have recommended for your consideration the immediate adoption of the Bretton Woods Agreements and suggested other measures which will have to be dealt with in the near future. They are all parts of a consistent whole. That whole is our hope for a secure and fruitful world, a world in which plain people in all countries can work at tasks which they do well, exchange in peace the products of their labor, and work out their several destinies in security and peace; a world in which governments as their major contribution to the common welfare are highly and effectively resolved to work together in practical affairs, and to guide all their actions by the knowledge that any policy or act that has effects abroad must be considered in the light of those effects.[10]

Havana Charter

A third international institution was envisaged to complement the Fund and the Bank—an International Trade Organization (ITO), which was discussed by representatives of 53 nations at Havana, Cuba, in 1947. As proposed in the Havana Charter, the ITO was to govern trade barriers, but in addition it contained a chapter on "Economic Development and Reconstruction," covering private foreign investment, infant industries, and other issues of concern to primary producing countries. Another chapter dealt with intergovernmental commodity agreements, and another focused on restrictive business practices.

Political delays had made the ITO subordinate to consideration of the Fund and Bank. The ITO also proved more controversial in content because it covered in detail a whole range of commercial policies that went beyond mere tariff reductions. At Havana, the LDCs differed with the more developed countries on provisions for international commodity agreements, state trading, cartels, and restrictive business practices.

The General Agreement on Tariffs and Trade (GATT) was originally designed to serve as a temporary expedient until ratification of the Havana Charter. But the ITO met congressional opposition in America and was never born. The GATT became the narrower substitute, becoming permanent in 1955. When the ITO did not absorb the GATT, the "Economic Development and Reconstruction" chapter of the Havana Charter became moot. As a result, the GATT allowed less special treatment for LDCs than had been proposed by the Havana Charter. But the question of whether there should be different trade rules for countries according to their different stages of development has persisted. Special and differential treatment for LDCs is now a dominant question in the North-South dialogue and the call for a New International Economic Order.

Aspiring Nations

Following Bretton Woods, the postwar period was characterized by a revolution of rising expectations as Roosevelt's vision of "freedom from want" spread throughout the underdeveloped world of Africa, Asia, and Latin America. At the Nyasaland Symposium, the new Parliamentary Secretary of Nyasaland's Ministry of Finance conveyed the "temper and aspirations" of his contemporary Africa:

> In Colonial Africa the dominant sentiment is the urge to be free. It is no exaggeration to say that the African in this part of Africa is in a state of general revolt. He is revolting against colonial rule.
>
> In free Africa the dominant sentiment is different. Here the main desire is to found modern nations, modern states—in which the indigenous people will have the right to manage or mismanage their own affairs; in which everyone will enjoy freedom from want and fear; and a sense of security and belonging that will accord economic modernization the primacy it deserves.[11]

Dr. Banda could also declare: "What those people who were saying we should not demand self-government and independence because we were poor did not realize is that we were poor because we were not independent . . . It is only when a country becomes independent that real development begins." [12]

In 1945, the United Nations was established with only 51 nations, almost none from Asia and Africa. In the next two decades, 65 nations became independent—and they considered themselves to be not only primary producing but also less developed countries. Colonial peoples became aware that far higher standards existed for a minority of the world's peoples and that some "catching up" might be possible for others as well. With growing nationalism, people who were formerly "natives" became nationals who believed they might start along the road of equality with former alien rulers. The state became the means. A reliance on the state also followed from a belief in planning, social welfare measures, and collective controls as instruments of planned development.

In the emergent nations, the economics of development was initially an economics of discontent—discontent with the old order, discontent with the legacy of colonialism, and discontent with economic dependence. The emergent nations became aspiring nations that sought to move the world quickly toward both political and economic equality. Their aspirations were now to meld with the aspirations of the new international institutions and the efforts of the international development community.

In 1960, as Nyasaland was about to become independent, a newly elected African official conveyed these thoughts to an American economist:

> I am certain that we can do quite a great deal with the executive power which we have been granted to influence the pace and course of development. It thrills me to think that we shall soon have the opportunity of trying out the ideas which you and the United Nations' economic experts have so fervently advocated. Looked at in this light, the fluidity and underdevelopment of our economy turns out to be a blessing in disguise. It is not easy to redirect the course of development of a relatively mature economy. There are, undoubtedly, Himalayan tasks ahead of us. I am confident that we shall address ourselves to the problems that confront our country with enthusiasm, drive, and determination. I hope you and your colleagues will come to our assistance should our government need—and I feel certain it will—your advice and expertise. [13]

2

Efforts

An Evolving Development Agency

In 1946, when the World Bank rented the ninth and tenth floors of a Washington office building at 1818 "H" Street, it was questionable whether it would be a permanent institution. In quarters that had no rugs, no safe, and only borrowed furniture, the Executive Directors of the Bank held their first meeting. Only $750,000 of the capital subscribed by 38 countries had so far been received. The Bank's first loan was $250 million to France; and the first public offering of its bonds was launched. Not until 1948, however, was the first loan made to a less developed country—Chile.

When Chile first submitted a loan request in 1946, it was simply a seven-page application by the Corporación de Fomento de la Producción for what a Bank official called "a completely undigested list of projects," including hydroelectric, forestry, harbor, urban and suburban transport, and railway projects. Two years later, after considerable study of project feasibility, the first loan was granted to Chile for $13.5 million for electric power facilities and $2.5 million for the import of agricultural machinery.

A Bank officer has described how the World Bank from the outset sought a more effective use of resources:

24

We began to discover the problem with our first mission which went to Chile in 1947 to examine a proposal that we finance a power project there. The presentation of this proposal had been made in a book handsomely bound in black Morocco leather, and I remember that one of the senior people in the Bank at the time expressed a belief that we would be able to make a loan for the project in about a week. But when we opened the book, we found that what we had really was more of an idea about a project, not a project sufficiently prepared that its needs for finance, equipment, and manpower resources could be accurately forecast.

We found it necessary to visit Chile several times to get information about the project and its economic setting. Before the loan was finally made, members of the Bank staff had made suggestions about the financial plan, had contributed to the economic analysis of the scheme, had advised on changes of engineering, and had helped study measures for improving the organization of the company which was to carry out the scheme. When we finally made the loan, the project had been modified and improved, the borrowing organization had been strengthened, and the foundation had been laid for a power expansion program in Chile which has been proceeding steadily ever since.[1]

Other early loans to LDCs were for railroads and power projects in India, roads and a development bank in Ethiopia, electric power projects in Mexico, Brazil, and El Salvador, irrigation in Thailand, and flood control in Iraq. By 1950, however, only $100 million had been disbursed to LDCs.

From its tentative beginning, the World Bank has emerged as the most influential development institution in the world. When Robert S. McNamara retired as President of the Bank in 1981, he could look back on 13 years of remarkable growth. Borrowings for the Bank had increased from under $1 billion a year to over $5 billion. Annual financial commitments had risen from under $1 billion in 1968 to $12.3 billion in 1981.[2] And the Bank now owned not only 1818 "H" Street, but it also owned or had space in seven other buildings in Washington, housing a professional staff of over 2,550, representing more than 100 nationalities.

Even more significant than the expansion in lending and the

supervision of projects has been the reshaping of the Bank's development strategy over the years. The Bank has evolved from a narrowly conceived lending institution to a comprehensive development agency that provides broad support for the problem-solving activities of borrowing countries. At the same time, it has taken the lead in some aspects of development thought, and it has been foremost in applying analytical techniques to operational problems of development.

During the 1950s, the Bank's philosophy of development focused on the release of private initiative and private domestic and foreign investment. But it recognized that this first required an adequate complement of public overhead capital—roads, railways, power plants, ports, major irrigation works, and communication facilities. To finance this capital infrastructure, foreign exchange resources would be necessary, and the recipient government would have to plan and program public-sector investment. The Bank concentrated on the selection and preparation of projects in the field of basic utilities—"vitally important facilities" that the Bank believed to be "the first step in the gradual industrialization and diversification of the underdeveloped countries." This would create the institutional framework for the effective functioning of privately owned productive enterprises. Loans from the Bank were to be a temporary arrangement, to be superseded in time by the assumption of lending from private sources through the purchase of bonds issued by the governments of developing countries themselves. The Bank's support of "planning" was not a way of creating centrally planned economies but simply a way of assuring that through efficient programming the limited resources available for the financing of infrastructure investment would be put to their best possible use. The objective was to maximize the services that the public sector could render to the private sector, where directly productive activities would be determined by private enterprises operating in a market economy.

The Bank's charter specified that the Bank had to satisfy itself that, under prevailing market conditions, its borrowers would not be able to obtain loans elsewhere on terms that "in the opinion of the Bank" were reasonable. The Bank was also charged to act "prudently in the interests both of the particular member in whose territories the project is located and of the members as a whole." Because the paid-in subscriptions by member countries of the Bank were limited, and the Bank had to obtain its resources mainly from private capital markets, it adopted conservative lending policies. The Bank financed only specific projects that promised profits sufficient to repay the initial investment, covered only foreign exchange (not local currency) costs, concentrated on the traditional "public utility" investments, and lent at 0.5 percent above the cost of its borrowing.

To many, the Bank appeared unduly conservative and cautious. The Bank's management, however, pointed to "the lack of well-prepared and well-planned projects ready for immediate execution" and low debt servicing capacity as limiting the loan operations of the Bank. Early Bank reports complained about the lack of domestic capital, a shortage of technical and managerial personnel, mounting inflation and chaotic monetary conditions, low education level of the mass of the people, strong vested interests that resist social reforms, and unsettled political conditions.

But the Bank itself was not yet willing to help remove these obstacles to accomplish a greater volume of lending. In one area, however, the Bank did attempt to assist the private sector more directly by establishing in 1956 the International Finance Corporation through which the Bank could make equity investments directly to private enterprise without government guarantee. At the same time, the Bank refused to finance state-owned industrial projects: the very few publicly controlled industrial projects that the Bank financed in its early years were all designed to be turned over to private control at a specified stage.

After a decade of operations, 60 member nations had contributed a total capital of nearly $10 billion to the Bank, and the Bank had negotiated 153 loans amounting to a total of $2.8 billion for 44 countries. Most of the Bank's financial assistance had taken the form of direct loans instead of the earlier envisaged operation of private loans guaranteed by the Bank. It had become easier for the Bank to market its own bonds rather than to sell the Bank-guaranteed bonds of its member countries.

The 1960s saw the Bank double its subscribed capital and also introduce a soft loan window through the International Development Association (IDA). Recognizing that the poorest of the poor countries could not service debt on the terms on which Bank loans were normally made, governments contributed to IDA to allow grant-type assistance—longer grace period (usually 10 years), small annual service charge (0.75 percent), and long maturity (50 years).

The Bank also moved away from its traditional emphasis on infrastructure investment and expanded its lending for agriculture and industry through loans to development finance companies. Financial support also began for education in recognition that human resources and investment in human capital could be as important as physical capital for the development process. (Significantly, the Bank's first loan to China in 1981 was $200 million for the development of higher education in science and engineering.)

Not only did the Bank assume a wider view of development strategy, but its President also emphasized the long-term character of the development process: he referred to the "century of development" in contrast with the notion of the Development Decade promoted by the United Nations. Another notable change was the Bank's insistence that the "performance" of potential borrowers, as determined by the efficacy of their own policies, be the criterion for the allocation of Bank funds. Since performance was already related to the quality of the developing country's national economic management, the Bank began offering advice on public policies that affected the country's mobilization and allocation of resources. Foreign trade policies, interest rate policies, and exchange rate policies became critical areas of concern to the Bank. Policy advice, technical assistance, and lending for projects, sectors, and programs all began to be interrelated as the Bank moved from being a narrow lending institution to undertaking a broader role in development policymaking.

During the McNamara years of the 1970s, the Bank departed sharply from previous practice by now viewing development as a process of social change. In his first speech to the Governors of the Bank, McNamara said: "I have always regarded the World Bank as something more than a Bank, as a Development Agency." The Bank began to emphasize population control—the sociocultural changes that were necessary to bring about the acceptance of birth control and the provision of public support for various techniques of birth control. Even more boldly, the Bank began to focus on the critical question of who benefits from development. The Bank recognized that growth in a country's gross national product (GNP) often does not trickle down to the lower income levels. New policies were therefore needed to reach four target groups: (1) small farmers, (2) landless laborers and submarginal farmers, (3) the urban underemployed, and (4) the urban unemployed. Although growth in GNP is a necessary condition of development, it became apparent that it was not a sufficient condition. Economic growth does not assist the poor if it does not reach the poor. Action has to be taken that will directly benefit the poor.

Addressing the Bank's Governors in Nairobi in 1973, McNamara called world attention to the basic human needs of those in "absolute poverty." Although there may always be "relative poverty" in the sense of income differentials, McNamara wanted to focus on those in "absolute poverty" who suffer "a condition of life so degraded by disease, illiteracy, malnutrition, and squalor as to deny its victims basic human necessities." Those in absolute poverty were identified as roughly the lowest 40 percent of individuals living in the less developed countries—about 900 million with an average per capita income of less than $100.

Although 40 percent of the populations of the less developed countries have not been able to contribute significantly to national economic growth nor to share equitably in economic progress, they represent an immense, untapped human potential for increasing economic growth. Not welfare programs, but policies to increase the productivity of the poor were deemed necessary. If the Bank could help make the poor more productive, there might be a reduction in absolute poverty and a more equitable pattern of economic growth.

The Bank therefore altered its lending patterns by channeling more of the IDA resources to the poorest countries (about 50 countries with a per capita income of less than $370 in 1979 dollars), by allocating more to rural development loans where the objective is to provide benefits to the bottom 40 percent income group, and by lending more to the newer social sectors of education, population, urbanization, water supply, and nutrition. More attention was also given to the urban poor.

At the end of the 1960s, nearly 60 percent of Bank lending went to the development of infrastructure; by the end of the 1970s, such lending had fallen to one-third of the total, with nearly one-half of Bank lending directed to agriculture and rural development, education, population and nutrition, and urbanization. The Bank has also changed its lending policies for loans to government-owned Development Finance Companies to aid small-scale industries, and more loans have been made to state-owned industrial enterprises.

In 1980, the Bank began lending for "structural adjustment" to meet the balance-of-payments problems caused by rising oil prices, continued high rates of inflation, and slow growth in the industrialized countries. Structural adjustment lending was designed to help supplement, with longer term financing, the relatively short-term finance available from commercial banks and the IMF to meet balance-of-payments deficits.

Structural adjustment would entail the use of capital to increase domestic production of energy and economize its use, expand domestic output of food, and increase and diversify exports. For example, a $45 million structural adjustment loan to Malawi in 1981 was to support the government's program designed to diversify the export base, encourage efficient import substitution, adjust incentives and wage-price policies, improve the financial performance of the public sector, and strengthen the government's economic planning and monitoring capability.

In fiscal 1983, commitments of loans and investments from the World Bank group totaled more than $15 billion and financed more than 300 operations in 85 countries. This was a marked increase compared with 1971 when loans totaled less than $2.5 billion. By mid-1983, the Bank had committed since its inception nearly $90 billion for about 2,300 operations in 104 countries. IDA credits amounted to over $30 billion for nearly 1,300 operations in 79 countries. As a foundation for further expansion of the Bank's lending program in the 1980s, the Bank's authorized capital that serves as a guarantee for the Bank's bondholders was increased in 1980 from $41 billion to approximately $80 billion.

The real effectiveness of the World Bank, however, lies beyond these numbers. The Bank still provides barely 1 percent of the total investment in developing countries. Nevertheless, the leverage effect of the external capital is extremely important. Not only does the Bank's technical analysis frequently raise the rate of return on projects, but the very concept of "project" has widened to include sector support, promotion of new institutions, and broad program support. As a leader for lending consortia and consultative groups, the Bank exercises influence on other lenders. Most important, beyond its lending operations, the Bank has become influential in providing an incentive for countries to improve their national economic management and has actively helped countries improve their economic performance through policy advice and monitoring of the economy.

Moreover, the Bank remains the largest multilateral development finance institution, owned by governments of 146 countries. As a world institution, its leadership and influence on international policymaking can affect not only the future course of the development process but the cohesion and stability of the international system itself. From its tentative beginning, each year the Bank has assumed a more influential role by evolving into a wide-ranging development institution that has increasingly recognized the complexity of the analytic issues and the practical problems of development for which the solutions are neither simple nor immediate. More and more, the Bank's pronouncements and policies recognize that development is a long-term process with more dimensions and complexities than were recognized in the earlier decades of the 1950s and 1960s.

The Bank has outgrown its initial narrow banking approach, which was restricted to financing infrastructure projects, and has acquired the courage to emphasize basic human needs and growth with redistribution. It has demonstrated a broader activism in formulating and pressing remedial policies to meet the ultimate end of alleviating mass poverty and fostering growth with equity. In promoting these domestic and international policies, the Bank has become the main agency by which the thinking of development economists might be translated into action.

The wider role has not weakened the financial condition of the Bank. Indeed, the Bank's loan portfolio has never suffered one

penny of loss; there is a firm policy against any participation in
rescheduling of loans; annual net profits have been realized every
year since 1948; and the Bank's bonds have the highest AAA
quality rating on bond markets. As Mr. McNamara stated in his
keynote speech, so too did his successor A. W. Clausen (former
President of the Bank of America) state in his first speech:
"Judged, then, by conservative banking standards the World Bank
is a vigorous and healthy financial intermediary between its borrowers and lenders. But it is far more than that. It is also a unique
and immensely productive development institution."

In contrast with this positive evaluation of its activities, the Bank
has been subject to critical appraisals from both the left and the
right of the political spectrum.[3] From neo-Marxists and the school
of dependency come accusations that the Bank's activities are mere
palliatives or tokenism at best and probably counterproductive
for the developing countries. It is argued that the Bank supports
reactionary elites and bolsters political authoritarianism. Only a
revolutionary change of the dependent capitalist system can offer a real solution. (This criticism will be presented more fully in
Chapter 8.)

The conservative critique, however, contends the very opposite—that the Bank is too liberal in its lending, is promoting socialism, and is undermining capitalist development. Conservative critics argue against the support of state planning, against
emphasis on redistribution of income and wealth, and for more
reliance on free enterprise and the market-price system.

In view of both radical and conservative critiques, the Bank's
philosophy of operations might best be characterized as reformist. Economic, political, and social changes are promoted—but
far short of revolution or a too disruptive social upheaval. A
gradualist, long-run, patient view of the development process is
adopted. Grand recipes and quick cures are eschewed.

Although some observers accept this reformist approach, they
levy other criticisms. In a period of national budget-tightening
policies, the Bank appears to have grown too big and too fast.
Its bureaucracy is said to be overstaffed and cumbersome. Too
long a time is consumed on project studies; too narrow a view is
taken of the development process. Critics suggest that more attention be given to the context of the individual project, and that

the scattered nature of project support neglects the macro-aspects of the development process. It seems research studies have little operational relevance. Engineers and economists dominate the organization, with little attention given to the insights of political scientists, sociologists, or anthropologists. Performance is judged too much by amount of lending. Shouldn't more staff come from developing countries? Shouldn't a louder voice be granted to the LDCs themselves?

Such a range of criticisms is to be expected, given the extensive activities that the Bank is attempting to undertake, the many challenges of development, and the widely different perspectives from which the course of development can be viewed. In spite of these criticisms, it is fair to say that the Bank has been a predominant and constructive force in the international development community—even though it is still only a beginning.

IMF Resources

Although Bank activities have been clearly directed to the development objectives of its members, the IMF was not designed to give any special attention to developing countries and only acquired a development role in the course of its evolution. Originally designed to use its resources only "for monetary stabilization operations," the Fund has come to recognize the interdependence between monetary stabilization and development. The LDCs benefit indirectly if the Fund supports the more developed countries and thereby forestalls balance-of-payments restrictions on imports from LDCs or restrictions on capital exports to developing nations. More directly, in some of its policies on the use of its resources, the Fund has managed to give special consideration to the problems of its less developed member countries.

In 1963, for instance, the Fund established a compensatory financing policy to offer financing for fluctuations in the export proceeds of primary producing countries. Members having a balance-of-payments problem may draw on the Fund under this facility if the Fund is satisfied that the problem that caused the shortfall is a short-term one, that it is largely attributable to circumstances beyond the country's control, and that the country will cooperate with the Fund in an effort to solve its balance-of-payments difficulties.

The Fund also provides a buffer stock facility, designed to assist in the financing of members' contributions to international buffer stocks of primary products when members having balance-of-payments difficulties participate in these commodity stabilization agreements (tin, cocoa, sugar). Again, the member is expected to cooperate with the Fund in an effort to find appropriate solutions for its balance-of-payments problem.

By approving stand-by arrangements or extended arrangements for the drawing of other countries' currencies from the Fund, the Fund allows a developing country to secure temporarily the foreign exchange it needs while it gains time to deal with its balance-of-payments problems, without having to sacrifice its rate of development. Undrawn balances under stand-by arrangements or extended arrangements totaled 11.1 billion SDRs (special drawing rights) as of the end of 1982.[4] The Fund's approval of a stand-by or extended arrangement provides not only periodic installments of needed foreign exchange to the member country but also encourages other potential lenders to extend additional resources to the country as the installments from the Fund are made conditional on a specified performance by the drawing country. Drawings under the credit tranches, the extended facility, compensatory financing, and buffer stock facilities totaled 7.4 billion SDRs in 1982.

Recalling that India failed in its attempt at Bretton Woods to include a clause that would single out assistance for "the fuller utilization of the resources of economically underdeveloped countries," it is ironic that the Fund's loan of $5.75 billion in 1981 to India was then its largest to date—and for essentially development purposes. The extended arrangement over a three-year period was in support of India's structural adjustment program for investment in oil production and other industries to improve the country's balance of payments. It is also noteworthy that in recent years most of the loan commitments by the Fund have been to developing countries.

Although the Fund has adapted its activities to meet unforeseen problems that have arisen in developing countries, many of the LDCs remain disappointed. Greater voting power in the IMF organization, more financial assistance, less onerous conditions for access to Fund resources—these continue to be the demands of the developing countries.

In recent years, as the deficits of the non-oil-producing LDCs increased, these countries became more disturbed over the terms and conditions imposed by the Fund in allowing access to resources for financing their balance-of-payments needs. Before a country can continue to draw from the Fund, it must meet certain conditions of national economic management imposed by the IMF. This issue of conditionality came to a head in the case of Jamaica in 1980. After Fund assistance had already reached more than 12 percent of Jamaica's national income, the Fund insisted on further reductions in the central government's deficit. Prime Minister Michael Manley balked at this condition, and the question of continued negotiations with the IMF soon became a political issue. Although demonstrations on the streets of Kingston were directed against the IMF, the Fund refused to grant a waiver of its conditions. The Jamaican cabinet announced that it had concluded that the IMF's loan program would involve Jamaicans in more hardship than necessary and would not result in a viable economy. The government decided to proceed to a new election. Whether or not to oppose the IMF became the central issue of the election.

The opposition party, led by Edward Seaga, predicted economic collapse unless the conditions of the IMF were fulfilled. In the graffiti on Kingston walls, "IMF" also meant "Is Manley Fault" in Jamaican argot. But in a message to the Arusha Conference on the International Monetary System and the New International Order, Prime Minister Manley reiterated his conviction that

> IMF prescriptions are designed by and for developed capitalist economies and are inappropriate for developing countries of any kind; the severe suffering imposed on a developing society through IMF conditionality is endured without any real prospect of a favorable economic outcome and without an adequate foundation of social welfare provisions to mitigate the hardships experienced by the people.[5]

The result of the Jamaican election—or the first so-called "IMF election"—was a landslide victory for Mr. Seaga's opposition

party. The defeated Prime Minister told his party supporters that
"What we did wrong was to challenge the power of the Western
economic structure. I will remain unrepentant and unrecon-
structed."

Many developing countries would still like to respond to the
"Arusha Initiative"—a call issued by a conference in Tanzania in
1980 for a United Nations Conference on International Money and
Finance that "will provide a universal, democratic and legitimate
forum for the negotiation of a new monetary system." This new
international monetary order would have as its fundamental objective the support "of a process of global development, especially for the countries of the Third World, which contain the
majority of the world's poor." Until a new international monetary system can be established,

> Third World countries' access to the higher credit tranches of
> the IMF must be guided by an unambiguous recognition that a
> large part of the deficits they now experience is attributable to
> factors for which they are in no way responsible. These include
> high international inflation, weak and fluctuating export prices,
> low demand for their exports, deterioration of their terms of
> trade and high interest rates; all symptoms of the present in-
> ternational monetary disorder and more generally of an unjust
> international system. Financing such deficits by the IMF must
> be much more flexible and automatic; it must not be guided by
> present conditionality criteria.[6]

Although less political and ideological in tone, statements by
the "Group of 24," a group of Ministers from developing countries, also call for international monetary reform. The Group's
Program of Action proposes immediate measures to accelerate the
flow of concessional aid to developing countries, increases in the
allocation of SDRs and a link to additional development assistance, greater program lending by multilateral financial institutions, provisions for external debt reorganization, replenishment
of IDA, and an increase in the capital base of the multilateral financial institutions.

The controversy surrounding conditionality is unsettled. Inflation and balance-of-payments problems are both reflections of the
attempt of a society to absorb more resources than it can currently generate. If the country then has to draw foreign ex-

change from the Fund and confronts the restraints of conditionality, which involve reducing real incomes and the use of
resources, there is likely to be strong resistance when each sector of society fears that it may have to bear a disproportionate
share of the burden of cutting real income. As more of the developing countries have turned to the Fund in recent years, it
has come to be viewed as excessively orthodox, conservative, and
monetarist in terms of conditionality. Developing countries have
found the Fund's stabilization programs to be excessively onerous, often requiring unreasonably heavy deflation or massive
devaluation, and insensitive to the income distribution and internal social and political effects that the stabilization policies
produce. Although the IMF may not support the more extreme
proposals of the Arusha Initiative or even the more modest requests of the Group of 24, it is likely to provide more long-term
conditional resources and to become more flexible in imposing
its conditions. Indeed, the IMF has already issued new guidelines on conditionality that give more attention to early warning
of a possible payments problem, recognition of the need for longer
periods of stand-by arrangements, and "due regard to the domestic, social, and political objectives, the economic priorities, and
the circumstances of members, including causes of their balance-
of-payments problems."

Like the World Bank, the Fund has increasingly recognized its
role as catalyst. As the problems of developing countries change,
so too must the policies of the Bank and Fund adjust to the
changing circumstances. More than through the actual provision
of resources, the Fund's effectiveness is determined by the quality of its policy advice and the appropriateness of the adjustment
policies that it supports in developing countries. The policy action supported by the Fund will determine the future mobilization of domestic resources and can encourage other sources of
external financing for development. Reliance on the Fund's stand-
by arrangements will be of considerable importance in reducing
the risk of commercial bank lending to developing countries. From
a larger perspective, the role of the Fund in promoting order in
international monetary affairs will be crucial in enabling developing countries to benefit from more stable growth in world trade
and investment.

GATT

Although more subdued and prosaic in its operations, the General Agreement on Tariffs and Trade (GATT) also helped shape the postwar Bretton Woods order. The Bretton Woods Conference looked forward to the creation of an ancillary institution that would reduce obstacles to international trade and give effective power to the principle of multilateral nondiscriminatory trade. Although the initial plans for the Havana Charter and the creation of an International Trade Organization were not carried out, the GATT emerged as a multilateral agreement embodying commercial policy provisions. While the IMF was designed to repair the disintegration that had befallen the international monetary system prior to the war and the World Bank was designed to stimulate and support foreign investment, which had declined to insignificant amounts, the GATT was intended to reverse the protectionist and discriminatory trade practices that had multiplied during the prewar depression years.

The Fund, the Bank, and GATT were designed to help the advanced industrial countries achieve the multiple objectives of full employment, freer and expanding world trade, and stable exchange rates. But of what direct benefit were these postwar institutions to be to the newly emergent countries with their problems of development that were quite different from the prewar problems of the more developed countries? Many advocates for the LDCs contend that the institutions remain biased in favor of the more developed countries.

With respect to GATT, the debate begun over the Havana Charter still continues. A core issue of international economic regulation is whether international trade rules favor the growth of industrialized countries while inhibiting the development of the nonindustrialized nations.

In its initial provisions, GATT did not relieve less developed countries of some obligations. It referred specifically to the type of country whose economy "can only support low standards of living and is in the early stages of development." A country in this category was offered the privileges of withdrawing a tariff concession, increasing tariff rates to permit protection of an infant industry, and using quota restrictions on imports "in order to safeguard its external financial position and to ensure a level of reserves adequate for the implementation of its program of economic development." Under the last provision, the developing countries have been able to protect their domestic industries through quotas imposed under the guise of balance-of-payments support.

The most comprehensive recognition of the trade problems of developing nations was given in 1965 when the GATT added a new chapter on trade and development to the General Agreement. This chapter recognized that the less developed country need not reciprocate a tariff reduction on its exports with a tariff reduction on its imports. The chapter also acknowledged the objectives of LDCs to increase their export earnings, to gain more favorable access to world markets, and to improve access to markets for their processed and manufactured products. Furthermore, the chapter recognized the desirability of measures "designed to attain stable, equitable and remunerative prices." Although these statements were sympathetic to the special trade problems of the developing countries, they remained only statements of principles and objectives without the backing of any legal obligations or the formulation of actual policies to achieve the desired results.

At the same time that GATT was considering its new chapter on trade and development, the first United Nations Conference on Trade and Development (UNCTAD) convened in Geneva, despite opposition by the industrialized countries. Under the leadership of its Secretary-General Raúl Prebisch, a noted Argentine economist, this conference debated and adopted several propositions that were aimed at helping the developing nations. Although the votes of the conference split between the majority of less developed countries and the industrialized countries, the majority argued that GATT imposes overly burdensome obligations on the low-income countries and exercises more of a negative role in policing trading relationships than a positive role in promoting trade from developing countries. Questioning GATT's "classic concept that the free play of international economic forces by itself leads to the optimum expansion of trade and the most efficient utilization of the world's productive resources," the economies of the industrially advanced and the developing countries are altogether different. As Raúl Prebisch stated:

> There is no dispute about the need for a rule of law in world trade. The question is: What should be the character of that law? Should it be a law based on the presumption that the world is essentially homogeneous, being composed of countries of equal strength and comparable levels of economic development, a law founded, therefore, on the principles of reciprocity and non-discrimination? Or should it be a law that recognizes diversity of levels of economic development and differences in economic and social systems?[7]

That question is still being asked.

Believing that the newly developing countries are in a special situation that justifies a new trade policy for development, UNCTAD has continued to formulate proposals to allow more positive and definitive action than has been possible under the GATT. These proposals emphasize the removal of restrictions by the more developed countries (MDCs) on imports from the LDCs, commodity agreements to gain higher prices for primary product exports, and preferential treatment in tariff rates on imports of semimanufactured and manufactured products from the LDCs.

Compared with the UNCTAD proposals, the latest round of multilateral trade negotiations, the so-called Tokyo Round concluded in Geneva in 1979, yielded disappointing results for the LDCs. The Tokyo Declaration of 1973 stated that the negotiations were to

> secure additional benefits for the international trade of developing countries so as to achieve a substantial increase in their foreign exchange earnings, the diversification of their trade . . . and a better balance between developing and developed countries in the sharing of the advantages resulting from this expansion.

The spread of the "New Protectionism" since the Tokyo Declaration—especially the numerous quota restrictions in the form of Orderly Marketing Agreements and Voluntary Export Restraints under the guise of preventing "market disruption" by imports from the newly industrializing countries—intensified the

LDCs' desire for improved market access. So too did the rise in oil prices aggravate the need of non-oil-producing LDCs for greater export revenue.

The results of the Tokyo Round did not, however, measure up to the need. LDCs gained somewhat from the general tariff reductions. Some improvement in the tariff rate structure—that is, in the differential tariff rates that vary according to the degree of processing from the raw material to the finished product—was also achieved. But the developing countries still believe that tariff escalation according to the product's stage of production discriminates against potential exports of manufactured goods from these countries. Arguing that the developed countries' high effective rate of protection, yielded by their higher duties on processed imports than on imports of raw materials, condemn the LDCs to remain hewers of wood and drawers of water, the LDCs want this type of tariff escalation to be removed.

Another issue vitally important to LDCs will be the future interpretation and application of the new code on the use of export subsidies. Although the code exempts developing countries from the commitment of the developed countries not to use export subsidies on industrial and mineral products, the developing countries do agree not to use such subsidies "in a manner which causes serious prejudice to the trade or production" of another country. Developing nations are also subject to the imposition of countervailing duties if their subsidized exports cause "material injury to a domestic industry, threat of material injury to a domestic industry, or material retardation of the establishment of such an industry." As LDCs attempt to promote more exports, there will be intensified controversy about the right to use domestic subsidies and about their effects.

On another major issue—of when a country can invoke trade restrictions as "market safeguards" to prevent "domestic injury" from imports—no agreement was reached. Nor was any substantial progress made in resolving the lingering issue of whether more favorable treatment should be accorded the LDCs.

In spite of five years of intensive negotiations (1974–1979), the Tokyo Round did not live up to initial expectations. UNCTAD declared that the negotiations failed in every respect to achieve the objectives of the Tokyo Declaration. And the LDCs continue to debate the merits of GATT with questions and arguments over trade restrictions, preferential treatment, and commodity agreements that are reminiscent of those first raised with respect to the Havana Charter. Certainly it cannot be claimed that developing countries would have fared better without GATT and its efforts at trade liberalization. But the basic issue of whether developing countries should receive special and differential treatment will undoubtedly arise repeatedly in the future.

United Nations

With the rise in the number of member states, most of them developing countries (from 33 developing member countries in 1945 to 121 now), the United Nations system has become ever more identified with development problems. The activities of UNCTAD may be the most visible, but also significant are the various development assistance activities within the U.N. system, the work of the specialized agencies, and the General Assembly's resolutions bearing on development strategy.

As early as 1949, a U.N. Economic and Social Council report proposed combining technical assistance with soft financing for "schemes of development which cannot be financed from the country's own resources and for which loans cannot be asked on strict business principles." By 1953, there was a formal proposal for SUNFED—the Special United Nations Fund for Economic Development. This was a bold attempt to meet the desire of the LDCs for access to capital on easier terms than those of the World Bank. There was, however, strong opposition by the United States and Britain to the soft financing proposal as well as a fear of creating a politically vulnerable rival to the World Bank. SUNFED was therefore scrapped, but the advocacy within the United Nations of grant aid and soft loans had proved useful in paving the way for the establishment of the IDA and IFC in the World Bank group.

Within the United Nations, the Special Fund and later the United Nations Development Program (UNDP) undertook aid activities. The UNDP is active in providing technical assistance and preinvestment financing for development projects administered by the United Nation's specialized agencies. Various forms of technical assistance are also provided by the World Health Organization (WHO), the U.N. Educational, Scientific, and Cultural Organization (UNESCO), the Food and Agriculture Organization (FAO), the International Labor Organization (ILO), and the U.N. Industrial Development Organization (UNIDO).

Other special funds within the U.N. system also operate on development problems—the U.N. International Children's Emergency Fund (UNICEF), the U.N. Fund for Population Activities, the World Food Program, and the International Fund for Agricultural Development. The Regional Economic Commissions for West Asia (ECWA), Latin America (ECLA), and Africa (ECA) promote programs of development within these regions, undertake research, and provide advice and technical expertise.

The General Assembly has been increasingly active in passing resolutions relating to international development. In 1961, the General Assembly designated the 1960s as "the United Nations Development Decade" with the objective to

> accelerate progress toward self-sustaining growth of the economy of the individual nations and their social advancement so as to attain in each underdeveloped country a substantial increase in the rate of growth, with each country setting its own target, taking as the objective a minimum rate of growth of aggregate national income of 5 percent at the end of the decade.[8]

Again, in 1970, the General Assembly adopted a resolution establishing the International Development Strategy for the Second U.N. Development Decade, with a target growth rate in national income of 6 percent annually.

A series of U.N. resolutions has also been notable for successively expressing the demands of the developing countries for a greater transfer of resources from the MDCs to the LDCs, and for new international trading arrangements and monetary arrangements intended to be of more benefit to the LDCs. These demands were stated in a resolution in 1962 on permanent sovereignty over natural resources. The General Assembly declared that

> the right of peoples and nations to permanent sovereignty over their natural wealth and resources must be exercised in the in-

terests of their national development and of the well-being of
the people of the state concerned. . . . The free and beneficial
exercise of the sovereignty of peoples and nations over their
natural resources must be furthered by the mutual respect of
states based on their sovereign equality.

This resolution attempted to bring foreign investment under the
control of the host government's legislation and to place problems of nationalization or expropriation under the national jurisdiction of the state taking such measures.

The Charter on Economic Rights and Duties of States (1974)
was adopted in spite of the objections of the United States and
other industrialized countries. Many articles in the chapter call
upon the international community to give preferences to "developing countries" in various international economic and trade
matters. Articles address policies of nationalization or expropriation, transfer of technology, trade and tariff questions, exploitation of natural resources, commodity cartels, the needs and
problems of the least developed countries, regional groupings,
"just and equitable terms of trade," and the sharing of common
ocean resources. In all these articles, the "needs and interests"
of the developing countries are stressed, and advanced countries
are requested to adopt "differential measures" in ways that will
provide "special and more favorable treatment" to developing
countries.

The demands of the developing countries culminated in the
declaration on the establishment of a New International Economic Order (NIEO), adopted at the sixth special session (1974).
The resolution called for the establishment of an NIEO "based
on equity, sovereign equality, interdependence, common interest and cooperation among all states, irrespective of their economic and social systems which shall correct inequalities and re-
dress existing injustices. . . ." Several specific policies were called
for, including

Measures to provide a "just and equitable relationship" between
the prices of exports and the prices of imports in the developing
countries "with the aim of bringing about sustained improvement in their unsatisfactory terms of trade."

Preferential and nonreciprocal treatment for developing countries.

More favorable conditions for the transfer of financial resources to developing countries.

Promotion of transfer of technology and the creation of indigenous technology for the benefit of the developing countries.

Expanded role for producer associations.

A reformed international monetary system that would promote development and provide an adequate flow of real resources to the developing countries.

More international aid and external debt relief.

Following a declaration for a NIEO, the General Assembly's resolutions have continued to echo the demands of the LDCs in the Group of 77. But as long as these resolutions are unacceptable to the more developed countries, the General Assembly remains little more than a forum for the rhetoric of development from which few practical results can emerge. Among international organizations, the power to shape international development policies still lies with the Bretton Woods institutions and GATT.

Foreign Aid

Beyond the institutions of the Bretton Woods system and the United Nations, foreign aid has been another major force shaping the course of development. Although lending operations of the World Bank have expanded markedly, they still account for only a small proportion (less than 20 percent in the last five years) of total net aid to developing countries.

A strict interpretation of "aid" would limit foreign aid or public financial assistance to those capital flows from rich to poor countries that are offered at concessional terms—that is, at below market rates of interest and for longer grace periods and amortization periods, thereby providing some gift or grant element in the concessionary loan. Pure aid would be a grant that transfers resources without any requirement of repayment. Short of pure aid, loan terms that are more favorable than commercial transactions will have some grant element.

The provision of resources on concessionary terms has been unprecedented in scope and amount. Dwarfing the earlier periods of aid from the metropolitan countries to their colonies, official development assistance (ODA) grew rapidly in the late 1950s, followed by a slower growth trend in the middle 1960s. Although ODA from the industrial countries in the Organization of Economic Cooperation and Development rose from $4.6 billion in 1960 to approximately $28 billion in 1982 (current dollars), ODA as a percentage of GNP declined from 0.51 percent in 1960 to 0.39 percent in 1982, far short of the U.N. target of 0.7 percent of GNP. For the United States, ODA as a percentage of GNP was only 0.27 percent in 1982. (ODA has at least a 25 percent grant element.)

Since the first oil price crisis in 1973, the recycling of petrodollars through commercial bank lending has been an important source of foreign exchange. Total nonconcessional receipts of developing countries increased from $11 billion in 1970 to $68 billion in 1981. This primarily benefited the newly industrializing countries and other middle-income countries. While aid flows increased by 50 percent in real terms during the decade of the 1970s, nonconcessional flows from the private sector doubled.

In 1981, the "least of the less developed countries" received 21 percent of total ODA, amounting to approximately $24 per capita, 10 percent of their GNP, and 50 percent of their current imports. The "middle-income countries" obtained an average of $15 per capita, 2.2 percent of their GNP, and 10 percent of their imports.

The real value of the aid flows, however, may be only 50 to 70 percent of the face value because some of the grants and loans may be restricted in their use to purchases in the donor country whose prices may be higher than world market prices, or loans may be tied to specific projects or commodities. Inflation has made the real value even lower.

The sources of aid have been diverse—bilateral on a government-to-government basis (such as through the U.S. Agency for International Development), multilateral (for example, the U.N. Development Program and World Bank Group), through regional development banks (the Interamerican, African, and Asian Development Banks), and through commodity arrangements (such as Public Law 480 for surplus farm products).

Although one may agree that aid is neither a necessary nor sufficient condition for development, nonetheless, in many cases achievements can be attributed to the receipt of external economic assistance. For instance, aid played a significant role in the success stories of South Korea and Taiwan. In many countries, aid has been a substantial fraction of investment. Even where it has been a lower fraction, aid has still been crucial in mobilizing more domestic resources, breaking production and manpower bottlenecks, and providing imports for which there is no adequate available foreign exchange substitute. Moreover, aid has had qualitative impacts of an educative kind, helping to motivate and complement domestic efforts and to improve policy-making.

Several studies that examine the relationship between foreign assistance and development performance have concluded that a number of aid recipients have gone through the successful sequence of increased investment rates, structural transformation, and declining aid requirements. Although development depends heavily on internal effort, aid has played an important marginal role by bridging savings gaps and balance-of-payments gaps, and by providing resources for infrastructure and human capital formation.

The auditing of the performance of over 700 completed World Bank projects also indicates that more than 90 percent have fulfilled their original objectives. These annual audits of project performance examine procurement, management, cost recovery, economy in design, appropriateness of cost in light of benefits, and rates of return.

On the other hand, aid has not fulfilled expectations in several countries. In some, aid has substituted for domestic savings and has been offset by increased consumption. In others, aid has sustained misguided policies by the recipient governments, led to dependency, and fostered inefficiency by having disincentive effects. Nor has the record of aid been without instances of waste and some invitations to corruption.

But mistakes and failure should not distort an assessment of the entire aid effort. On balance that effort has been one of effectiveness, and aid agencies have gained experience in determining what particular kinds and patterns of aid are most efficient. Some of the disappointments can even be attributed to insufficient aid. If only the volume of aid had been greater, it could have succeeded in breaking resource bottlenecks and filling expertise gaps. In other instances, the donor has not been insistent on policy changes or self-help measures. As the record of foreign assistance in several countries shows, external assistance may be incapable of yielding significant results unless it is also accompanied by complementary domestic measures such as basic reforms in land-tenure systems, additional taxation, investment in human capital, and more efficient government administration.

Most significant, the cases of failure have frequently been those cases in which aid has been given for reasons other than the promotion of development. If the objective has been military or political, the assistance is likely to impair the development effort and be suboptimal in comparison with what would have been the distribution of aid to maximize the developmental payoff. Where aid has focused most closely on the true objective of development, aid has been most successful, as the record of World Bank activities indicates.

Development Planning

Interrelated with the Bretton Woods institutions and aid agencies has been the practice of national development planning. Beginning with India's creation of a central planning commission in 1950, many other developing countries followed suit, desiring the prestige of having a development plan. During the 1960s and 1970s, however, a retrenchment was to come, moving governments away from the earlier comprehensive type of central planning to a lighter type and to more reliance on market institutions.

India's First Five-Year Plan (1952–1956) expressed the logic of development planning. The plan was to permit a rational determination of priorities and to select the best means to achieve desired objectives. To do this, the plan established a set of quantitative targets. Given an estimate of population growth (say 2 percent), a target of GNP growth is set (say 5 percent) to achieve a target growth in real per capita income (3 percent). To achieve this growth target of GNP, investment is needed in a certain amount. The sources of domestic and foreign resources to support this rate of necessary investment are then identified. The allocation of investable resources is then specified among sectors (agriculture, industry, foreign trade) and to specific projects within a sector. The plan distinguishes between activities to be carried out in the public sector and those for which the private sector is to be responsible. A variety of calculations can be made to relate inputs of labor, capital, and raw materials with the resulting outputs. Other calculations can trace the interrelationships among the income to be generated and expended for consumption and investment in the private and public sectors, for imports and exports, and for various outputs. The plan also seeks a balance in the conditions of demand and supply, consistency between the availability of resources and financing, between income generated and expended, between sector programs and the comprehensive aggregate plan, and feasibility in both financial and physical terms.

The mystique of planning soon intrigued many LDCs. Criticizing reliance on the price system, desiring social reform along with development, and stressing the pervasiveness of the obstacles to development, the governments of poorer countries have been more attracted to central planning than ever was the case in the historical experience of the now advanced Western nations. Governments of emergent nations commonly turned to national planning as if this were itself a precondition for development. In Thailand, an official considered "economic planning a matter of necessity rather than choice." And the Prime Minister of Trinidad claimed from his long experience that "even if a politician in a developing country came into office without intending to plan, he would soon have to invent planning or something very similar."

Planning was also stimulated by the desire to receive external assistance from public international lending agencies. Many plans were prepared with the assumption that a certain percentage of the proposed investment in the plan would be financed from abroad, and requests for aid were presented accordingly. Calculations of the amount of external assistance needed were frequently presented in terms of the necessity to overcome the shortage in domestic resources to achieve targets of a development plan. Some donors also attempted to promote better planning to coordinate investment activities. Some aid programs, such as the Alliance for Progress in Latin America during the 1960s, stressed the desirability of national economic planning as an important means of devising self-help measures.

The economist's tool kit also provided some modern techniques that could support the formulation of a development plan—especially input-output analysis, dynamic programming, and simulation of growth models. These techniques provided tests for the consistency, balance, and feasibility of plans. Frequently, visiting missions and foreign advisors cooperated with local planning agencies in producing analyses and policy recommendations underlying development plans. It was not uncommon for groups of "eminent experts" to demonstrate the potential of the economist's techniques for planning. For instance, the U.N. Economic Commission for Asia and the Far East convened a group of experts headed by Nobel laureate Jan Tinbergen, who recommended in 1959 that even countries like Nepal, Afghanistan, Burma, and Thailand should try to plan through comprehensive growth models.[9]

So too did the Economic Commission for Latin America (ECLA) vigorously advocate detailed planning. During the 1950s, ECLA engaged a number of Latin American governments in the techniques of programming as it emphasized "programmed" industrialization and "healthy" protectionism, adequate controls over the use of foreign exchange, and the programming of import substitution. The implementation of these policies presupposed strengthening the decision-making and regulating capacity of governments in the "periphery nations" to alter the structural imbalance between "center" and "periphery nations" and reduce the gap between them.

At the same time, however, as planning became more prevalent, it was also becoming more and more evident that most plans were not being implemented. Too often the formulation of a plan was only an intellectual exercise, and plans remained impressive only on paper. Although economists improved their method of formulating plans, they gave little thought to overcoming the obstacles to the plan's implementation.

Failure to implement has been the result of several factors. Some plans have been based on policies that do not have much operational relevance. Targets and policy instruments have been unrealistic. Some plans have also been based on the expectation of wide-ranging reforms that prove to be politically unpopular. Without political support and political stability, the best formulated plan cannot be implemented. Implementation has also been thwarted by weak administrations with divided loyalties and uncoordinated decision-making techniques among ministries, departments, and agencies. There is also commonly a short supply of skilled administrators and technicians to execute and monitor the plan.

The government of Malawi, for example, boldly formulated a plan for the new nation. It stated that it was a development plan, not merely " a development survey report" and defined a development plan as "an outline of what can and is intended to be done with a specific amount of resources within a stated period." Priorities of the plan were building the economic infrastructure, development of human resources, and the modernization of agriculture. Targets were established for the rate of growth, per capita income, investments, employment, external trade, and various sectors (agriculture, commerce and industry, education, roads and bridges, urban development). Numerous projects were also outlined. The plan's formulation met the tests of balance and consistency. But when the plan's section on manpower listed professional persons in the new country, the number of economists and accountants was dismal: "African—6, Asian—nil, European—nil"; the number of statisticians was equally discouraging: "African—nil, Asian—nil, European—nil."

The Minister of Development and Planning remarked that his Ministry contained "only four officers and none of them an expert in planning."

Even with a highly competent civil service such as India's, plans may be difficult to implement. The multiple objectives of a plan may be incompatible as they were in India's First and Second Five-Year Plans. They included a large increase in national income to raise the level of living, rapid industrialization with emphasis on heavy industries, a large increase in employment opportunities, as well as a reduction in the inequalities in income and wealth. It proved impossible to attain these multiple objectives simultaneously. An increase in the level of living may cause resources to be shifted away from investment to consumption, and hence lower the increase in national income; concentration on heavy industry may go against a higher rate of employment; and reduction in inequalities of income and wealth is possible only over the long run.

Not unlike the experience in other countries, India's plans have fallen short because political objectives have often taken precedence over economic objectives. Political compromise in the planning process has been at the expense of an emphasis on economic rationality. The plan, once set forth, has not adjusted to changing sociopolitical conditions. Projections have been overly optimistic, and readjustments have not been made when anticipations were not fulfilled. The plans have also concentrated too much on big public investment aggregates to the neglect of small-scale, local analysis and planning. Nor have policies and measures been sufficiently well designed from an operational standpoint to achieve the objectives. A leading Indian development economist, Jagdish Bhagwati, concluded that "experience has now shown that these premises of our policies have been either misguided or inadequate or unrealistic in our political framework."[10]

From a comparative analysis of development planning in over a hundred countries, a World Bank official concluded that

> Political instability, economic uncertainty, formalistic acceptance of plans and administrative friction largely explain why it has been possible for the rates of growth in the country without much planning experience to decline as planning techniques have improved.[11]

The conclusion is skeptical about the prematurely introduced comprehensive development plan and shows a clear preference for "planning-from-below" in the sense of improving information, instituting an effective planning approach in the operational ministries and agencies, improving budgeting techniques, and developing proper public investment programs.

At the same time that some countries encountered difficulties in implementing their comprehensive plans, other countries—such as Mexico, Israel, and Puerto Rico—were demonstrating their capacity to develop without a comprehensive plan. The functions of markets came to be more and more appreciated as a means to stimulate both economic efficiency and growth.

Now more governments recognize that there is no magic to a plan. The design of a development plan has not proved difficult—but the execution has. It has been increasingly recognized that a central, comprehensive, "heavy-type" plan is still premature for most of the LDCs. A more balanced role for government has been sought. Even in China, the slogan appeared: "The market is a good school for everyone."

For many, planning is now to be valued as a process, even if it does not lead to the writing of a plan. The value of planning lies in its contribution to improving the policymaking process. Objectives are made explicit, priorities ordered, and policy premises articulated. The interrelationships among the different sectors and projects are recognized, and the interdependence of a set of policies is determined. The policies, however, might involve a "lighter" type of planning, with more of a reliance on decentralized decisions operating through the market mechanism as well as a greater attention to devising policies that might make private action more effective.

In seeking a greater use of the market mechanism, governments have realized that, although their role is different from that in comprehensive planning, it is not necessarily a diminished role. Governments that embark on programs to enlist more private-sector activity have come to recognize that they must undertake programs of reform to remove the distortions caused by arbitrary, direct administrative controls of the past. Governments have also assumed a more extensive role in building market institutions such as banking systems, monetary and capital markets, agricultural cooperatives, labor organizations, rural credit institutions, and training institutes. Moreover, governments have realized that they may affect individual action by changing the legal and institutional framework, including land-tenure legislation, commercial law, and property rights. As governments have retrenched to a "lighter" type of planning with more use of the market price system, they have had to become more sensitive to maintaining a proper balance between state-owned enterprises and private enterprises, to promoting individual activity, to improving public-sector management, and to implementing as well as choosing development strategies.

Development efforts have depended on both the operation of international economic institutions and domestic policy measures. The IMF, World Bank, and GATT have had to respond to problems of development not contemplated when the institutions were originally designed. The strength of these institutions has been in their capacity to evolve and to meet new problems as they emerged.

So too have the governments of newly developing countries had to undertake self-help measures and improve the quality of their policymaking. At the same time, they have had to adjust to changing conditions in the international economy.

Over the past four decades, the international and domestic responses to the challenges of development have yielded achievements and disappointments—both in abundance. To a recollection of some of these, we now turn.

3

Achievements

The development mood is now one of stocktaking and reassessment—a questioning of what has gone right and what has gone wrong as countries during the past four decades have tried to emerge from their persistent poverty. Not surprisingly, an appraisal of such a multidimensional process as development in such a diversity of countries can only be mixed. As to how the development efforts have actually fared, perhaps the judicious verdict is "failure within success." We will first examine some of the achievements that support the verdict of success and then discuss in the next chapter the disappointments that tilt the record toward failure.

Aggregate Performance

Some of the aggregate indices point to success. After the preceding centuries of near stagnation, there has been unprecedented growth in national output and the value of output available per person in poor countries. Most of the LDCs fulfilled the target of 5 percent growth in GNP during the U.N. Development Decade I (1960s), and during Development Decade II (1970s) the 6 percent growth target. During the slower growth period of the 1970s, the developing countries still averaged an annual growth rate of 5.3 percent compared with the industrialized countries' average of 3.2 percent. About 30 non-OPEC, non-communist countries achieved real economic growth from 1960 to 1979, exceeding 6 percent per year and thereby tripling the size of their economies.

On a per capita basis, the growth rate of GNP per head has also more than fulfilled the targets of the two Development Decades. Indeed, the average rate of growth in GNP per head for all LDCs for the period 1955–1980 was 3.1 percent (including China)—a remarkable rate. Although the rate for low-income countries (per capita income less than $410 in 1980 dollars) was 2.0 percent, the rate for middle-income countries (per capita income more than $410) was 3.3 percent. During the same period, the per capita rate of growth in the United States was 2 percent. The growth rates for GNP per head were only between 1 percent and 2 percent for the United States and Western Europe during the half-century before the World War I, their period of fastest growth. Even for Japan, the long-term growth rate in GNP per head between 1880 and 1960 was below 2.5 percent. With the high growth rates in the middle-income developing countries, GNP per person rose almost two and one-half times in real terms during the past 30 years—from approximately $640 in 1950 (1980 dollars) to $1,580 in 1980. By 1983, about 27 low-income countries had graduated to a higher level of per capita income, at which point they were no longer eligible for IDA assistance.

Compared with their own past records and the records of presently developed countries in their initial phases of development, many LDCs have exceeded expectations in the growth of GNP and GNP per head. In spite of the obstacles confronted, the absence of components believed essential for accelerated development, and population growth rates that have been substantially higher than those with which the now developed countries had to contend during their periods of industrialization—in spite of these handicaps—many LDCs have achieved considerably more than would have been expected in 1950. The period since 1950 can certainly be viewed as the best period in history for people in the poor countries of the world.

Beneath the statistical aggregates are real improvements in health, education, and nutrition that are most meaningful to men, women, and children struggling to emerge from poverty. The infant mortality rate (ages 0–1) declined in low-income countries from 165 per 1,000 in 1960 to 99 in 1981, and in middle-income countries from 127 in 1960 to 81 in 1981. Between 1960 and 1981, life expectancy at birth increased in middle-income countries from 50 to 60 years, and in low-income countries from 41 to 58 years. Comparable accomplishments in Europe took a century. In 14 developing countries, life expectancy is now 70 years or more—close to the average level (74 years) in industrialized countries.

In 1950, only one-third of the population of LDCs was literate. By 1979, this proportion had risen to 56 percent. The adult literacy rate in the low-income countries rose from 20 percent in 1950 to 52 percent in 1980, and in the middle-income developing countries it rose from 48 percent in 1950 to 65 percent in 1980. The adult literacy rate rose between 1960 and 1980 from 2 to 60 percent in Somalia, from 10 to 79 percent in Tanzania, from 39 to 62 percent in Indonesia, from 39 to 63 percent in Bolivia, from 38 to 60 percent in Turkey, and from 54 to 82 percent in Taiwan.

From 1960 to 1980, the percentage of primary school age children attending school rose from 75 percent of boys to nearly 100 percent in middle-income countries, and from 80 to 93 percent in low-income countries. The number enrolled in secondary schools rose from 14 to 39 percent in middle-income countries, and from 18 to 29 percent in low-income countries.

Many nations can claim achievements in their struggle against poverty. The success stories have been written in a variety of ways. Some examples of successful performance can be illustrated by the newly industrializing countries of East Asia, the export-led development of the Ivory Coast, foodgrain self-sufficiency in India, the basic needs program of China and Sri Lanka, and the progress in Malawi.

South Korea's Achievement

When the Korean War ended, South Korea was left with a half-economy in ruins—a subsistence economy with 60 percent of its cultivated land laid waste, most of its limited industrial capacity destroyed, and more than a fourth of its population homeless refugees. The country had fewer natural resources and a higher population density than Holland, the literacy rate was only 30 percent, in 1961 per capita income was about $80, manufacturing accounted for less than 10 percent of GNP, and exports were only $41 million. During the following 17 years, 1962–1978, real GNP grew by almost 10 percent per annum, exports in dollar value by more than 40 percent per annum, and industrial production by about 20 percent per annum. By 1978, per capita income was more than $1,000 and exports were above $10 billion. Within a single generation, South Korea had emerged from abject poverty to a modern industrial economy.

A number of poor countries—about 20—have graduated into the category of newly industrializing countries—the NICs. These countries have become semi-industrialized and middle-income countries, with important manufacturing sectors and the substantial export of manufactures. Among the NICs, the gang of four in East Asia—Singapore, Hong Kong, Taiwan, and South Korea—are often cited as unique success stories for having managed to combine high rates of growth with a high degree of equality in income distribution and a rapid expansion of employment.

Korea's achievement is instructive. During the 1950s, American foreign aid to Korea, averaging approximately 15 percent of Korea's GNP, allowed modest growth in GNP, but was more important in helping control inflation, in supporting political stability, and in increasing Korea's stock of both physical and human capital. The level of human resources—measured by literacy rate and education—became exceptional for a country at Korea's low per capita income level. As the economy grew in the 1960s, foreign aid was able to be replaced by an increase in domestic savings and foreign exchange earnings.

Since the 1960s, GNP growth in Korea averaged more than 10 percent per year (at constant prices), thereby doubling real national income every seven years. Only Korea, Taiwan, Singapore, and Japan belong to the record group of countries that has achieved more than 10 percent a year growth in national output for more than a decade. Per capita income rose from $160 in 1950 to more than $1,300 in 1981 (in 1975 dollars). At the same time, the distribution of income has been among the more equal distributions in the developing world. A far-reaching land reform program in the late 1940s produced a relatively egalitarian distribution of assets. The export-led development strategy has also been employment intensive, favoring a more equal distribution of income. The share of the top 20 percent of income recipients compared to the lowest 20 percent has been about 8:1, a much lower differential than in most of the developing countries. The differential between rural and urban incomes has also been much lower than in most developing countries. Employment expanded rapidly, with labor-intensive production allowing employment to grow at more than 3.5 percent per annum. And the real wages of workers doubled every decade.

This remarkable growth record was achieved by the combination of a set of appropriate governmental policies and indigenous efforts that took advantage of the high level of human resources and a favorable external environment. Labor absorption was encouraged by relatively low wages compared with productivity, the absence of bias against labor-intensive products or processes, a well-educated and achievement-oriented labor force, and industrial discipline. Labor was absorbed into industry at a rate exceeding 10 percent a year—one of the highest rates ever recorded in any country.

In the early 1960s, the government changed the industrialization strategy from an inward-looking, import substitution strategy to the promotion of export of manufactures. Tax concessions and subsidies were given as incentives to exporters. The foreign exchange rate was changed in conformity with home-to-foreign price movements, and the periodic devaluations of the domestic currency (the won) kept Korean exports internationally competitive. Restrictive monetary and fiscal policies also restrained inflation. Policies to support the attainment of export targets were announced and maintained with sufficient stability and certainty to induce investment in the export sector. As a set, the government's policies liberalized the foreign trade regime to make it as attractive to produce for the export market as for the home market.

Other governmental policies were deliberately chosen to improve the allocation of resources. Price distortions were removed and prices were brought closer to a reflection of real costs. Interest rates were raised to check inflation, to stimulate savings, and to stretch the use of capital. From 1958 to 1962, the domestic saving rate was actually negative but, by 1976, almost a quarter of national income was being saved and invested; in 1981, the proportion was up to 30 percent. For many years the absolute increase in investment has been greater than the increase in consumption. The efficiency of investment has also increased, with better utilization of capital.

The Korean strategy has succeeded in making Korea an outstanding case of export-led industrialization. Exports have risen from only 3.3 percent of GNP in 1960 to nearly 50 percent. From 1960 to 1975, exports rose at the remarkable rate of 30 percent per annum, at constant prices. The share of exports in gross manufacturing output was nil in 1955, 6 percent in 1965, and more than 40 percent in the mid-1970s. In the decade 1965–1975, the ratio of exports to GNP more than trebled. Total exports grew from $1.7 billion (current prices) in 1972, to $7 billion in 1976 (1975 prices), and to $15 billion in 1981 (1975 prices). Manufactured exports came to account for almost 90 percent of exports and became more and more diversified—ranging from the initial growth of exports in textiles, clothing, and plywood to transport equipment, electrical machinery and appliances, and various manufactures of metal and nonmetallic minerals. Export growth has clearly accounted for an increasingly large proportion of the growth in total production, and the export growth became more important than even growth in domestic demand.

Since Korea has now reached a stage of development about where Japan was only 20 years ago, it is not surprising that comparisons are made between Korea's and Japan's course of industrial development. To many observers of the development process, the Korean achievement is a lesson in the pursuit of appropriate policies, a capacity to administer, and a political commitment to growth reflected in the stability of policies.[1]

Taiwan's Development Success

In undertaking a development strategy similar to Korea's, Taiwan has achieved a growth rate higher than any other country (except possibly Japan) and a greater degree of income equality than any of the developing economies. Many economists would interpret Taiwan's record as the most successful of the developing countries.

At the start of its development effort in the early 1950s, Taiwan was the world's second most densely populated country (after Bangladesh), with increasing population pressure on the land, of which only a quarter was arable. Two decades later, Taiwan's per capita income had tripled, the country had undergone a structural transformation from primary production to manufacturing, and had moved from being a labor-abundant to a labor-scarce country with a marked upward trend in real wages in manufacturing. At the same time, absolute poverty had been removed, the distribution of income had become more equal, and employment had expanded rapidly.

As in Korea, a set of appropriate policies was fundamental to Taiwan's success. During the 1950–1960 decade, fiscal and tight money policies were introduced to reduce inflation. The policy of high real interest rates was especially effective in encouraging domestic savings and the use of labor-intensive methods of production. From about 5 percent of national income in the 1950s, Taiwan's domestic savings rose to over 30 percent by the mid-1970s. Since the mid-1960s, Taiwan has been able to finance its entire gross domestic capital formation out of domestic savings.

Agricultural policies also promoted land reform measures that supported small farms, intensive cultivation, technological innovation, and institutional change. Agricultural output grew at the exceptionally high rate of 4.4 percent annually between 1954 and 1967. The productivity of agricultural labor increased at 6.6 percent a year during the 1960s, compared with 4.9 percent during the 1950s. These gains allowed the prices of foodstuffs to remain low, despite the pattern of rapid industrialization. The farm laborer's average wage was never substantially below the average urban wage, and the gap was eventually eliminated. Small landholders also had good opportunities for off-farm rural earnings. By 1980, almost three-quarters of the income of rural families came from nonagricultural income. In the decade 1966–1976, the percentage of the labor force employed on farms declined from over 43 percent to 29 percent.[2]

Taiwan followed policies of import substitution of nondurable consumer goods for only a short initial period (1953–1961) and then only in a moderate way. Beginning in the early 1960s, Taiwan shifted its strategy for industrial development from the domestic market to international markets. The foreign trade sector was stimulated by a number of policy measures designed to liberalize restrictions on imports, to make it equally attractive to produce for the export market as for the home market, to encourage the employment of the abundant labor supply, and to improve Taiwan's competitive position in world markets by maintaining a realistic exchange rate and restraining domestic inflation.

Deliberate policies of export promotion have supported export-led industrial expansion, and Taiwan's exports, valued in U.S. dollars, grew at an average annual rate of 27 percent during the period between 1965 and 1981. Manufactured exports (textiles, electronics) rose at a rate of nearly 30 percent a year, and the composition of exports was transformed from traditional primary exports of rice and sugar at the outset of the development program to 90 percent manufactured exports. Although industrial exports accounted for only 10 percent of total exports in 1952, they were 50 percent in 1962 and more than 80 percent by 1972. The ratio of exports to GNP rose from less than 10 percent in the early 1950s to nearly 40 percent in the early 1970s, and it is now nearly 55 percent—one of the highest in the world.

The rapid growth in manufactured exports supported the fast expansion of manufacturing production and the rise of manufacturing employment, doubling every seven years. In spite of high rates of population growth, the reserve of surplus labor was absorbed in productive employment by the end of the 1960s, and real wages began to increase at an accelerated rate. By 1971, full employment was achieved. Between 1961 and 1976, employment increased by 2.3 million persons, which was equivalent to 60 percent of the 1961 employment—a remarkable increase. Through the expansion of domestic and export markets, employment was able to grow twice as fast as population, at the high annual rate of 4.8 percent from 1965 to 1981.

Income distribution in Taiwan is much less unequal than in other developing countries and, according to statistics, is probably the most egalitarian of all capitalist countries. There has been a favorable change in nationwide income distribution ever since the development process accelerated. The ratio of the income share of the richest 20 percent of the population to that of the poorest 20 percent fell from 20.47 in 1953 to 4.18 in 1980. The share of wage income in the national income increased from about 40 percent in 1951 to over 60 percent in 1979. The share of property income dropped accordingly. This has been the result of a great increase in the earnings of labor and the relatively rapid rate of employment generation for members of the lower income groups, initially, and the rise in their wages in later years. As the economy grew, unskilled labor became relatively more scarce in terms of the reduction in its excess supply, and the wage rate of unskilled labor rose more rapidly than that of skilled labor. The gap in income between farm and nonfarm families was also restrained by an increasing share of off-farm income in the total income received by farm families.

Taiwan's emphasis on growth through export expansion together with its development of a labor-intensive agricultural sector and promotion of labor-intensive manufacturing yielded remarkable structural change and "growth with equity."

The Strategy of the Ivory Coast

While Korea, Taiwan, Hong Kong, and Singapore have demonstrated the success of export-led growth in manufacturing, the Ivory Coast has achieved remarkable growth in exports of primary products. By 1975, its exports of cocoa, coffee, and timber were, respectively, 4, 5, and 30 times the 1950 exports in volume. The Ivory Coast now ranks third among world coffee and cocoa producers. Between 1958 and 1967, export earnings grew at a compound rate of 10 percent annually. Commodity exports averaged as much as 35 percent of national income in 1970–1975.

And yet, when the Ivory Coast became independent from France in 1960, with a per capita income of around $70, it was among the poorest of nations. By 1976, income per head had reached $680. Over the period 1960–1975, the real growth in national output averaged a remarkable 7.5 percent per annum. Real income per capita increased by 3.6 percent over the same period. Over the last two decades, gross domestic investment grew by more than 13 percent a year, reaching more than 30 percent of national income in 1979.

After independence in 1960, the outward-oriented development strategy underlying the "Ivorian miracle" was based on a deliberate policy decision by the government to promote the export-oriented agricultural sector and utilize foreign capital and know-how. Exports grew by nearly 9 percent a year during the 1960s and over 5 percent a year in the 1970s. An inflow of managerial and skilled labor was encouraged, mainly from France. Political stability and the government's steady commitment to growth attracted capital and labor from abroad. Sixty-five thousand French people now live in the Ivory Coast—four times as many as at independence.

Agriculture was encouraged through public investment in infrastructure and by direct incentives to production, especially the maintenance of relatively high and stable producer prices for the main agricultural products. Continued efforts toward agricultural diversification gave the Ivory Coast a clear advantage in the production of coffee, cocoa, oil palm products, copra, pineapple, and bananas. It has also become economically feasible to produce cotton, groundnuts, rice, and maize.

The central government has provided incentives for agricultural production through favorable trade and other taxes, officially regulated producer and consumer prices, credit policies, general extension services, and a publicly financed infrastructure. Specialized governmental institutions operating in the agricultural sector also influenced output and input prices, granted credit on favorable terms, and provided subsidies. The main policies have been to support farmers with reasonable and stable prices, keep wages in agriculture relatively low, create an efficient organizational structure, and promote employment in agriculture.

Policies have been effective in encouraging the growth in production of both industrial crops and food crops. Farmers have responded positively to price signals and incentives transmitted through market forces. Industrial crops grew by 5 percent a year between 1965 and 1976, at the same time as diversification continued. Food crop production grew about 3 percent a year in 1965–1970, and by 4 percent in 1970–1975, surpassing the most optimistic forecasts of government policymakers. From 1965 to 1975, the rural population increased 27 percent, but produced 42 percent more food, and imports of foodstuffs declined. In spite of the marked growth in the urban population and the rise in per capita incomes, the sizable increase in the marketed surplus from rural food producers allowed the country to become less dependent on food imports.

The government has also attempted to use agricultural development as a basis for more industrial development. Because of an increase in population, greater productivity in agriculture, and education that provides higher skills, jobs have to be created outside agriculture. The government has therefore encouraged industries based on local raw materials, and it has attempted to shift the emphasis from import-substituting industries to the export-oriented processing of local raw materials. The result has been rapid industrial development to support the strategy of outward-looking growth.

The Ivory Coast's success represents a strong case in support of the focus on peasant agriculture, the potentials of a diversified agricultural export sector, a reliance on the private sector for a directly productive activity, and the use of foreign resources in aid flows, technical assistance, and private foreign investment.

Self-sufficiency in India—A Foodgrain Policy

On the stroke of midnight on 14th August, 1947, the Tricolour was hoisted to the strains of the national anthem. India became independent.

The monsoon night was starless but aglow with the brilliant illuminations below. Every man, woman and child was out to witness the supreme, historic moment and the air was filled with jubilant cries of *Jai Hind!"*

An elemental force had burst its confines and swept like a flood across the land. Would it also wash away the cobwebs, the inertia and deadness of centuries? Would it create overnight a brave new country in which everything would be perfect? Anything seemed possible.

Next morning, the sun rose in the sky to reveal the same squalor, the staggering poverty and hunger, the deep inequalities as the day before. Myriads of flowers, yellow and orange marigolds and pink rose petals, lay scattered on the ground, stale, scentless, trampled.

The municipal sweepers came and swept the streets, and the blossoms mingled in the dust.

An age and a journey had ended. In the same moment, however, another had begun.

Of the momentous events in the decade following independence, perhaps one of the most important in the long term perspective was the decision of the Indian Government to direct and regulate the pattern and tempo of future economic development in the country by state planning, followed by a declaration by the Indian Parliament, in December 1954, that the broad objective of economic policy should be to achieve a "socialist pattern of society."

The central objective of planning in India at the present stage was defined in the First Plan: "to initiate a process of development which will raise living standards and open out to the people new opportunities for a richer and more varied life." The problem of development of an under-developed economy is one of utilizing more effectively the potential resources available to the community, and it is this which involves economic planning. But the economic condition of a country at any given time is a product of the broader social environment. . . .

The basic problem, therefore, of how to bring about rapid change in a people's social and economic values, within the framework of democratic planning, remains. It requires fresh thinking, and is a challenge to the government, the politicians, the social scientists and the economists engaged in planning in India. It is a difficult problem. But it should not be an impossible one. Given the will, there seems to be no reason why it should not be possible to tackle it.

So wrote Kusum Nair in 1961 in her book entitled *Blossoms in the Dust*. Her skepticism was widely shared. And since independence, India's population has doubled. The country is now responsible for 15 percent of the world's population, second only to China, with a projected increase of 1 million people per month for the next 20 years, reaching a population of 1 billion by the year 2000. More than three-quarters of the people still live in rural areas, in about 600,000 villages. Food production is obviously of paramount concern.

In the past, food production has been a major bottleneck in the development process, droughts have produced famine and soaring food prices, and scarce foreign exchange has had to be spent on food imports. In the early 1970s, India was importing over 10 million tons of grain each year.

By the second half of the 1970s, however, yields in wheat and rice had expanded so much that it allowed India to be nearly self-sufficient in these crops. In the northwest part of India, which accounts for about 90 percent of the nation's marketable surplus of wheat and over 60 percent of the marketable rice, the output of these grains tripled between the mid-1960s and the late-1970s. Dispelling not only the earlier fears of pessimists but also surpassing the expectations of even the optimists, India has managed to achieve near self-sufficiency in foodgrains.

How has this been done? By 1961, new high-yielding varieties of dwarf wheats from Mexico and rice varieties from Taiwan had been imported and tested under Indian conditions. Two severe droughts in 1965–1966 and 1966–1967 reduced foodgrain production by millions of tons and led the Indian government to react to the crisis with a "New Strategy of Agricultural Development."

The key elements of the New Strategy were widespread introduction of the new high-yielding varieties, a package of complementary farm inputs adapted to local conditions, incentive prices to farmers, as well as programs in research, extension, and rural credit. Within a year, foodgrain production rose almost 10 percent above the previous record output. By 1974–1975, high-yielding varieties were sown on 62 percent of the total wheat area and on 30 percent of the total rice area. This rapid spread of the new technology exceeded even the spread of hybrid corn in the American Midwest.

The government pursued a number of supporting policies: land consolidation programs that resulted in contiguous small-farmer holdings with established tenure, the building of roads to link villages and market towns, the deregulation of the distribution of fertilizer, minimum procurement prices, and a provision of credit for small farmers. As a "package," the policies had physical, technical, logistical, and economic dimensions. Together the policies allowed the farmer to expect higher net income from the adoption of the new varieties. Production costs per ton were comparable to those for older varieties, but the new varieties produced 50 percent higher yields with the application of modern inputs. Although larger farmers were the first adopters of the new practices, small farmers and tenants soon followed.

The way in which India rode out the 1979 drought demonstrated how much progress had been made. Because of the drought, the 1979–1980 foodgrain production fell 17 percent below the 1978–1979 record level. In the 1966 drought, when foodgrain production dropped by a comparable amount, there was severe and widespread famine and dislocation followed by foodgrain price increases of about 30 percent, notwithstanding foodgrain imports of over 10 million tons. In 1980, however, instead of becoming a comparable international disaster, the similar drop in production resulted in hardship but there was no widespread famine, foodgrain prices increased only about 17 percent, and the government still managed to export about half a million tons of grain. During 1980, the government was able to increase the amount of foodgrains available for consumption to about 114 million tons, about 5 million tons more than what would have been available from that year's production alone. It did this by distributing almost 15 million tons of grain through public channels.

Efforts are continuing to ensure that higher production is sustained and that the gains are extended to other foodstuffs and other irrigated regions. The foodgrain production target of the Sixth Plan is ambitious but technically feasible to a growth rate of 3.8 percent per year.

India's achievement in approaching self-sufficiency in foodgrains is important in its own right, but it also has other favorable consequences. The government can promote diversification of crops as per acre yields increase: more production of oilseeds may reduce the need to import edible oil, sugar cane may be cultivated for domestic needs and even possibly for export, and cotton might also become a valuable export item. Potential surpluses of foodgrains would also allow exports of foodgrains, if prices are competitive with world market prices, or lower foodgrain prices may allow increased consumption and diversification into nonfoodgrain crops. Expansion of the agricultural sector will also stimulate the industrial sector, directly through an increased demand for industrial products and indirectly through the saving of foreign exchange that might allow liberalization of imported inputs for industry. Beyond feeding the world's second largest population, India's achievement in foodgrain production has widespread significance for the economy's development effort.

China and Sri Lanka—Fulfilling Basic Human Needs

What does it profit a nation to gain an increase in its GNP if its poorest inhabitants are still unable to fulfill their basic human needs? A few countries have chosen to concentrate during their early phases of development on meeting needs in nutrition, education, health, shelter, water, and sanitation. And some have achieved this without a trade-off between growth and basic needs. China and Sri Lanka are notable examples—and so again are Taiwan and South Korea—all countries that have managed to achieve above average improvements in basic needs accompanied by above average growth rates in GNP. The achievement resulted from calculated and determined public policy in China and Sri Lanka, countries among the poorer countries in a list of developing countries.

China's most remarkable achievement during the past three decades has been to make low-income groups far better off in terms of basic needs than their counterparts in most other poor countries. They all have employment. Whether voluntarily or not, the labor pool has been mobilized so that both urban and rural populations are hard at work throughout the entire year. Agricultural land resources have also been fully mobilized, and three-fourths of the labor force are members of rural communes, brigades, and teams. No longer is there a large class of destitute peasants without land and without employment opportunities. Inequalities in income have been narrowed, to a greater extent than in other developing countries (although significant differences in urban-rural incomes remain).

The food supply is guaranteed through a mixture of state rationing and collective self-insurance. Public distribution systems introduced the rationing of basic necessities at relatively low prices, and the rations favor those performing the most strenuous work. In urban areas, staple foods have been rationed at very low prices with monthly entitlements that vary with age, sex, and occupation, but which provide for an adequate level of consumption. In rural areas, the government has guaranteed to sell enough grain to households to fill any gap between the amount of grain distributed as income in kind by their production team and a floor level of grain per person per year. The food rationing system has eliminated acute malnutrition, a contributing cause of between one-third and two-thirds of all child deaths in other developing countries.

Most of the children are in school and are being comparatively well taught. Widespread primary education, especially of women, has also contributed to improved nutrition and health practices in child-rearing.

Life expectancy—reflecting many other social and economic variables—has risen over the past three decades from 36 years to nearly 69 years, an exceptionally rapid advance to an outstanding figure for a country at China's low per capita income level. The dramatic decline in the death rate has given the Chinese a life expectancy that would be expected only of a country with several times its per capita income. The infant mortality rate of 56 per 1,000 contrasts with the 100 to 200 deaths in other low-income countries. The causes of death in China are now comparable to those in the more developed countries.

China's success in reducing mortality is related to its success with population control that has facilitated higher nutritional and environmental health standards. The attainment of greatly improved nutrition levels has undoubtedly promoted better health. China's massive efforts to provide access to regular water supplies and hygenic sanitary facilities have also contributed to the reduction of mortality.

By controlling infectious and parasitic diseases, China's health service has played a dominant role in reducing mortality. Its health policy strongly emphasizes preventive measures and the improvement of the general health environment. China has devoted a substantial amount of resources to promoting public preventive services over curative health services. The fame of China's barefoot doctors and public health workers in cooperative medical stations attests to the widespread diffusion of basic curative care and the mass participation in the health delivery system. A clinical referral system provides at least minimal access to curative care for most of the population, and the ratio of population to medical personnel is exceptionally favorable for a poor country. Rising incomes, expanding basic education, the food distribution policy, and the improving water supply and sanitation have all contributed indirectly to the program for better health. The fields of health and education have both had a pro-rural bias, reaching the poorest of the massive rural population. The virtual universal coverage is unique.

China has succeeded in effectively fulfilling minimum needs for all through a variety of measures that have raised entitlements so that poverty can be eradicated. At the same time as minimum needs have been fulfilled, China's economy has managed to grow at a rate above the average of developing countries: over 6 percent in the aggregate and about 4 percent for income per head between 1952 and 1978.

If China represents the achievement of basic needs of its people through a planned economy, Sri Lanka represents the achievement in a private enterprise economy within a democratic society using welfare intervention by the government. Although income per capita is less than $200 a year, life expectancy in Sri Lanka is 69 years (up from 43 years in 1946), almost 85 percent of the adult population is literate (up from 58 percent in 1946), almost 90 percent of children ages 5 to 14 are enrolled in school (up from 41 percent in 1946), infant mortality per 1,000 is down to 46 (compared with 141 in 1946), and the death rate per 1,000 is 7.7 (compared with 19.8 in 1946). These values are far better than would be expected for such a poor country.

The reduction of mortality has followed dramatically from antimalaria campaigns, the spread of maternity care, and the widespread medical coverage of the population through primary health care facilities staffed by paramedical workers and a strong backup referral system of clinics and hospitals. The low mortality statistics also indicate that the relatively equitable distribution of foodgrains, based on the government's food ration and subsidy program, has allowed Sri Lanka to avoid the high degree of malnutrition-related deaths common in most low-income countries. Although subsidy programs can be very expensive and mismanaged, Sri Lanka has focused foodgrain subsidies on the poorest who need them, avoiding disincentive effects on agricultural production.

Education has been promoted by high expenditures, with high enrollment rates at all levels of education, and priority has been given to the education of women. If women are educated, many benefits follow—good nutrition practices, preventive health care and family planning, even the transmission to children of changes in values. The improvement in education has carried over to the fulfillment of other basic needs. Literacy, for instance, has an important impact on life expectancy and infant mortality, since literacy increases the knowledge and ability to screen and evaluate new information about home hygiene and other health and nutrition practices. The rising rate of literacy has also had other favorable effects—from raising rice yields by increasing the utilization of improved agricultural practices to contributing to lower fertility rates by increasing life expectancy and the expectation that children will survive into adulthood.

Students of Sri Lanka's economy have concluded that the basic needs program has actually contributed to growth. With less progress in health and education, Sri Lanka would have worse current prospects for growth in per capita income: population growth would be higher, and the labor force less educated and less healthy. In the first half of the 1970s, Sri Lanka's social expenditures were approximately $15 per capita per year, split about equally between the food subsidy program and social services. The $15 overstates costs of direct basic-needs programs because it includes both benefits to those basic needs that have already been substantially met and social programs with objectives other than basic needs, such as higher education. But even the $15 figure is not high by the standards of domestic poverty programs in aid-donor countries, or even by the standards of donor-funded development projects in poor countries. Because Sri Lanka has accomplished more in meeting basic needs than most countries with three or four times its per capita income and appears to have average or better growth prospects, its achievement certainly merits attention.

Tanzania is another country with remarkable achievement in literacy. The raising of the adult literacy rate from under 10 percent in the early 1960s to about 79 percent by 1980 is a historically unique record. In 1970, the government announced a national literacy program to eradicate illiteracy by the end of 1975. The government also set a target of universal primary education. The majority of the instructors for the adult literacy campaign were volunteers, responding to the call for the removal of illiteracy. By the summer of 1975, 90 percent of the estimated number of illiterates were in fact enrolled in the program. During the short period between 1967 and 1975, the effective literacy rate doubled.

Although they represent different types of economies and different sociopolitical environments, the examples of China's mitigation of absolute poverty, Sri Lanka's program of social welfare, and Tanzania's literacy program all illustrate how much can be achieved by determined public effort, sensibly directed toward specific goals. Under diverse circumstances, the governments have successfully removed particular aspects of poverty and deprivation by deliberate public policy.

Malawi's Progress

Few, if any, of the development economists at the Nyasaland Symposium in 1962 would have predicted the achievements that were to be realized during the next decade and a half by the new nation of Malawi.[3] The Honorable Dr. H. Kamuzu Banda had wanted to bring economists to see a typically underdeveloped country, a poor country. And mass poverty was certainly to be seen. With political independence at hand, the country was to inherit problems of a colonial history and limited human, physical, and financial resources.

At independence, the country had fewer than 1,000 individuals who had completed a secondary education (about two-thirds of them only since 1961); there were only 16 African teachers with a few years of schooling; over 50 percent of the teachers were from the Peace Corps; only about 30 Africans had any type of postsecondary education; there were only three African doctors (including Dr. Banda?), one African engineer, one African agricultural officer, and no African geologists or surveyors. An ambitious development program was to be launched without experienced African administrators, technicians, or entrepreneurs.

The handicaps were many and as severe as in any newly independent country. Landlocked with no significant natural resources, very little infrastructure, no transportation network, and no banking and financial sector, the economy had advanced little beyond the stage of subsistence agriculture. Nearly 95 percent of the population was in agriculture. Aside from a few plantations, agricultural production was confined to traditional subsistence agriculture by small holders. Only a minority of the population derived cash income from the sale of their own produce. Most were self-employed in small-scale agriculture, growing in their gardens their own food requirements with a small surplus of cash crops for sale (maize, tobacco, cotton, groundnuts, and rice).

The smallholders offered their labor for varying periods in wage employment on tea and tobacco estates, but domestic employment opportunities were extremely limited. Only about 130,000 Africans were in wage employment. Almost 250,000 migrant workers were being attracted, however, to employment under contract in the mines and plantations of South Africa, Northern Rhodesia (Zambia), and Southern Rhodesia (Zimbabwe). Manufacturing output was only about 5 percent of national output. The domestic market was very narrow with a population of under 4 million (a guess, since no census of Africans existed), but the population was dense and rapidly growing. Fertility and mortality rates were extremely high.

Per capita income was only $60 in 1964. Gross national saving was actually negative (the country was spending more on consumption than it earned from production). Investment was only about 8 percent of national income. Imports amounted to nearly one-third of national income, but exports were less than one-fifth.

Government revenue was low, amounting to only a fraction of government expenditures, and had to be supplemented by British budgetary grant aid (covering nearly half of total government expenditure at independence).

What the economists would call the country's "initial conditions" were scarcely auspicious for development. And yet the new government declared that it had

> every intention of pursuing a vigorously expansionist policy aimed at increasing agricultural productivity [and] to provide the basis on which a simultaneous growth of industry may take place in partnership with foreign capital. . . . To balance the economy and to raise living standards is the challenging task for the new Malawi nation. In facing the responsibilities that independence has brought, the Malawi government has the incalculable advantage of the enthusiastic and united support of the entire country which has manifested itself not only at the polls but in the numerous self-help schemes that are being carried out all over the country.

Two decades later, many of the expectations have been translated into substantial achievements. The growth rate in real national income has been among the highest of any country—7.5 percent a year between 1964 and 1975, and even as high as 6.1 percent between 1970 and 1980 when stagnation and the energy crisis markedly lowered the growth rates elsewhere. GNP per capita rose from approximately $60 at independence to over $200 in recent years, growing at a rate of about 4 percent per year at constant prices. This rate has been considerably above the average for developing countries. Domestic investment as a percentage of national income increased from only 8 percent at independence to nearly 30 percent in 1979. At the same time, from negative domestic savings at independence, gross domestic savings have risen to nearly 20 percent of national income. The government's expenditure on its development budget rose from about Malawi Kwacha (K) 5 million in 1964 to almost K 150 million in 1979–1980. Although all of the capital accumulation in Malawi at independence was being financed from external capital inflows, almost 60 percent of the investment was being financed from domestic savings by 1979.

Much more of the economy has been monetized, and subsistence agriculture now amounts to less than 30 percent of national output. Wage employment grew between 1968 and 1978 by nearly 9 percent a year—one of the fastest growth rates for employment recorded anywhere. The volume of exports tripled from the early 1960s to the mid-1970s. Even during the slowdown in the world economy, export volume grew by an annual 14.6 percent rate during the 1970s.

How was this progress achieved? Primarily, the appropriate policies pursued by a stable government strongly committed to growth were responsible. A high rate of growth was considered necessary not only to increase employment and incomes, but also to yield foreign exchange earnings, domestic savings, and government revenue for additional capital accumulation and further growth. The growth strategy was agro-based and export oriented. Governmental policies also supported a market orientation, avoided price distortions and inflation, and took advantage of international market opportunities.

The cornerstone of the government's development program has been the development of the agricultural sector—the sector that employs most of the population and accounts for 90 percent of export earnings. Emphasizing the priority of agriculture, Dr. Banda became not only the President, but also the Minister of Natural Resources. The government's aims in agriculture have been to maintain self-sufficiency in food and to expand agricultural exports.

Farming methods of the small holders are extremely labor intensive, with the majority of farmers working with simple hand tools such as hoes, knives, or axes. The use of work oxen or ox carts is still rare. To increase the supply of food staples, the government provided agricultural inputs and farm services and began a number of rural development programs in the small holder subsector. To expand agricultural exports of tobacco, tea, and sugar from the estate subsector, the government provided a favorable investment climate and restrained wage increases to maintain the competitiveness of Malawi's exports in world markets.

The general approach has concentrated on a gradual improvement of extension, land husbandry, and farmer-training services throughout the country, supported by small rural development programs in four specific areas that encompass 20 percent of Malawi's population. These projects have provided infrastructure (roads, markets, water, and health facilities), supported land improvement and conservation measures, improved extension and other services, and instituted credit facilities. One such comprehensive program—the Lilongwe Land Development Program—involves a 13-year development program for 1.2 million acres. The benefits from the project are expected to include an increase in farm family income, an exportable surplus, increased government revenues and taxes, the establishment of a commercially oriented and stable pattern of agriculture, and the formation of a corps of experienced development officers.

Since the mid-1970s, emphasis has shifted from the intensive and costly capital investments characteristic of the earlier major projects to a program of agricultural services that benefit smallholders over the entire country in order to improve the productivity of already cultivated areas. Special attention is given to extension services, adaptive research, input supply, marketing, and credit services. The government has become more and more aware that adequate price incentives, improved techniques to raise yields on the limited supply of arable land, and supplies of consumer goods in rural areas are necessary to provide incentives for the sale of cash crops on the market.

Much of the economy's growth has depended on the rise in exports of tobacco, tea, and sugar from the estates—from less than K 10 million in 1964 to over K 150 million in recent years. The output from estates has expanded in real terms at the exceptionally high annual compound growth rate of more than 17 percent since independence. Accounting for 70 percent of Malawi's exports, the expansion of the estate subsector has been an important source of income growth, foreign exchange earnings, and employment. Between 1966 and 1977, almost 350,000 migrant workers returned from South Africa, Zambia, Mozambique, and Zimbabwe—equivalent to 15 percent of the economically active population in 1977. The returning migrants were successfully reabsorbed in the rapidly growing estate sector. Employment on estates more than tripled during the 1970s and now provides about 45 percent of the country's total wage employment. The advantages of appropriate soil, climate, high yields, and cheap labor

have enabled Malawi to be highly competitive in producing tobacco and tea for export.

The agricultural program has taken advantage of the relatively
abundant labor supply while economizing on the scarce factors
of capital and foreign exchange. Unlike many other developing
countries, Malawi has not subsidized inefficient, high-priced,
import-replacement industries. The government avoided sad-
dling agriculture with a high-cost parasitic industrial sector that
would have taxed agriculture through the higher cost of inputs
and the higher cost of consumer goods. Nor did the government
maintain an overvalued exchange rate that would have made it
more difficult to export.

The avoidance of an excessive differential between urban and
rural incomes has also minimized the rural-urban migration and
has not been a disincentive to agricultural production. Malawi's
National Wages and Salaries Policy introduced an incomes policy aimed at constraining wages to encourage the expansion of
labor-absorbing manufacturing firms and agricultural estates, to
restrain inflation and maintain Malawi's competitiveness in world
markets, and to moderate the rural-urban income gap. The government has held the line on urban wages and wages in the public
sector while increasing rural welfare through projects that raised
the productivity of subsistence agriculture and through the expansion of estate employment. This restrained the amount of
rural-urban migration. Nor did urban wages outstrip productivity so much so that they would lead to higher prices on manufactured goods vis-à-vis agricultural products.

The wage policy has also had a favorable effect in encouraging
labor-intensive industries and labor-intensive techniques of production. The increases in wage employment have been remark-
ably high in relation to increases in domestic output. Wage employment throughout the economy has increased at a faster rate
than the increase in the real value of domestic output. The increases in agricultural estate employment and manufacturing have
been especially high, indicating success in promoting labor-intensive patterns of production. Private-sector employment has
grown at a much faster rate than that of government.

The private sector has been encouraged. The government's expenditure program has been directed mainly toward sectors and

activities outside the realm of private enterprise—to smallholder agriculture, infrastructure, public utilities, and social services. Estate agriculture and manufacturing have been left to private enterprise. In the absence of local entrepreneurship at independence, the government created a hospitable environment for foreign investors. Foreign capital and management were attracted by the low wages in Malawi, liberal trade and external payments policies, moderate tax levels, and various incentives that included exemption from customs duties for imported materials used in manufacturing and capital allowances for tax purposes. There has, however, been an attempt to increase the local participation in foreign enterprise. Through the government-owned Malawi Development Corporation, the government has promoted greater Malawian financial and managerial participation in the private sector. The government has also bought out parts of foreign-owned estates for settlement by Malawians, and the number of locally owned tobacco estates has expanded rapidly.

Although not heavily protected or subsidized, the manufacturing sector has grown at a high rate parallel to the agriculture-oriented development strategy. Since independence, the manufacturing sector has expanded at an annual average rate of nearly 10 percent, increasing its share in domestic output from about 5 percent to 12 percent. Agroindustrial processing (food, tobacco, tea, and sugar processing) accounts for a large proportion of industry. The growth in manufacturing output has been matched by that in employment, indicating a labor-intensive pattern in manufacturing.

The government's budgetary position also improved from independence until the mid-1970s. Through increased taxes, better tax collection, and restraint in government spending, the government was able to achieve a balance on its revenue account by 1973 and to do without foreign budgetary support to cover recurrent deficits. Over the period 1967–1980, government revenue increased somewhat faster than the growth in total domestic output.

At the same time that investment has become a larger share of national income, a greater proportion of the investment has been financed from domestic savings with less reliance on foreign capital. Between 1967 and 1969, gross national savings were sufficient to cover only about 7 percent of domestic investment, and most of the capital formation had to be financed from foreign sources. In recent years, private-sector savings have financed over 90 percent of private-sector investment, and public enterprises have been able to self-finance about 60 percent of their own investment programs.

Although there have been current account deficits in Malawi's balance of payments, these deficits relative to domestic output declined from about 7 percent in the mid-1960s to about 4 percent in the mid-1970s. Through 1977, net capital inflows were more than sufficient to cover the current account deficits, allowing Malawi in those years to build up its official foreign reserve holdings. Until recent years, most of Malawi's external debt was owed to multilateral and bilateral agencies on relatively soft terms—low interest charges with long grace and repayment periods. Debt service payments as a percentage of export revenue were only 7 percent in 1977.

The country's exceptional political stability has also allowed the government to pursue its policies in a decisive manner ever since independence. His Excellency, the Life President, H. Kamuzu Banda, as head of the only political party, has enjoyed the power to appoint and dismiss cabinet ministers and all civil servants. All citizens are expected to participate in the development effort, and Dr. Banda's personal leadership rallied support in keeping with the traditional African concept of the communal village society. Strong organizational links between central government and district and village levels of operation have also been used to advantage. Considering its pursuit of appropriate policies, the allocation of public investment, and the operation of public enterprise, the government has managed the public sector in a creditable fashion while it has encouraged private enterprise and foreign investment.

Finally, the role of economists in government policymaking is an active one. An Economic Common Service was headed early by a Chief Economist, who is also in charge of the Economic Planning Division in the Office of the President and Cabinet, now staffed by about 50 professional economists. Other economists are in the various ministries, but all communicate through the Economic Common Service. Although not charged with formulating any grand five-year development plan, the Economic Planning Division is closely integrated with the policymaking machinery of other ministries. Economists are looked to for daily analysis and advice. Communication among different ministries is good, and decisions based on economic analysis are made regularly and quickly. The integration of economists into the machinery of government in Malawi is probably the most effective in all of ex-British Black Africa.

As Malawi and many other success stories illustrate, the achievements of development have depended not on a country enjoying favorable initial conditions but on its pursuit of appropriate public policies that take advantage of the opportunities provided by the world economy. At the end of the 1970s, however, small developing economies were extremely vulnerable to external shocks. If a successful development record during the first generation of the development effort was achieved by the combination of appropriate domestic policies and a favorable international environment, the continuance of a strong development momentum during the 1980s will depend not only on appropriate domestic policies, but also on the restoration of a favorable international economic environment and the capacity to adjust rapidly to external shocks when the external environment becomes adverse.

4

Disappointments

The first generation of development economists in the 1950s were optimistic about development prospects. As we have seen, several achievements have vindicated their optimism. But, at the same time, various aspects of the development record have turned out to be disappointing. Especially disconcerting have been the lagging growth of the poorest countries, the unexpected rise in population growth, the failure to reduce the number in absolute poverty, the increasing numbers in unemployment and underemployment, the persistence of inequality in the distribution of income, the sluggish agricultural performance, and the existence of political authoritarianism.

The Poorest Countries

Although the average growth rates in GNP and income per head in the LDCs have exceeded most expectations, the least developed countries have suffered the lowest growth rates. Theirs has not been a record of development but only the deepening pain of poverty.

Among the poorest is Bangladesh—the eighth largest country in the world with one of the highest densities of population. Ninety percent of the population lives in rural areas, and 30 percent of the labor force suffers from unemployment and under-employment. And yet, with a high rate of population growth of about 3 percent, population continues to press on limited resources. During the 1960s (as East Pakistan) per capita income at best stagnated, and during the 1970s it actually declined. The poverty is aggravated by substantial inequality in income distribution: the top 20 percent of the population receives nearly one-half of the national income, and the lowest 20 percent receives only 8 percent. Widespread malnutrition, a high rate of illiteracy, low life expectancy, extremely low rates of saving and investment, large balance-of-payments deficits—all these characterize the country.

As one report on Bangladesh states:

> Constant food shortage and recurrent famine, devastating floods and cyclones, disorder, violence and corruption, an uncontrollable population explosion, failure of government and administration, a malfunctioning economy beset with financial crisis, a begging bowl to the rest of the world. In the face of such a catalogue, what hope is there for Bangladesh?

> In Bangladesh, it is nature not man that is in control. Can man's ascendency be established? Is there hope for Bangladesh? Can population be controlled? Can malnutrition be eliminated and health improved? Can the people of Bangladesh look forward to more in the way of material possessions than a bamboo home, a bed, a chair or two and a few cooking utensils? Are they to be forever deprived of access to the world's knowledge and its application to ameliorating their way of life?

> The outlook is grim, the odds are unfavorable; yet there is a path that Bangladesh could follow to reach the goal of a stable population and a standard of living which offers little in luxury but enough in meeting the fundamental requirements of life to make existence more bearable. . . . If development can be made to succeed in Bangladesh there can be little doubt that it can be made to succeed anywhere else. It is in this sense that Bangladesh is the test case for development.[1]

The countries of Sub-Saharan Africa have also been bypassed. Of the 36 poorest countries in the world, 22 are African. Over the period from 1960 to 1980, per capita income in 19 countries in Sub-Saharan Africa grew by less than 1 percent per year. During the last decade, 15 countries actually suffered a negative rate of growth of income per head. Output per person rose more slowly in Sub-Saharan Africa than in any other part of the world, particularly during the 1970s, and it rose more slowly during the 1970s than the 1960s.

These are small open economies, heavily dependent on agricultural exports. Of the 45 states in the region, 24 have fewer than 5 million people. Only Nigeria has a national income greater than Hong Kong's. In the 1970s, agricultural output per capita declined 1.1 percent per year, and the volume of exports fell by 4.5 percent per year. Food production per person stagnated in the 1960s and actually declined in the 1970s. Adult literacy remains only 26 percent; only 25 percent of the population have access to safe water; the death rates are the highest in the world; life expectancy is the lowest in the world (46 years); and the death rate among African children is 67 percent greater than in South Asia and three times higher than in Latin America.

According to a World Bank report, "Africa's disappointing economic performance during the past two decades reflects, in part, internal constraints based on "structural" factors that evolved from historical circumstances or from the physical environment. These include underdeveloped human resources, the economic disruption that accompanied decolonization and postcolonial consolidation, climatic and geographic factors hostile to development, and a rapidly growing population.

> Growth was also affected by a set of external factors—notably adverse trends in the international economy, particularly since 1974. These include "stagflation" in the industrialized countries, higher energy prices, the relatively slow growth of trade in primary products and—for copper and iron ore exporters— adverse terms of trade.

> The internal "structural" problems and the external factors impeding African economic growth have been exacerbated by domestic policy inadequacies, of which three are critical. First, trade and exchange-rate policies have overprotected industry, held back agriculture, and absorbed much administrative capacity. Second, too little attention has been paid to administra-

tive constraints in mobilizing and managing resources for development; given the widespread weakness of planning, decision making, and management capacities, public sectors frequently become overextended. Third, there has been a consistent bias against agriculture in price, tax, and exchange-rate policies.[2]

Population Growth

Another disappointment has been the unanticipated high rate of population growth in most of the LDCs. Some countries have enjoyed success with family planning programs—countries as diverse as Indonesia, Singapore, Colombia, and China. But the average rate of population growth in developing countries is about 2.2 percent (with a country range from 1 percent to over 3 percent), down somewhat from the 2.4 percent rate of 1960–1965 but considerably higher than the earlier rate of 1.9 percent in the 1950–1955 period. The least developed of the developing countries in Asia and Sub-Saharan Africa have also tended to have the highest population growth rates. Although the population growth has not been the sole cause of their poverty nor the inevitable consequence of the poverty, the future task of emerging from mass poverty would be lightened for these countries if their rates of population growth could be reduced.

Population has grown rapidly because of falling rates of mortality as a consequence of the introduction of new public health technologies while fertility rates have remained high. The result is population growth in the LDCs that is two to three times greater than was typical for the presently developed countries when they were undergoing their industrialization and modernization in the nineteenth century. Today mortality differences between developing and developed countries are much smaller than fertility differences—crude death rates of about 13 and 9 in the developing and developed countries, in contrast to a more than two-to-one ratio for fertility. The demographic transition—the change from high preindustrial birth and death rates to low modern rates—has not yet been reached for most of the LDCs. Fertility is declining slowly in many countries, and with the future improvement in life expectancy the rates of population growth will not fall rapidly. Moreover, because of past high fertility, developing countries have very young-age distributions. When a high proportion of women are in child-bearing ages, even with a rapidly declining fertility a high rate of population increase must still be expected.

When the rate of population growth is between 2 and 3 percent, as in most developing countries, the population doubles every 20 to 35 years. The age structure of the population is also concentrated in young age groups. Whereas the average age of an industrialized population is 35 years, Sub-Saharan Africa's population has an average age of 22 years. In general, in the LDCs about 17 percent of the population is below the age of 5, a little more than a quarter is between 5 and 14, and only a little over one-half is of working age. In contrast, in North America and Europe, less than 8 percent of the population is under 5, only about 17 percent is in the 5 to 14 age bracket, and nearly two-thirds of the population is of working age.

With the younger age structure, the ratio of dependents to workers increases; in the United States there is one dependent for every two potential workers, but in a high-fertility country such as Mexico or Nigeria there is one dependent for every potential worker. This dependency burden may cut into savings as more income is spent in supporting the consumption of the young. In allocating savings into investment, a greater proportion must be allocated to human-resource investments. In education, for instance, over 20 percent of the population of a typical developing country is of primary school age compared with 10 percent in a developed country. Growth in the school age population—doubling in most Latin American countries, for example, every 20 years—requires more educational investment, or else smaller educational inputs per enrolled child, or lower enrollment ratios.

The employment problem is clearly intensified when population is growing more rapidly. According to the International Labor Organization, between 1980 and 2000, the world's labor force will increase more than 40 percent from 1.8 billion to over 2.5 billion. Of this increase of 700 million workers, nearly 90 percent of the total increase, or more than 660 million, would be added to the labor force in the developing countries. In countries such as Mexico, Pakistan, and Nigeria, people under 15 years already comprise almost 50 percent of the population. As these young people start to seek employment, jobs will be increasingly scarce.

With high population growth and a faster growing labor force, a greater proportion of investment has to be allocated simply to equip new entrants to the labor force with the same amount of equipment. Over the past 25 years, the working age population in most developing countries has doubled or more. Even if all the national investment were concentrated on new entrants to the labor market, it would amount to less than $4,000 per entrant in countries such as Kenya, India, Tanzania, and Sri Lanka, in contrast to $150,000 to $250,000 per entrant in the United States, Japan, and France.[3] Again, it is disappointing that the lowest rates of growth in per capita income have occurred in the poorest countries, and that these countries have the lowest rates of investment to cope with the highest rates of growth in population and labor force.

The surprisingly high rate of urbanization in the developing world is also partly the result of the high rate of population growth. Large cities are doubling every 10 to 15 years. The urban population of Asia has more than tripled since 1950. There are now 28 African cities of over 500,000 people, where only 20 years ago there were only three. Much of the growth in urban and metropolitan centers is from natural increase. But large-scale, rural-urban migration has also added significantly to urbanization, dominating over natural increase in the fastest growing cities. As population increases on a limited amount of cultivatable land, rural income remains below urban income, and the push from the rural sector is added to the pull of urban attractions. Urban growth is, however, extremely expensive in the amount of investment needed for capital-intensive housing, public utilities, and social infrastructure. Not to mention the social costs of the favelas, barriadas, and bidonvilles for huge numbers of migrants. The percentage of urban population can be over 50 percent in the matting huts of the Peruvian barriadas of Lima, the pavement settlements of Indian cities, or the shacks and shanties of Dakar and Accra.

Another important consequence of population growth is, of course, the increased demand for food. The growth in a country's population is more important than growth in national income in determining the demand for food. The danger of food production falling below consumption levels threatens the development effort—not simply by placing more pressure on the country's balance of payments through imports of food, but also by affecting nutrition and productivity. The number of what the Food and Agriculture Organization terms "severely under-nourished" people in LDCs (excluding China) rose from around 350 million in 1969–1971 to almost 490 million in 1980. For developing countries as a whole, food production managed to grow faster than population in the 1960–1975 period at annual rates averaging 3 percent. But in many LDCs, demand has been fulfilled more and more by food imports. And this has been so in some of the poorest countries, especially Sub-Saharan Africa where food imports are now five times greater than in the 1960s. To avoid diminishing returns to land as their population increases, these countries must mobilize additional investment, develop new land, and introduce new agricultural techniques to increase yields.

Absolute Poverty

Average rates of growth in GNP for the LDCs and rates of growth in per capita income mask the persistent problems confronted by the most underprivileged groups in the most underprivileged countries. In spite of respectable achievements in rates of growth in GNP, it has been tragic that the low-end poverty groups below a poverty line, based on minimum standards, have not received more of the benefits of this growth. Instead of a "trickling down" of income to the poorest and a reduction in the numbers below a poverty line, there has actually been an increase in the enormous number of people suffering from what the World Bank terms "absolute poverty." Relative poverty in the sense of being at the lower end of a nation's income distribution will exist in any country. But the existence of large numbers in absolute poverty is the agonizing condition of a poor country.

Those in absolute poverty can be identified as approximately the bottom 40 percent of the population, those whose per capita incomes are less than one-third of the national average per capita income. The absolute poor are mainly small subsistence farmers, tenant farmers and sharecroppers, landless workers in agriculture, unemployed and underemployed urban laborers.

Too few of the benefits of economic growth have reached these groups. The failure of these groups to attain a minimum level of income above the poverty line is now of more concern than that of relative poverty, or a "widening gap" between rich and poor countries. With the increase in population, the number of people in absolute poverty has grown and is now in the order of 800 million. For these millions, development has failed. The less developed economies may have done well in terms of GNP growth rates, but hundreds of millions of people in the lowest income groups have not been able to emerge from their poverty.

Malnutrition is especially prevalent among the absolute poor. Fifteen to 20 percent of mankind still suffer from moderate to severe chronic undernutrition. Evidence of serious protein-caloric malnutrition for several hundred million people comes from estimates of food consumption, medical studies, and data on child mortality. Consumption by large sections of the population is still far below what is needed for a minimally satisfactory diet. Undernutrition is most widespread in Africa and South Asia. About 70 percent of all hunger is in nine countries (India, Pakistan, Bangladesh, Indonesia, Philippines, Kampuchea, Zaire, Ethiopia, and Brazil). Moreover, there is evidence that the size of the malnourished population has grown. Studies by the Food and Agriculture Organization and World Bank estimate that the number of malnourished in the world has grown at a rate that exceeds population growth.

Why do people go hungry? Contrary to the common belief that the cause is a failure of food supply relative to the population, malnutrition is largely a reflection of poverty. People simply do not have enough income for food that will provide adequate calories and protein requirements. Undernutrition has persisted even when food supplies meet market demand at acceptable prices. Not deficiencies in food supplies but inadequate entitlements through inadequate incomes are most important in accounting for hunger. A World Bank Report estimates that at the global level, if income were distributed differently, present output of grain alone could supply every man, woman, and child with more than 3,000 calories and 65 grams of protein per day—far more than the highest estimates of requirements. Eliminating malnutrition would require the redirection of only about 2 percent of the world's grain output to the mouths that need it.

To reduce hunger, the employment and income effects of agricultural development are much more important than increasing food output per se. To the tourist, poverty and hunger are more visible in urban areas, but the vast numbers of undernourished people are actually in the countryside. Many of these people have no direct access to land to grow more food or to income to purchase it. Agrarian reforms have not been forthcoming to ameliorate their lot, nor have sufficient productive jobs been created. The lack of income generation and the inequitable income distribution have kept more people in hunger than has a failure to expand food production.

The absolute poor tend to be concentrated in the least developed countries of South Asia and Africa, and mainly in rural sectors. Some 200 million of the absolute poor are in cities, unemployed or underemployed in self-employed pursuits of very low productivity that yield a precarious and meager income. For the 600 million subsistence farmers, tenants, and landless laborers in the rural areas, the weakness of rural development has provided no escape from absolute poverty.

Why have there not been greater benefits from growth for the bottom 40 percent? In part, the failure is related to the other disappointments of failure in agricultural development and the explosive population growth. But there are also other explanations. The pattern of growth, with its emphasis on capital accumulation instead of human-resource development, has failed to raise the productivity of the poor. Those in absolute poverty have not had sufficient access to essential public services such as education and health. Illiteracy, malnutrition, and ill-health keep too many entrapped in absolute poverty. There have not been the necessary opportunities for access to productive assets—land, credit, and education. And employment opportunities have been limited in the face of a growing labor force and rural-urban migration.

Children of Poverty

Absolute poverty takes its greatest toll in denying a future for the children living in poverty. Some 1.6 billion individuals in the world are age 15 or under; most of them—1.3 billion—live in developing countries. These individuals were born with 1 chance in 6 of not living a year. Mortality rates among children age one to four years in low-income countries are frequently 20 to 30 times those in Europe or North America. Even in a country with as good a development record as Brazil, 48 percent of all deaths as late as 1975 occurred among children under five years. The main causes of child mortality today are diarrhea and respiratory infections. These are diseases of the poor, in which the lack of adequate diet, lack of clean water, and lack of basic health services are contributing factors. Eighty percent of the cases of infections or parasitic disease among children could be avoided if only their families had access to clean water.

The fraction of children in poverty is larger than the fraction of adults. In urban Latin America, for example, it is estimated that 50 percent of young children are in absolute poverty.[4] Of the 220 children who are born each minute in poor countries, a large percentage will never have access to medical care. The majority will be undernourished—the incidence of malnutrition among children less than 10 years is almost 70 percent in Asia and over 55 percent in Latin America.[5] Nutrition deficiency is an underlying or associated cause of death in more than half the deaths of children at the ages between 1 to 4 years in developing countries. The consequences of infant malnutrition endure even after the period of undernourishment is passed: malnutrition stunts growth, and there is now evidence that it may retard mental development and limit the individual's learning abilities and educational achievement at later stages in life.

For those who do enter school, 60 percent will not complete more than three years of primary school. The quality of schooling is poor, repeaters occupy 15 to 20 percent of school places, and the school leaver and dropout rates are high. In the low-income countries, less than 10 percent of the secondary school age population is enrolled.

Far removed from the classroom, the poor child is often a

working child who endures long days on farms, in mines, in workshops, or in street trades such as cleaning shoes, selling chewing gum, washing cars, or collecting rubbish in the urban centers. The International Labor Organization estimates that 75 million children under 15 years of age are working at a fixed job. Some 17 million Indian children have gone straight from "swaddling clothes into working gear." The child is obviously obliged to accept simple jobs that call for no previous experience or training. These jobs are by their nature low-productivity jobs, and they yield only an irregular and inadequate income. Moreover, children doing this kind of work remain no more qualified for a better job after years of cleaning shoes or selling lottery tickets than they were when they started. But the conditions of child labor have stunted their physical and mental growth—their future has been mortgaged.

Unemployment and Underemployment

Associated with the rising number in absolute poverty is the rising number in unemployment and underemployment. In spite of high rates of investment and growth in national output, the growth process has not provided sufficient employment opportunities. A large labor surplus remains underutilized in many poor countries; the problem of labor absorption is still as acute as three decades ago.

The continuing labor surplus is evidenced not only by open involuntary unemployment—people willing and able to work at the prevailing wage but unable to find a wage-paying job. More significant, in many of the developing countries, the majority of workers tend to be self-employed or unpaid family workers. The underutilization of their labor takes other forms besides open unemployment. Although they may be working—and even for long hours—they are engaged in very low-productivity activities that yield only a small and precariously variable income. Others are in employment of less than normal duration and would like to work for a longer period of time if employment were available. If we were to calculate the average income of a fully employed worker and then take one-third to one-half of this average and identify those groups of workers whose incomes fall below this average, we would identify large numbers of under-employed. The underemployed earn an income, but it is below a cutoff level—below a minimum wage level or a poverty line.

The underemployed abound in the rural areas where some of the family workers could be removed from the land without a loss in output if the remaining workers would only sacrifice some leisure and work "normal" hours. The underemployed also abound in the urban areas where the high-productivity indus-trial sector has not provided sufficient employment opportuni-ties. Having deserted the countryside in hopes of securing a wage-paying job in the city, the latest wave of migrants soon drifts into the marginal settlements of the urban area. Unable to secure wage employment, however, many of the migrants turn to self-em-ployment as street hawkers, shoeshine boys, photographers, and betja drivers. Necessity drives people to create work in every conceivable way—from the making of furniture from old crates, sandals from tires, pans and paraffin lamps from old metal con-tainers, to activities of "spivvery." They swell the ranks of the working poor.

Comprehensive data on the numbers in open unemployment and underemployment are difficult to obtain. The International Labor Organization, however, estimates that in Latin America, while only 5 percent of the labor force was in open unemploy-ment, 30 percent were underemployed in 1975; in Africa, nearly 38 percent were underemployed; in Asia, approximately 36 per-cent. A recent Rockefeller Foundation report estimates that 40 percent of the labor force in LDCs is unemployed or underem-ployed—nearly one-half billion people with no jobs at all, or employed only sporadically.

Most disappointing is the fact that the labor utilization prob-lem has intensified in some countries. The rates of growth in industrial employment have been low; there have been high rates of unemployment for new entrants to the labor force; and low levels of labor productivity have persisted. Although there has been growth in GNP and rising per capita income, employment has not expanded sufficiently to absorb the surplus labor. Nor has the structure of demand been sufficiently upgraded to gen-erate higher wage employment for those currently employed at low wages. Nor has there been a sufficient rise in productivity and income for the self-employed among the working poor in order to raise them above the poverty level.

The unusually fast growth in the labor force in many developing countries is only part of the explanation of the disappointing record of labor utilization. Also significant has been the widening gap between the urban and agricultural wage levels. The employment problem in the urban areas has resulted in part from a premature increase in the industrial wage combined with a premature reduction in agricultural employment. It might be thought unreasonable that urban wages should rise while alternative earnings in agriculture have not, and while the supply of labor coming to the cities is still greater than the demand. But the institutional determination of wages by minimum wage laws, social security legislation, trade union activity, and growth of public-sector employment have created a high-wage sector. Being two or three or more times higher than agricultural earnings, the high urban wage has continued to "pull" the rural to urban migration at the same time as rural employment opportunities have not expanded to reduce the "push." Techniques of production have also been biased toward more capital-intensive production methods, either through the introduction of labor-saving machinery in response to rising wages or through improvement in personnel and production management practices that have trimmed labor requirements. The maintenance of too low a rate of interest and too low a price for foreign exchange have also promoted the use of capital-intensive methods of production. The more intensive use of labor has also been restrained when the government has been attracted to the most modern capital equipment and when foreign enterprises continue to use advanced production techniques more suited to their home countries where labor is scarce.

The urban employment problem is, in turn, a reflection of the rural employment problem—the failure of agriculture to hold and provide sufficient income for all the people whom the urban sector is not yet ready to employ. The urban "pull" was not offset by lessening the "push" through rural development. Many countries failed to follow a labor-using, capital-saving approach to agricultural development. And many failed to realize the employment potential in rural modernization. Without the absorption of more workers in agriculture, and without rising productivity and rising earnings in agriculture, which accounts for 70 to 80 percent of employment, it has not been possible to generate sufficient demand and opportunities for the unemployed and underemployed. The rise of the numbers in absolute poverty and the persistent underutilization of surplus labor are thus related to the neglect of agriculture. The development strategies of the 1950s and 1960s that emphasized rapid capital accumulation and industrialization led to the employment problems of the 1970s and 1980s.

Inequality

Also disappointing has been the persistence of a highly unequal distribution of income in many developing countries, and even an increasing inequality in some countries that have had high rates of growth. Much of the poverty problem is a reflection of low levels of per capita income, but highly unequal distribution patterns are also important. For example, because of the more unequal income distribution in Colombia than South Korea, the proportion of the population below the poverty line is twice as high in Colombia than in South Korea, even though the average incomes of the two countries are close. The development strategies of some countries have succeeded in raising the level of per capita income markedly without having much impact on the poverty problem because of the deterioration in relative income shares. The growth in income has been concentrated in the higher income levels.

A typical distribution of income in a less developed country shows that more than 50 percent of total income is received by the top 10 percent of the population, while the bottom 20 percent receives less than 5 percent. About three-quarters of the total GNP goes to the top 40 percent of the population, while the bottom 40 percent receive only about 10 to 15 percent of the total national income. Even in countries such as Mexico and Brazil, with impressive rates of growth in GNP, the richest 10 percent receive six to eight times the share of income of the poorest 40

percent. The level of employment and remuneration to the own-
ers of capital, land, and labor explain only part of the distribution of income. The low income for the bottom 40 percent is to
be explained by underemployment, self-employment in low-productivity activities, and especially the lack of productive assets
owned by the lowest income groups—land, physical capital,
access to public capital goods, and human capital embodying
education and skills.

Agricultural Development

Closely connected with the other disappointments of the development record is the weakness of agricultural development in
most of the LDCs. It should not be surprising that the slower
rate of growth in the poorest countries and the problems of population explosion, unemployment and underemployment, inequality, and absolute poverty should all be associated with the
disappointing agricultural record. Since the poorest countries tend
to be more agricultural, and since agricultural development has
lagged behind industrial development, the overall growth rate has
also been lower in the poorest countries. The most pervasive and
persistent problems of mass poverty are to be found in the rural
regions of the low-income countries. The problems created by the
population explosion stem from the pressure put on agricultural
resources. An increasing number of marginal farm households
and landless households bear the brunt from the increasing
pressure of population on the land. It has clearly been disappointing that in almost one-half of the developing countries food
production per head was lower at the end of the 1970s than a
decade earlier. Population growth also intensifies the need for
agricultural progress to reduce urbanization pressures and contain unemployment and underemployment by absorbing more
people in agriculture. With a large percentage of the population
already in agriculture, a young age distribution, and a high rate
of natural increase, it would call for a phenomenal increase in
industrial production and an unrealistically large increase in
nonagricultural employment to bring about an absolute decline
in the agricultural labor force. It is impractical to think that the

labor absorption problem can be completely solved through industrial employment.

Inequality in the distribution of income will also be more pronounced if agriculture is neglected. If most of the labor force is in agriculture, and agricultural incomes are the lowest, then greater equality in distribution depends on improving farm incomes. So too does the removal of absolute poverty insofar as some 80 percent of the absolute poor are in the rural areas. Small farmers, tenants, and landless laborers are the largest target groups among the absolute poor.

What accounts for the deficiencies in rural output? Numerous country studies have argued that inappropriate governmental policies have favored industrialization to the neglect of agriculture. The strategy of industrialization via import substitution has been especially harmful to agricultural development by raising the prices of industrial inputs to agriculture, while keeping the prices of foodstuffs and raw materials low. Protection of home industry acts as a tax on agriculture because it raises the price of manufactured goods relative to agricultural goods in the home market. The other side of the subsidization of industry has been the implicit taxation of agriculture. State procurement has lowered producer prices to ensure lower prices to urban consumers; taxes on agricultural exports have reduced incentives to produce; so too has an overvalued exchange rate hurt the competitive position of agricultural exports and given agricultural producers less domestic currency for a given quantity of their exports. Prices have been twisted against farmers: if the farmers had instead been able to sell their products at world market prices and been able to buy their production inputs and consumer goods at world market prices, they would have done so at more favorable terms than under the existing domestic price distortions.

Moreover, although many countries have provided cheap loans and subsidized some agricultural inputs such as fertilizer and irrigation, these benefits have gone to large, labor-replacing farm units, leaving the small farmer, tenant, and landless laborer unbenefited. Middle- and upper-income farmers buy most subsidized inputs, while the poorer farmers usually lack the money to buy adequate amounts of fertilizer and pesticides, and are usually unable to obtain credit except at near-prohibitive interest rates of often 60 to 100 percent a year. Credit and subsidy programs for tractors, tube wells, and other fixed investments also go mostly to the largest and richest farmers. Overvalued exchange rates have also stimulated imports of machinery that have preempted more labor-intensive production. The Green Revolution, which introduced higher yield varieties of foodgrains, fertilizer, and irrigation, also primarily benefited the large farmers. And research and development in tropical food production has only just begun. The Green Revolution has yet to come to the rain-fed zones, which contain most of the world's farmers.

To explain policies that neglect or actually harm agriculture, some political economists look to the power structure that influences these policies, and they find an urban bias in policymaking. The distribution of power within the developing country favors the urban elite. Powerful urban interests have succeeded in biasing the allocation of resources toward urban areas. The share of investment in the urban-modern sector has been high, while the 60 to 80 percent of the population dependent on agriculture are allocated only some 20 percent of public resources. The urban bias underlies policies that have deliberately raised nonfarm prices relative to the prices of farm goods to support a structural transformation of poor economies through industrialization.[6] The farm sector is squeezed by transfers of resources from it and by prices turning against it.[7] As one economist aptly notes, "In tax incidence, in investment allocation, in the provision of incentives, in education and research: everywhere it is government by the city, from the city, for the city."[8]

A country's overall agricultural strategy must encompass a host of substrategies—including agricultural research into new techniques of cultivation, more rural education and farmer training to adopt technological change at the farm level, investment in roads and water resource development, rural works projects, worker mobility, improvements in marketing, provision of low-cost credit, distribution of farm inputs, and policies related to agricultural taxation, land tenure, and prices. Very few of the developing countries have demonstrated the political commitment and ability to design and implement a comprehensive agricultural strategy that does justice to the set of substrategies that must be pursued if agricultural development is to result.

Political Underdevelopment

Beyond the purely economic disappointments, it is also unfortunate that efforts to achieve economic development have produced political disorder. Economic development has been a politically destabilizing process, marked by instability and violence. Those who had hoped that economic development would bring political freedom, individual rights, and democratic institutions have been disappointed by the exercise of arbitrary political power in many developing countries. Many believed that economic development would bring a widening of economic choice, and that this, in turn, would promote an extension of individual rights and freedoms. Unfortunately, however, only too often economic development has not led to political development but, instead, to political decay and political instability. Ethnic and class conflict, military juntas, the dominance of unstable leaders, corruption among civil servants, coups d'etats, insurrections, and guerilla warfare have continued to characterize political underdevelopment.

The rate of political organization and institutionalization has been low in most of the LDCs. In very few developing countries have there been marked achievements in political development. Juntas and coups, military regimes, and dictatorships of the right and left have eliminated or drastically controlled elections, and systematic repression of political dissent has been practiced in many countries. The loss of civil liberties, the censorship of media, and restrictions on political parties have been common. Too often an elite controls policy without any desire to encourage a broader participation in the political process. It is readily apparent in many countries of Latin America, Asia, and Africa that political development has not followed economic development in the way that many writers during the 1950s and 1960s looked forward to an interdependent development of economic, political, and social influences moving in the direction of the institutions and participatory values of Western industrial democracies.

It might be contended that Western political forces and ideals are simply not appropriate or even relevant for the new states of Africa and Asia. Although replication of the Western model is not necessary, the movement toward authoritarian regimes can scarcely be called political development or political modernization. Social change and economic modernization have had disruptive effects on politics and political institutions, intensifying political disorder and giving rise to political authoritarianism instead of political development. Political scientists and political economists offer a variety of explanations for the emergence of authoritarianism. The reasons may differ among countries—being related to purely political, ideological, cultural, or personality factors. Different reasons may explain political authoritarianism in Argentina, Brazil, Chile, Uruguay, Uganda, Ghana under Nkrumah, Indonesia under Sukarno, and South Korea under Park.

There has, however, also been an attempt to seek some common economic determinants for the rise of authoritarianism. One explanation for the emergence of authoritarian regimes in the major Latin American countries focuses on the increasing difficulties of import-substituting industrialization and the recurring inflationary and balance-of-payments crises. These contribute to sociopolitical disintegration, and political instability and disorder give way to authoritarianism after demands from the "popular sector" reach a "threat level." Reform movements, supported by politically active workers and radicalized sectors of the middle class, develop to correct the imbalances and inequities that have arisen in the course of development. The gap between demands and performance may lead to crises. Perceiving the political and economic crises as a threat to the existing order, military regimes may then establish "bureaucratic-authoritarian" regimes that use repression and coercion to exclude and deactivate the popular sector of lower-, middle-, and working-class groups whose demands are viewed by the ruling technocrats as an obstacle to economic growth.

More broadly, the desire to impose an orthodox, market-oriented set of policies has prompted authoritarian regimes to resist populist pressures and to adopt an antiplanning posture. Governments have sought to introduce policy measures to tighten up the economy and increase economic efficiency—especially through changes in taxation, public service pricing, labor markets, and capital markets. But increased taxes, the removal of subsidies, lower real wages for industrial labor, higher interest rates, devaluation of the domestic currency in terms of foreign currency—all these policies arouse popular concern and run counter to the preferences of the majority of the politically conscious people. The adoption of economic policies that will cause serious losses to some organized groups is difficult in a politically unstable environment without the imposition of a repressive regime. As one student of Latin American economies concludes, "Personal freedom may be taken away to make free markets possible."[9]

Some argue that the transition to conservative economic strategies that rely on economic rationality and the market mechanism requires the political elites to devise state structures that insulate them from the pressures of competitive politics. It is claimed that authoritarianism is necessary to avoid distributivist policies that are incompatible with rates of investment necessary for rapid growth and with anti-inflationary stabilization programs. Authoritarian regimes may also guarantee the political stability and tranquility that are essential for attracting foreign capital and for satisfying international financial institutions. The authoritarian regime, it is also contended, gives proper scope to the technocrats to devise rational policies and implement them in an efficient manner. The record of development in authoritarian regimes, however, belies these contentions, Authoritarianism is neither a necessary nor sufficient condition for economic development. Not sufficient, as the poor record of development in many authoritarian countries shows. And not necessary, as demonstrated by other countries in which a transition to more orthodox and efficient policies has been undertaken without the severe repression of authoritarian regimes (for example, Colombia, pre-Allende Chile, Venezuela, and Mexico to make comparisons in Latin America in contrast to Argentina, Brazil, Chile, and Uruguay). Authoritarianism has often been too inhumane as well as counterproductive. Reform, rather than repression, may be the better alternative to revolution. It is possible, as East Asian countries have demonstrated, to introduce policies that heed efficiency criteria while also increasing equality and maintaining low degrees of repression.

Regardless of the explanation of authoritarianism, the problem remains: the development of political institutions has lagged behind social and economic change. Political fragility has been offset by authoritarian governments, but at high political and social cost. As much as it is necessary to combine equity with economic development, so too must freedom from repression be combined with improved economic performance to overcome the disappointing record of political development.

II
VISION

The preceding chapters stand in danger of being read as merely a description of what has happened—an economic travelogue without much interpretation beneath the surface. To do more than report and describe, we need to focus not on the story of development but on the plot of the development process—the how and the why. For this purpose, we need some analytical insights, some theoretical framework within which we might sort out the crucial variables and the strategic relationships that govern the development process.

Economists have been attempting to do this ever since Adam Smith inquired into the *Nature and Causes of the Wealth of Nations*. Their task, however, became more urgent with the revolution of rising expectations after World War II. In the mid-1950s, on the occasion of the first course offered by the World Bank's Economic Development Institute, the Director Alec Cairncross said:

> The human intellect, like nature, abhors a vacuum, and if it cannot devise a rational explanation of events that trouble it, will turn to myth and magic for comfort. Economic development does trouble the world as never before and people are all too willing to listen to the medicine men who claim to have the spells and rituals to command it. So long as economists fail to provide intelligible explanations of growth and development, the medicine men will hold the field. Why do the people, in the words of Holy Writ, imagine a vain thing? Because they are offered hope where the economist must often show scepticism; and because they are offered quick returns where the economist is bound to underline the continuity and gradualness of things. It is the business of economists to seek out and bring into the light the true sources of the wealth and economic prosperity of nations; but their task is not an easy one. . . .

Interlocking with the record of development over the past three decades has been a sequence of ideas that has dominated the thinking of the development professionals—be they trustees for the poor or guardians of rationality. The progress of events has shaped ideas, and ideas have shaped the reality of development. The interplay between development experience and the evolution of development thought provides valuable insights into the problems of development.

The earliest ideas stemmed from the classical economists, from Adam Smith to John Stuart Mill. Among these economists of the eighteenth and nineteenth centuries, the search culminated in the magnificent dynamics—the analytical framework within which classicists studied the growth of wealth (what we now call the gross national product) in the "progressive state." Although a new development economics was to be fashioned in our time, it can best be understood in terms of its antecedents in the old growth economics. What some interpret as change in economic thinking is often a rediscovery of an earlier idea.

We begin with an exposition of these earlier ideas (Chapter 5) and then proceed to the development thought that began in the 1950s and 1960s (Chapter 6), followed by the revision of development ideas that took place in the 1970s (Chapter 7). Finally, we examine the completely different lineage of thought associated with the school of dependency and the neo-Marxists (Chapter 8).

In presenting these perspectives on development thought, we will want to consider the interaction between thought and reality and the capacity of economic thought to offer policy advice to the developing countries.

5
Old Growth Economics

Why the very early interest in growth? Let Adam Smith have the first word:

> It is in the progressive state, while the society is advancing to the further acquisition, rather than when it has acquired its full complement of riches, that the condition of the laboring poor, of the great body of the people seems to be the happiest and the most comfortable. It is hard in the stationary, and miserable in the declining state. The progressive state is in reality the cheerful and the hearty state for all the different orders of society. The stationary is dull; the declining melancholy.[1]

Smith and the Progressive State

Smith's was an optimistic outlook on the progressive state. Not only would it be for the Professor of Moral Philosophy "the cheerful and hearty state," but one could identify and promote various sources of growth that would support the "progress of opulence." According to Smith, the level of output per head, together with its growth,

> must in every nation be regulated by two different circumstances: first, by the skill, dexterity, and judgment with which its labor is generally applied; and, secondly, by the proportion

between the number of those who are employed in useful labor, and that of those who are not so employed.[2]

The major sources of growth are (1) growth in the labor force and stock of capital (machinery and equipment), (2) improvements in the efficiency with which capital is applied to labor through greater division of labor and technological progress, and (3) foreign trade that widens the market and reinforces the other two sources of growth.

Smith assigned a major role to capital accumulation or investment in the growth process. For capital is the main determinant of "the number of useful and productive laborers" that can be set to work. Labor is "put into motion" by capital. Capital accumulation allows population and the labor force to increase, provides workers with better equipment, and, most important, makes possible a more extensive division of labor. Capital accumulation therefore serves to increase both total output and output per worker (labor productivity). An economy's rate of progress is proportional to its rate of investment: more investment leads to more employment and output, and faster growth in living standards.

> When we compare, therefore, the state of a nation at two different periods, and find, that the annual produce of its land and labor is evidently greater at the latter than the former, that its lands are better cultivated, its manufactures more extensive, we may be assured that its capital must have increased during the interval between those two periods.[3]

Underlying the process of capital accumulation is thrift or saving—Smith's stipulation that the "exchangeable value of the annual produce" must exceed "that of the annual consumption." In Smith's world, people save—that is, do not consume all their income—through the desire of bettering their condition. What is saved is then invested, provided that a "neat or clear profit" can be earned: "[E]very prodigal appears to be a public enemy, and every frugal man a public benefactor."[4] But even though wages exceed subsistence in a progressive state, the margin is hardly sufficient to allow saving by laborers. Most of the addition to a nation's capital stock must therefore originate with "undertakers" (businessmen) or with landlords. As for the policy of forc-

ing savings through taxation by the state, Smith gave no support
to this. Indeed, public prodigality was considered the enemy of
private parsimony, and "The whole, or almost the whole public
revenue, is in most countries employed in maintaining unpro-
ductive hands." In contrast, Smith believed that capital accumulation would proceed most rapidly when capital was "employed in the way that affords the greatest revenue to all the
inhabitants of the country, as they will thus be enabled to make
the greatest savings."[5] Such employment would result when
investors were left free to invest according to their self-interest
in seeking the best attainable returns. It was "the highest imper-
tinence and presumption, therefore, in kings and ministers . . .
the greatest spendthrifts in the society . . . to pretend to watch
over the economy of private people."[6]

Once begun, the growth process becomes self-reinforcing in the
progressive state. As long as the growth in wealth (GNP) favors
profits, there are savings and additional capital accumulation, and
hence further growth. And with capital accumulation, the demand for labor rises, and the growing labor force is absorbed in
productive employment.

Smith attributed overwhelming importance to the division of
labor, in the broad sense of technical progress: "It is the great
multiplication of the productions of all the different arts, in consequence of division of labor, which occasions, in a well-gov-
erned society, that universal opulence which extends itself to the
lowest ranks of the people."[7] The division of labor entails improved efficiency of labor, and increasing specialization leads to
rising per capita income. By increasing the division of labor, improvements in production would reduce the amount of input per
unit of output.

> This great increase of the quantity of work, which, in conse-
> quence of the division of labor, the same number of people are
> capable of performing, is owing to three different circum-
> stances; first, to the increase of dexterity in every particular
> workman; secondly, to the saving of the time which is com-
> monly lost in passing from one species of work to another; and
> lastly, to the invention of a great number of machines which
> facilitate and abridge labor, and enable one man to do the work
> of many.[8]

Smith also emphasized that

> the division of labor is limited by the extent of the market. . . .
> When the market is very small, no person can have any en-
> couragement to dedicate himself entirely to one employment,
> for want of power to exchange all that surplus part of the pro-
> duce for his own labor, which is over and above his own con-
> sumption, for such parts of the produce of other men's labor
> as he has occasion for.[9]

The division of labor increases wealth, and this in turn widens
the market, which enables the division of labor to be carried further forward. An increase in buying power through a rise in average income and numbers would enlarge the division of labor,
and this enlargement would further expand buying power. This
view of the progressive and cumulative changes associated with
increasing division of labor is the basis for Smith's optimism with
regard to economic growth.

Foreign trade would also contribute to growth. The gains from
trade take several forms. As an extension of the division of labor
on an international scale, Smith viewed overseas trade as a way
to allow a country to purchase goods more cheaply.

> It is the maxim of every prudent master of a family, never to
> attempt to make at home what it will cost him more to make
> than to buy. . . . What is prudence in the conduct of every
> private family, can scarce be folly in that of a great kingdom.
> If a foreign country can supply us with a commodity cheaper
> than we ourselves can make it, better buy it of them with some
> part of the produce of our own industry, employed in a way
> in which we have some advantage.[10]

Foreign trade also provides a "vent for surplus" by furnishing
an outlet for surpluses of particular goods above domestic requirements. Another view of trade was that it increases productivity. By widening the extent of the market, foreign markets encourage domestic division of labor. Finally, through trade a
country (such as Holland) could overcome its shortage of land
and resources. Any restriction on free international trade should
therefore be opposed. The "mean and malignant" trade regula-
tions of the earlier mercantilist system should be disbanded in

favor of trade liberalization that would widen the extent of the market and promote growth.

If capital accumulation, division of labor, and foreign trade are sources of a nation's economic growth, then growth can be promoted through the extension of market institutions and the activity of competition. Competition promotes economic evolution. Structural development is enhanced by competition that extends the division of labor and expands markets, and hence leads to the establishment of new trades. And technological development is promoted by expanding markets that facilitate the further exploitation of technology, land, and improvements in machinery and in techniques of production. The strategic class that is to be the agent of development comes from society's middle and lower ranks that stand to benefit most. Not to a few creative entrepreneurs innovating in a bold manner did Smith look for his agents of change. Instead, economic change is primarily the product of a vast number of minor changes introduced by a multitude of comparatively small "undertakers."

What role did Smith assign the state in development? A minimum, because the system of "natural liberty" permits change and development, while government intervention would handicap the positive forces of growth. Individuals should be free to act on their "propensity to truck, barter, and exchange one thing for another" and to pursue self-interest. Competition and market forces would act as an invisible hand to bring self-interest into harmony with public interest.

> As every individual, therefore, endeavors as much as he can both to employ his capital in the support of domestic industry, and so to direct that industry that its produce be of the greatest value; every individual necessarily labors to render the annual revenue of society as great as he can . . . he intends only his own gain, and he is in this, as in many other cases, led by an invisible hand to promote an end which was no part of his intention.
>
> The natural effort of every individual to better his own condition, when suffered to exert itself with freedom and security, is so powerful a principle, that it is alone, and without any assistance, not only capable of carrying on the society to wealth

and prosperity, but of surmounting a hundred impertinent obstructions with which the folly of human laws too often incumbers its operation; though the effect of the obstructions is always more or less either to encroach upon its freedom, or to diminish its security.[11]

Individuals should therefore be freed from governmental policy that had the effects, according to Smith, of limiting capital formation, using capital unproductively, conferring monopoly privileges, and sapping the vitality of competitive forces. Public spending should be kept to a minimum, and production in the public sector should be limited to that small share that could not be supplied by private enterprise. The sovereign's duties were limited to defense, administration of justice, and the maintenance of some public works, the profit from which could never repay the expense to any individual. According to Smith, "Little else is requisite to carry a state to the highest degree of opulence from the lowest barbarism, but peace, easy taxes, and a tolerable administration of justice."

Smith's language may now be quaint, but his insights still retain much relevance. To Smith and the modern economist, growth is the outcome of a logical process; both share the mutual search for some laws and generalizations. Modern economists still emphasize, as did Smith, capital accumulation as a driving force in the growth process. So too do they concentrate on increasing productivity. They also point to the possibilities for development based on foreign trade. And, at the forefront of development discussions, economists seek to find the proper division between a reliance on the market-price system and governmental actions.

With two centuries of hindsight, however, we can question Smith's optimism. Within his own system of thought, the optimistic view of development might be justified. But Smith wrote before the Reverend Thomas Malthus raised the spectre of population outstripping the supply of resources. Smith did not worry about population. In Smith's progressive state, the demand for labor is increasing, and the supply of labor is increasing, but with a time lag, so that an expanding economy was likely to be associated with rising real wage rates.

Nor did Smith believe that machinery would displace labor. The introduction of machinery was regarded as a complement of, rather than a substitute for, labor. Indeed, the division of labor depended on a prior increase in the labor supply, and the number of workers also increased with the division of labor. No Malthusian overpopulation, no Marxian reserve army of the unemployed, no Keynesian problem of less than full employment worried Smith. Capital would simply outdistance population in the progressive state. The benefits of growth would be shared by all orders of society. No problem of inequality would arise.

Smith's analysis was also restricted to Western capitalist countries about to enter the industrial revolution. Only a few casual references were made to China and India, and then only to illustrate that these countries were either in a stationary state or declining state. Other members of the British classical school of thought were to remain as parochial. But their thought is worth recalling for the ways in which they extended Smith's analysis of growth.

Malthus and Redundant Population

The doctrine of Malthus that population could outstrip the means of subsistence was to reduce economics to a dismal science. But the Reverend Malthus (1766–1834) was variously described as cheerful, with a mild and easy temper. The literary editor Sydney Smith wrote this description to a friend:

> Philosopher Malthus came here last week. I got an agreeable party for him of unmarried people. There was only one lady who had had a child; but he is a good-natured man, and, if there are no appearances of approaching fertility, is civil to every lady. . . . Malthus is a real moral philosopher, and I would almost consent to speak as inarticulately, if I could think and act as wisely.[12]

And the author Harriet Martineau wrote of him:

> A more simple-minded, virtuous man, full of domestic affections, than Mr. Malthus could not be found in all England. . . . Of all people in the world, Malthus was the one whom I heard

quite easily without my trumpet;—Malthus, whose speech was
hopelessly imperfect, from defect in the palate. I dreaded
meeting him. I was delightfully wrong. His first sentence—slow
and gentle with the vowels sonorous, whatever might become
of the consonants—set me at ease completely. I soon found that
the vowels are in fact all that I ever hear. His worst letter was
L, and when I had no difficulty with his question—"Would not
you like to have a look at the lakes of Killarney?" I had nothing
more to fear.[13]

Earlier writers had anticipated his leading idea, but with the
exaggerated emphasis of a youthful genius Malthus captured the
public's attention by arguing that population was actually and
inevitably increasing faster than subsistence, and that this was
the reason for the misery observed: "Population, when un-
checked, increases in geometrical ratio. Subsistence increases only
in an arithmetical ratio." He illustrated this by the juxtaposition
of the series:

$$1,2,4,8,16,32,64, \ldots$$

and

$$1,2,3,4,5,6,7,8, \ldots$$

for population and food, respectively. Only through the operation of "misery and vice" could there be "a strong and con-
stantly operating check on population from the difficulty of subsistence." This was Malthus' view in the first edition of his *Essay
on Population* (1798).

In his second edition (1803), however, he offers an entirely
different theory. For now Malthus introduces the prudential check
of "moral restraint." (It may be that Malthus discovered from his
own experience that a deferment of marriage until the year following the second edition, when he was 38 years old, did not
involve either misery or vice.) The possibility of "moral restraint" meant that, given suitable institutions and social habits,
the possibility of improvement could not be absolutely denied as
under the population spectre of the first edition.

In 1804, Malthus became the recipient of the earliest chair in
political economy to be established in England, with no less a

prodigious title than "Professor of General History, Politics, Commerce, and Finance." Interestingly enough, the position was at the newly established East India College at Hailebury—an institution for the training of administrators in the East Indian Company. He was, however, no longer the center of controversial pamphleteering. His students called him "Pop," and he had three children while writing his second book on *The Principles of Political Economy, Considered with a View to Their Practical Application.*

It is only too easy, but an injustice, as Keynes notes, to let Malthus appear

> as a symbol of the sophisms of the economists—the ingenious and hateful tautologists who, out of the bowels of their humanitarianism, can prove, by means of truisms, that all attempts to mitigate poverty and misery are destined to increase it; that impulsive charity is a lesser social virtue than enlightened self-interest; and that all will be for the best possible in a miserable world if the businessmen are left with the least interference to get on with their beneficient pursuit of the survival of the fittest—meaning those financially most gifted.[14]

Keynes rightly makes a distinction between the first and second editions of the *Essay on Population* and points out that, whereas in the first edition the stress is on the *difficulty* of curtailing the supply of labor, in the later editions the emphasis is on the *importance* of curtailing its supply. As Malthus said in the second edition:

> The structure of society, in its great features, will probably always remain unchanged. We have every reason to believe that it will always consist of a class of proprietors, and a class of laborers; but the condition of each, and the proportion which they bear to each other, may be so altered as greatly to improve the harmony and beauty of the whole. It would, indeed, be a melancholy reflection, that, while the views of physical science are daily enlarging, so as scarcely to be bounded by the most distant horizon, the science of moral and political philosophy should be confined within such narrow limits, or at best be so feeble in its influence, as to be unable to counteract the increasing obstacles to human happiness arising from the progress of population. But however formidable these obsta-

cles may have appeared in some parts of this work, it is hoped that the general result of the enquiry is such, as not to make us give up the cause of the improvement of human society in despair. The partial good which seems to be attainable is worthy of all our exertions; is sufficient to direct our efforts and animate our prospects.

By "moral restraint," Malthus did not mean deliberate control of conception. By his classification, contraceptive practices amounted not to "moral restraint" but "vice." Other classical economists, however, advocated birth control as the way to emancipation and progress by restraining population growth below the rate of capital accumulation. As Francis Place said in his *Illustrations of the Principle of Population* (1822),

> If it were once clearly understood, that it was not disreputable for married persons to avail themselves of such precautionary means as would, without being injurious to health or destructive of female delicacy, prevent conception, a sufficient check might at once be given to the increase of population beyond the means of subsistence; vice and misery, to a prodigious extent, might be removed from society, and the object of Mr. Malthus, Mr. Godwin, and of every philanthropic person, be promoted by the increase of comfort and intelligence and of moral comfort, in the mass of the population. . . . It is time . . . that those who really understand the cause of a redundant, unhappy, miserable, and considerably vicious population, and the means of preventing the redundancy, should clearly, freely, openly and fearlessly point out the means.

Ricardo and the Stationary State

The most elegant of the British classical theorists was David Ricardo, one-time stockbroker from the early age of 14, gentleman farmer, member of Parliament, and author of *The Principles of Political Economy and Taxation* (1817). Concentrating on three major groups of actors on the economic scene—capitalists, laborers, and landlords—Ricardo analyzed how the relative income shares of these three groups—profits, wages, rent on land—vary in the course of the development process.

Capitalists play the key role in the economy. In undertaking production, they rent land from the landlords and provide the laborers with tools and implements of production and advance as wages the food, clothing, and commodities consumed by workers during the production period. They promote development by continually searching for the most profitable investment opportunities, and they reinvest their profits in the accumulation of capital.

Labor is the largest group and is dependent on the capitalists for employment. The wage rate is simply the total amount of funds that capitalists advance to the workers for their maintenance (the "wages fund"), divided by the number of workers. There is a certain subsistence real wage, fixed by custom and habit, at which the laborers just perpetuate themselves. If the actual wage rises above this "natural" subsistence real wage, population increases; and below it, numbers decrease.

As population expands and capital accumulates, the most fertile types of land become more and more scarce. In meeting the higher demand for food, the labor and capital are employed on successively poorer grades of land. This brings about diminishing returns in agricultural output: doubling the inputs of labor, capital, and land will yield less than a doubling of agricultural output. As poorer lands are brought into cultivation, competition among the capitalists for the better grades of land causes a "rent" to be gained by the landlords on the more fertile land. The rent arises when demand exceeds supply, and it is simply a surplus to the landlord. Because land is fixed in amount, the rent cannot induce a larger supply of land: it is a return to the landlord that covers no cost and is merely "that portion of the produce of the earth, which is paid to the landlord for the use of the original and indestructible powers of the soil."

In the classical tradition, Ricardo's analysis assigns overwhelming importance to capital accumulation as the prime force of development. By saving and increasing the wages fund, the capitalists set in motion the forces that increase ouput. Ricardo improves on previous theories, however, by emphasizing how the distribution of income affects the development process, and how the distributional pattern is, in turn, a consequence of development.

Ricardo also demonstrates how, under a free trade regime, the pattern of international trade would be based on each country's comparative advantage, with each country specializing in its most efficient production. His celebrated example of Portugal trading wine for cloth from England demonstrates that there are mutual gains from trade for all trading nations if the principles of division of labor and specialization are followed internationally. Each trading country—whether primary producing or industrial—enjoys a higher real income. The game of trade is not zero sum, but of benefit to each trading country. There is a natural harmony of interests under free trade.

Ricardo's analysis is also notable for envisioning the dynamic evolution of the economy, ultimately culminating in the advent of the stationary state. The process takes place in the following manner. Capitalists save a portion of their income and invest it when they recognize profit opportunities. The rate of capital accumulation is governed by the ability to save and the will to save. The ability depends on the amount of the economy's surplus—that is, the difference between the value of all commodities produced minus the value of the commodities needed to just sustain the labor force that produced this output. The larger this surplus or "net income," the greater the means to save. Thus, "out of two loaves I may save one, out of four I may save three." The will to save will be determined by the prospects for profit, and

> While the profits of stock are high, men will have a motive to accumulate. . . . The farmer and manufacturer can no more live without profit, than the laborer without wages. Their motive for accumulation will diminish with every diminution of profit, and will cease altogether when their profits are so low as not to afford them an adequate compensation for their trouble and the risk which they must necessarily encounter in employing their capital productively.[15]

As long as capital accumulates, additional workers are hired. If the wage rate is assumed initially to be at its "natural" subsistence level, the addition of the savings to the wages fund, which already exists for the purpose of hiring labor, causes the wage rate to be bid up above its "natural" price. Initially, "it is prob-

able that capital has a tendency to increase faster than mankind." Gradually, however, the Malthusian population demon
takes over. There is a greater demand for agricultural commodities that are produced under conditions of diminishing returns.
Because the price of food rises, the workers are forced to spend
more on food to secure their customary standard of living. The
real wage rate returns to its customary, near-subsistence level.
But, in money terms, the wage rate is higher because the price
of food—the major component of the worker's budget—is higher.
This implies that the rate of profit is lower, because profits "depend on high or low wages, and on nothing else." As recourse
is had to less fertile land, rents also rise on the superior grades
of land. Technological improvements and the opening up of new
land overseas may for a time mitigate the downward pressure
on the rate of profit. But eventually in a mature economy the redistribution in favor of landowners will cause the rate of profit
to fall so low that it does not afford the capitalists adequate com-
pensation for their trouble and risk. The rate of growth in national income then ceases. The economy becomes stationary. Rents
are high, the real wage rate is at its minimum subsistence level,
the profit rate is near zero, no further capital accumulates, population is at a maximum, and total output remains stationary. Such
are the characteristics of Ricardo's stationary state—a marked
contrast to Smith's progressive state.

Mill and Antigrowth Theory

John Stuart Mill (1806–1873), the last representative and the most
popular of the classical economists, sums up the classical interpretation of growth, but he also anticipates the neoclassical view
that the progressive, growing economy loses importance if population can be controlled. Unlike Smith and Ricardo, Mill envisages a stationary state that can actually be quite pleasant.

Before Mill's stationary state could be attained, however, there
would first have to be a high level of development. And such
development was to be achieved through the classical forces of
capital accumulation and technical progress.

Mill learned about these classical forces at an early age. When only 13 years old, he received lectures on political economy from his father James Mill. From the lectures during their daily walks, the son prepared abstracts of the lessons which served as notes for the father as he wrote his *Elements of Political Economy*. About the same time, the young Mill wrote that "Mr. Ricardo invited me to his house and to walk with him in order to converse upon the subject." At age 16, he was publishing articles in defense of the Ricardian analysis. And the last thing Ricardo wrote on the day he was stricken with his fatal illness was a letter in which he corrected an essay written by the 17-year-old Mill.

Steeped in the classical system, Mill devoted himself in his *Principles of Political Economy* (1848) to an analysis of "the nature of wealth, and the laws of its production and distribution, including: directly or remotely, the operation of all the causes by which the condition of mankind . . . is made prosperous or the reverse." Again he emphasized capital accumulation, "without which no productive operations beyond the rude and scanty beginnings of primitive industry are possible."[16]

An increase in the amount of capital formation in a country depends on two circumstances: (1) the magnitude of "the produce of industry," or "the amount of the fund from which saving can be made"; and (2) "the strength of the disposition to save," since capital is "the product of saving, that is, of abstinence from present consumption for the sake of the future good." "The strength of the disposition to save" depends, in turn, on the rate of profit or return to be made on savings, and upon "the effective desire of accumulation," which reflects the willingness of individuals to sacrifice "a present, for the sake of a future good."

Mill also recognizes that the law of diminishing returns on land can "be suspended or temporarily controlled by whatever adds to the general power of mankind over nature, and especially by any extension of their knowledge, and their consequent command of the properties and powers of natural agents." Drawing a greater distinction than most classicists would between the laws of production and distribution, Mill states that, while the "laws and conditions of the production of wealth partake of the character of physical truths," the distribution of wealth "is a matter of human institution solely. . . . Society can subject the distribution of wealth to whatever rules it thinks best."

Although Mill was officially associated for 35 years with the India Office, his writings about Indian affairs were confined to routine administrative details, and he showed no general concern with problems of development in non-European countries.

Perhaps his most interesting observation, "principally applicable to an early stage of industrial advancement," relates to the role of international trade in stimulating development:

> [A] people may be in a quiescent, indolent, uncultivated state, with all their tastes either fully satisfied or entirely undeveloped, and they may fail to put forth the whole of their productive energies for want of any sufficient object of desire. The opening of a foreign trade, by making them acquainted with new objects, or tempting them by the easier acquisition of things which they had not previously thought attainable, sometimes works a sort of industrial revolution in a country whose resources were previously undeveloped for want of energy and ambition in the people: inducing those who were satisfied with scanty comforts and little work, to work harder for the gratification of their new tastes, and even to save, and accumulate capital, for the still more complete satisfaction of those tastes at a future time.[17]

Although Malthus and Ricardo were pessimists about the course of development, Mill had no reason to look on the future of the masses "as otherwise than hopeful." But this was only because he believed mankind was heeding the Malthusian lesson and that voluntary birth control would allow capital to win the race against population. Although he too envisioned the emergence of a stationary state, he had none of the misgivings of Ricardo because he had eliminated the spectre of overpopulation. To Mill, if population can be controlled, there is no need for the economy to go on expanding in order that wages should be above the subsistence level. If labor is fixed in amount, some of the surplus production can then go to wages. Mill's stationary state represented a state in which a high level of development had been achieved by technical progress and capital accumulation, held at that level by a stationary population. As such, it would actually be an agreeable state—the very objective toward which policy should be aiming. If population can be controlled, there is no need for the economy to go on growing. In this, there is an early vision of the neoclassical, static analysis that was to follow.

In contrast, under conditions of growth, the "quality of life" could actually be inferior. As Mill says in his *Principles of Political Economy*,

> I cannot regard the stationary state of capital and wealth with the unaffected aversion so generally manifested towards it by political economists of the old school. I am inclined to believe that it would be, on the whole, a very considerable improvement upon our present condition. I confess I am not charmed with the ideal of life held out by those who think that the normal state of human beings is that of struggling to get on; that the trampling, crushing, elbowing and treading on each other's heels, which form the existing type of social life, are the most desirable lot of human kind, or anything but the disagreeable symptoms of one of the phases of industrial progress. The northern and middle states of America are a specimen of this stage of civilization in very favorable circumstances; having, apparently, got rid of all social injustices and inequalities that affect persons of Caucasian race and of the male sex, while the proportion of population to capital and land is such as to ensure abundance to every able-bodied member of the community who does not forfeit it by misconduct. They have the six points of Chartism, and they have no poverty; and all that these advantages seem to have done for them is that the life of the whole of one sex is devoted to dollar-hunting, and of the other to breeding dollar-hunters. This is not a kind of social perfection which philanthropists to come will feel any very eager desire to assist in realizing.[18]

Marx on Colonialism

The last of the classical economists, Karl Marx (1818–1883) worked with classical tools of analysis to lay bare the "laws of motion" of modern society—but after settling in the British Museum Library for some 20 years, he reached conclusions completely contrary to the classical tradition. Marx initiates a divergent line of thought, emphasizing the conflict of interests among classes within a country and among nations in the international economy, in contrast with the classical emphasis on harmony of interests within a country and mutual gains from trade in the world economy.

Although based on elements of classical economics, the Marxian theory involves other psychological and sociological assumptions and implies deep structural changes in the evolution of an economy that were not recognized by Marx's predecessors.

Marx argues that capitalism is the most brutalizing and dehumanizing system history has known, but capitalism is still a necessary stage toward final salvation, because only capitalism can create the economic and technological infrastructure that will enable society eventually to liberate its members: "What the bourgeoisie, therefore, produces is, above all, its own grave-diggers." Within a capitalist economy, Marx envisages progressive impoverishment, increasing severity of economic crises, intensification of class war, and the final expropriation of the expropriators and the advent of full communism.[19]

Like other classical economists, Marx's system of thought was also directed essentially to the European world. But he did write about Asia and the implications of colonialism. Marx maintained that the ultimate victory of socialism rested on the prior universalization of capitalism. European colonial expansion must therefore be endorsed as a brutal but necessary step toward this victory. If the horrors of industrialization are dialectically necessary for the triumph of communism in Europe, so too are the horrors of colonialism dialectically necessary for the world revolution of the proletariat since without them the colonies will not be able to emancipate themselves from their stagnant backwardness. Through the impact of Western bourgeois society, non-European nations are drawn into the orbit of universal capitalism.

> The need for a constantly expanding market for its products chases the bourgeoisie over the whole surface of the globe. It must nestle everywhere, settle everywhere, establish connexions everywhere.

> The bourgeoisie has through its exploitation of the world-market given a cosmopolitan character to production and consumption

in every country. . . . All old-established national industries have been destroyed or are daily being destroyed. They are dislodged by new industries, whose introduction becomes a life and death question for all civilized nations, by industries that no longer work indigenous raw material, but raw material drawn from the remotest zones; industries whose products are consumed, not only at home, but in every quarter of the globe. In place of the old wants, satisfied by the products of the country, we find new wants, requiring for their satisfaction the products of distant lands and climes. In place of the old local and national seclusion and self-sufficiency, we have intercourse in every direction, universal interdependence of nations. And as in material, so also in intellectual production. The intellectual creations of individual nations become common property. National one-sidedness and narrow-mindedness become more and more impossible, and from the numerous national and local literatures there arises a world literature.

The bourgeoisie, by the rapid development of all instruments of production, by the immensely facilitated means of communications, draws all, even the most barbarian, nations into civilization. The cheap prices of its commodities are the heavy artillery with which it batters down all Chinese walls, with which it forces the barbarians' intensely obstinate hatred to foreigners to capitulate. It compels all nations, on pain of extinction, to adopt the bourgeois mode of production; it compels them to introduce what it calls civilisation into their midst, i.e., to become bourgeois themselves. In one word, it creates a world after its own image.

The bourgeoisie has subjected the country to the rule of the towns. It has created enormous cities, has greatly increased the urban population as compared with the rural, and has thus rescued a considerable part of the population from the idiocy of rural life. Just as it has made the country dependent on the towns, so it has made barbarian and semi-barbarian countries dependent on the civilised ones, nations of peasants on nations of bourgeois, the East on the West.[20]

The costs of colonialism were to be endured because they paved the way to eventual emancipation. The introduction of private property and of industrial production were to be welcomed as the foundations for the transition to communsim. Imperialism is, according to Marx, the highest stage of capitalism. Not, however, as Lenin maintained, because it must lead to a world war that will ultimately destroy capitalism and lead victors and vanquished alike into socialism, but because there is no chance for socialism to emerge unless its foundations are first laid down by capitalism itself.

> England it is true, in causing a revolution in Hindustan, was actuated only by the vilest interests, and was stupid in her manner of enforcing them. But that is not the question. The question is: can mankind fulfill its destiny without a fundamental revolution in the social state of Asia? If not, whatever may have been the crimes of England, she was the unconscious tool of history in bringing about that revolution.[21]

> The bourgeois period of history has to create the material basis of the new world—on the one hand the universal intercourse founded upon the mutual dependence of mankind, and the means of that intercourse; on the other hand the development of the productive powers of man and the transformation of material production into a scientific domination of natural agencies. Bourgeois industry and commerce create these material conditions of a new world in the same way as geological revolutions have created the surface of the earth.[22]

Considering Britain and India, Marx maintained that Britain had a "mission" to perform. The British mission was twofold: "The annihilation of old Asiatic society, and the laying of the material foundations of Western society in Asia." In pursuing this mission, Englishmen were the unwitting instruments of history. The "moneyocracy" shut out India's finished textiles from British markets, and the "millocracy" flooded India with products of Britain's power looms. "British steam and science uprooted, over the whole surface of Hindustan, the union between agriculture and manufacturing industry." But there was no turning back to the misconceived idealism of traditional village life. Ultimately, Britain's intervention in India would sow the seeds of its own destruction.

Later the followers of Marx departed from his unusual view of colonialism and adopted arguments more familiar to us. Lenin in particular saw imperialism as

capitalism in that state of development in which the dominance of monopolies and finance capital has established itself;
. . . in which the division of the world among the international trusts has begun; in which the division of all territories
of the globe among the great capitalist powers has been completed.[23]

The Marxists argue that, at this point in the development of
mature capitalist countries, the forces of stagnation become more
acute in the form of a low rate of profit and chronic overproduction. The older industrial countries therefore turn increasingly to
stimulation of the foreign trade sector to postpone their final destruction. The export of capital to emerging areas overseas where
the rate of profit is higher becomes significant in the attempt to
offset the tendency toward stagnation. This also becomes a means
for encouraging the export of commodities which relieves the
pressures of overproduction at home.

According to the Marxist view, further domination of the poorer
countries by the advanced capitalist countries accompanies the
export of capital. There are resistances to be overcome within these
areas if foreigners are to find profitable outlets and to exploit the
people. Each capitalist power also desires to exclude competition
from other capitalist nations. The governments of the great powers therefore intervene and forcibly create conditions favorable
to the process of exploitation. In all this, the people of the poorer
regions do not benefit. On the contrary, traditional habits and
customs are destroyed; handicraft industries are wiped out by
cheap manufacturing imports; and the masses are stripped of their
means of production. In short, "Finance capital and the trusts
are increasing instead of diminishing the differences in the rate
of development of the various parts of world economy."[24]

The Static Interlude

About 1870, there was a definite shift in the main current of economic thought—away from the classical economist's vision of an
evolving economy, which was thought to progress in a dynamic
fashion as a result of cumulative forces, to the neoclassical economist's preoccupation with the static allocation of given re-

sources at a given period of time. This shift was primarily the result of the successful realization of growth: with real wages considerably above the subsistence level and rising, the rate of profit high, and technological and resource discoveries continuing to outstrip population growth, there was no fear of the advent of a stationary state. Short-run problems came to the fore.

By 1871, in his *Theory of Political Economy*, W. S. Jevons could dismiss "the doctrine of population" because "it forms no part of the direct problem of Economics." Instead, he defined the "great problem of Economy" as follows: "Given, a certain population, with various needs and powers of production, in possession of certain lands and other sources of material: required, the mode of employing labour which will maximize the utility of the produce."[25]

Focusing on the search for the conditions of efficiency in utilizing existing resources in the economy, economists totally ignored economic growth as a policy objective for several decades, from about 1870 to the 1930s. The theory of value and resource allocation dominated economic thought. Economic action became the exercise of the logic of choice. Price became the coefficient of choice par excellence, showing the rate at which one commodity could be exchanged for another. In maximizing the satisfaction from consumer choice, or minimizing the cost of the producer's choice, the economist became the guardian of rationality. Economic analysis concentrated on the conditions that would make possible various optima rather than on the conditions that would allow an economy to achieve ever-changing optima of ever-increasing range. Not the movement of aggregate output in the entire economy, but the movement of particular lines of production toward an "equilibrium" position became the neoclassicist's concern. To tighten up the economy and avoid inefficiency was the neoclassicist's objective. Rigorous analysis of individual markets and of price formation was the neoclassicist's hallmark.

One price, however, brought the neoclassicist close to growth problems—the rate of interest. The return to loanable funds is a price that connects the present with the future. It becomes relevant in dealing with the choice between consumption and investment, between present consumption and future consumption, or the willingness to sacrifice present satisfactions for future satisfactions. Because the rate of interest determines the rate of saving and also the rate of investment, it is for the neoclassical economist the key price in the subject of capital accumulation.

For the most part, however, neoclassical writers shortened their time horizon as they considered interrelationships among the various sectors of the economy at a particular moment of time, the determination of prices, the operation of markets, and the distribution of income. In the static world of the neoclassicist, history drops out, time becomes irrelevant, past and future are identical. The subject is the static allocation of resources, not the dynamic growth of an entire economy.

This static interlude of neoclassical economics continued for about seven or eight decades until the end of World War II. During that period, neoclassical economics was in too narrow a groove to incorporate the problems of development. As late as 1948, the first edition of the best-selling textbook on *Economics* by Nobel laureate Paul Samuelson, on which hundreds of thousands of students were to be raised, had only three brief—almost parenthetical—allusions to matters of development: a sentence comparing the steady improvement in Western living standards with "more backward nations, two-thirds of whose inhabitants were badly undernourished"; a paragraph on the International Bank for Reconstruction and Development, with the observation that "South America, the Orient and other regions of the world could profitably use our capital for their industrial development"; and the statement that the infant industry or "young economy" argument "has more validity for present-day backward nations than for those who have already experienced the transition from an agricultural to an industrial way of life. In a sense such nations are still asleep; they cannot be said to be truly in equilibrium."

Writing on *The Theory of Economic Growth* in 1952, Nobel laureate Arthur Lewis would say "no comprehensive treatise on the subject has been published for about a century. The last great book covering this wide range was John Stuart Mill's *Principles of Political Economy*, published in 1848." Only three years earlier, Lewis' own *Economic Survey 1919–39* had scarcely mentioned the less developed countries, referring only to the terms of trade for primary producing countries, although the focus was on world

economic events of the interwar period and the need for cooperation in international economic policy.

A minor stream of writing did exhibit some interest in the less
developed countries during the neoclassical interlude—the writing on colonial economics. But these writings were only too often
little more than descriptive travelogues, without the analytical
span of the earlier growth economists. Also influenced by the
neoclassicists, many of the books on colonial economics and the
multitude of official reports on colonial policy were devoted to
fragmentary topics on economic organization, the workings of
markets, and the formation of prices. Although cultural anthropologists and sociologists were more at home in their study of
colonial societies, their noneconomic observations were not
blended into the works of the economists. No indigenous economics arose during the colonial period.

Another feature of much writing on colonial policy was what
Nobel laureate Gunnar Myrdal calls "the colonial theory"—apol-
ogetic writing attempting to absolve the colonial regimes from
responsibility for the state of underdevelopment. Tropical climate, population pressure, lack of resources, or values and institutions that made the people unresponsive to opportunities for
improving their incomes and living standards were all frequent
excuses for the lack of development in colonial economies.

The postwar wave of decolonization changed all this. The study
of development of former colonies acquired a new urgency. In
the late 1940s and 1950s, the early development economists incorporated some of the insights of the Old Growth Economics
but moved on to new territory, both in thought and space.

Old Growth Economics: Refrain

Turning to the Early Development Economics, we consider how
elements of classical thought have been incorporated in the more
modern thinking about development. That it should still retain
some relevance is not surprising if it is realized that classical economics arose when most people in Western Europe were poor,
living under conditions similar to those that now prevail in low-
income countries.

At the back of modern analysis is still some vision of economic evolution—of the cumulative forces that lead to what the classicists called "the progressive state." The focus is on variables that change over a long period of time, culminating in a rise in per capita income. The economic problem is one of scarcity, and the objective is to have man succeed in overcoming the niggardliness of nature. In analyzing the course of economic progress, development economists are still concerned with the "heavy" variables of classical analysis—capital accumulation, technical progress, and population growth. Of special relevance is the classical concern that there should be enough capital to provide employment for everybody—that the labor surplus be absorbed productively. So too is there interest in the concept of the stationary state: the classicist's desire to avoid the stationary state now becomes the developing country's desire to emerge from conditions resembling a stationary state. And the prospects for development through international trade are very much at the forefront of development thought. Indeed, Ricardo's Portugal-England example has modern overtones in the North-South dialogue, a developed northern industrial country and an underdeveloped, primary producing, southern country.

Although elements of the classical vision of the economic future reappear in the modern vision, there are vast differences in the techniques of analysis. It is interesting to see how modern techniques of analysis illuminate development programs. Particularly challenging will be the economist's attempt to be both the trustee for the poor and the guardian of rationality.

6

Early Development Economics

After World War II, scores of countries in Africa and Asia gained their freedom from colonialism and sought policy advice on how to accelerate their national development. So too did aspiring Latin American countries look to economists for development advice. Western economists responded with an optimism derived from the experience of New Deal reforms during the Great Depression in the United States, the wartime mobilization of resources, and Marshall Aid for the postwar recovery of Europe.

The Formative Period

The World Bank's first economic mission was to Colombia in 1949. As head of that mission, Lauchlin Currie, a former Harvard economist and official in the Roosevelt administration, recalls his attitude toward the Colombia mission:

> I don't know where in my conservative Canadian background I acquired a reformer's zeal, but I must admit that I had it. I just happen to be one of those tiresome people who can't encounter a problem without wanting to do something about it. So you can imagine how Colombia affected me. Such a marvelous number of practically insoluble problems! Truly an economic missionary's paradise. I had no idea before I came what

the problems were but that did not dull for a moment my enthusiasm nor shake my conviction that if only the Bank and the country would listen to me I could come up with a solution of sorts to most. I had had my baptism of fire in the Great Depression. I had played some role in working out the economic recovery program in the New Deal for the worst depression the United States had ever experienced. I had been very active in government during the Second World War."[1]

The wartime mobilization of resources demonstrated what could be achieved once a nation was given an overriding national objective and a sense of priorities. So too had the Marshall Plan stimulated national planning of the postwar recovery programs. To finance these programs, nations calculated the requirements for external resources through loans and grants based on the shortfall between national needs and the domestic resources available to fill these needs. The combination of reform, national mobilization of resources, and foreign aid now carried over to the needs of the newly developing countries.

But there was no distinct body of development economics, awaiting application to Colombia and other underdeveloped countries. As Currie states,

> When, in 1949, I was asked to organize and direct the first study mission of the World Bank there were no precedents for a mission of this sort and indeed nothing called development economics. I just assumed that it was a case of applying various branches of economics to the problems of a specific country, and accordingly I recruited a group of specialists in public finance, foreign exchange, transport, agriculture, and so on. I did, however, include some engineers and public health technicians. What emerged was a series of recommendations in a variety of fields. I was at pains to entitle it "the basis of a program" rather than a socioeconomic plan.[2]

The initial emphasis in all development programs was on increasing gross national product (GNP) at a faster rate than population growth. The index of development became a rise in per capita real income. To be sure, population growth made this achievement more difficult; but population pressure was not viewed as the cause of underdevelopment. Instead, economists considered population pressure as merely associated with pov-

erty: to say a poor country has population pressures is equivalent to saying it has a low level of development. Rather than being
the cause of the problem, population pressure was interpreted
as the problem: a higher rate of development through an increase in GNP was needed. Where population growth was high,
the need for accelerated development was intensified. To raise
per capita income, economists thought it more expeditious over
a short period of time to raise the numerator of national income
instead of attempting to lower the denominator of population.
And to raise national income, capital accumulation was necessary. It looked as if the Early Development Economics was back
to the prescription of the Old Growth Economics. And so it was—
but with some modifications and extensions.

The Early Development Economics was uneasy with both the
neoclassical system and the Keynesian system that had arisen
since the Old Growth Economics. Development economists
questioned the relevance of the market-price system of neoclassical economics for the poor countries. The price system in the
less developed country (LDC) existed in only a rudimentary form:
markets were fragmented and localized; market imperfections
were pervasive; and there was little range for the sophisticated
exercise of the logic of choice as in a well-defined price system.
Moreover, large changes in the economy were the very essence
of development—not the incremental or marginal changes of
neoclassical economics. Substantial transformation in the structure of the economy was needed. A widening of the economy
was required—not simply the tightening up of the economy
through the application of neoclassical principles of resource allocation. For economists concerned with the larger issues of development, the neoclassical analysis was believed silent.

Even though the University of Chicago's economics department was the stronghold of neoclassical economics, its chairman
Theodore Schultz observed that

> In most poor countries there is not much economic growth to
> be had by merely taking up whatever slack may exist in the
> way the available resources are being utilized. To achieve eco-
> nomic growth of major importance in such countries, it is nec-
> essary to allocate effort and capital to do three things: increase
> the *quantity* of reproducible goods; improve the *quality* of the

people as productive agents; and raise the *level* of the productive arts.[3]

A notable dissenter among the pioneering development economists was the Cambridge don Peter Bauer who warned that the analysis of development problems should not be "price-less," that the functions of prices should not be ignored, that the economic responses to individual incentives should not be overlooked, and that government should not intervene with the market-price system. But from Oxford, Ian Little could critically say of Bauer's book on *Indian Economic Policy and Development* (1961) that "One would like to dismiss this book as the obvious outpouring of a political adolescent with an economic *idée fixe*."[4]

The Early Development Economics also found the Keynesian analysis of national income determination wanting in relevance since Keynes had been concerned with the unemployment of labor and the underutilization of capital during depressions in advanced industrial countries as a result of oversaving. The cyclical type of unemployment that worried Keynes was not the type of unemployment that pervaded the poor countries. Theirs was a chronic surplus of labor, indicated by not only persistent unemployment, but also widespread underemployment, disguised unemployment, and employment with low productivity. Many of the underemployed would be willing to work longer hours if jobs were available. Some in disguised unemployment appeared employed but were actually adding nothing or very little to total output. Many were among the "working poor," laboring long hours but at low-productivity tasks, yielding incomes below a poverty level. The unemployment problem was related to a deficiency of capital—not to too much savings, as in the Keynesian diagnosis of an advanced capitalist economy suffering from a short-run cyclical depression. The Keynesian remedy of increasing aggregate demand was not the remedy for poor countries; their task was to mobilize more savings and increase investment. They were not deficient in investment outlets, but in savings—in the availability of real resources.

Moreover, Keynesian analysis was limited to the short period of time. Its assumptions of static conditions violated the very nature of the development process. That process was scarcely Keynes' concern when he stated:

> We take as given the existing skill and quantity of available la-
> bor, the existing quality and quantity of available equipment,
> the existing technique, the degree of competition, the tastes and
> habits of the consumer, the disutility of different intensities of
> labor and the activities of supervision and organization, as well
> as the social structure.[5]

Keynesian analysis thereby paralyzed from the outset many of
the essential variables of the development process.

Rejecting neoclassical price analysis and Keynesian income
analysis, the development economist sought to establish more
relevant principles. The founding director of the Institute of Development Studies at the University of Sussex, Dudley Seers,
criticized the dominance of Anglo-Saxon economics with its
"special case" of the developed, industrial, private-enterprise
economy. To analyze the problems of nonindustrial economies,
he thought a major revolution in economic doctrine was essential.

So too did Nobel laureate Gunnar Myrdal call on the underdeveloped countries to produce a new generation of economists
who might create a body of thought more realistic and relevant
for the problems of their countries:

> In this epoch of the Great Awakening it would be pathetic if
> the young economists in the underdeveloped countries got
> caught in the predilections of the economic thinking in the ad-
> vanced countries, which are hampering the scholars there in
> their efforts to be rational but would be almost deadening to
> the intellectual strivings of those in the underdeveloped coun-
> tries.
>
> I would, instead, wish them to have the courage to throw away
> large structures of meaningless, irrelevant and sometimes bla-
> tantly inadequate doctrines and theoretical approaches and to
> start their thinking afresh from a study of their own needs and
> problems.[6]

The view of Seers and Myrdal were too far reaching. An entirely new subdiscipline of "development economics" did not
appear. Instead, modifications and additions were grafted to the
Old Growth Economics. The progress that has been made in de-

velopment economics has actually been mainly within the framework of traditional economic analysis. Although it is recognized that problems of underdevelopment are different in degree—and, to some extent, even in kind—from those encountered in developed countries, nevertheless it has not been necessary to forge entirely different economic tools and apply completely different principles of analysis. Many traditional tools and principles of accepted economic theory proved directly applicable to the problems of poor countries, and some conceptions and techniques could become more useful with some ready-made modification or extension.

What soon became clear, however, is that development economists must frequently depart from traditional assumptions and must alter the premises of accepted economic theory to make the theory relevant to countries that have a different social system and economic structure from those to which Western economists are accustomed. The task of development economists is initially difficult not because they have to start afresh with a completely new set of tools, but because they have to acquire a sense of the different assumptions that are appropriate to analyzing a problem within the context of a poor country. The development economist has to take special care in identifying different institutional relations, in assessing the different quantitative importance of some variables, and in allowing some elements that are usually taken as "given" in traditional economics to become crucial variables that are determined within the development process itself.

Unlike the neoclassical economists who assumed a smoothly working market-price system, the new development economists adopted a more structuralist approach to development problems. The structuralist approach attempted to identify specific rigidities, lags, and other characteristics of the structure of developing economies that affect economic adjustments and the choice of development policy. They identified supply bottlenecks that appeared in certain sectors of the economy through imbalances in the productive structure—particularly the supply shortfalls in the agricultural and export sectors.

On approaching development problems, the early development economists first thought of what "obstacles" to development had to be overcome, and what "missing components" of the development process had to be supplied. If the underdeveloped economy bore some resemblance to the classical stationary state, then the positive forces that classical economists had emphasized as delaying the advent of the stationary state—namely, capital accumulation and technical progress—could now also be emphasized as forces to accelerate development. From the classical tradition, a major obstacle to be overcome was the capital deficiency. And from the viewpoint of missing components, it was necessary to fill the "savings gap" and to foster technical progress. Supply-side economics is not new to the development economist.

It was evident that the amount of capital per head was low in the poor countries, and the current rate of capital accumulation was also very low. As early as 1951, the Secretary-General of the United Nations appointed a "group of experts" to consider measures to accelerate the economic development of underdeveloped countries. The group stated in its report:

> It is a commonplace that economic progress is a function, among other things, of the rate of new capital formation. In most countries where rapid economic progress is occurring, net capital formation at home is at least 10 percent of the national income, and in some it is substantially higher. By contrast, in most underdeveloped countries net capital formation is not as high as 5 percent of the national income, even when foreign investment is included. In many of these countries, the savings have been sufficient only to keep up with population growth, so that only a negligible amount of new capital, if any, has actually become available for increasing the average standard of living. How to increase the rate of capital formation is therefore a question of great urgency.[7]

Considering various domestic measures for mobilizing resources for capital formation, the report recognized the existence of surplus labor:

> In many underdeveloped areas, the population on the land is so great that large numbers could be withdrawn from agriculture without any fall in agricultural output and with very little change of capital techniques. If this labor were employed on

public works, capital would be created without any fall in other output, or in total consumption.[8]

Among this group of experts were Professors Arthur Lewis and Theodore Schultz—each of whom was to receive the Nobel Prize 27 years later for his contribution to development economics. In 1951, however, Lewis was yet to present his celebrated model of capital accumulation, and Schultz was yet to emphasize the value of human capital.

Before these contributions were to be appreciated, other economists followed the Old Growth Economics and emphasized capital accumulation but with some refinements in analysis. How to increase investment became the core of development strategy during the 1950s. For a growing number of academic and government economists, there were five major elements in the commonly advocated development strategy: (1) capital accumulation, (2) deliberate industrialization, (3) protection against imports, (4) development planning, and (5) external aid.

The Big Push and Balanced Growth

Before World War II ended, Paul Rosenstein-Rodan wrote a seminal article about "Problems of Industrialization of Eastern and South-Eastern Europe." Rodan was then studying problems of postwar reconstruction at the Royal Institute of International Affairs. A few years later he was to be the first Assistant Director of the Economics Department at the World Bank, and later a member of the panel of experts for the Alliance for Progress in Latin America. Foreseeing that the development of the "international depressed areas" of the world would be the most important task in the making of the peace, Rodan emphasized the need for a "big push" in investment to accelerate development. His analysis began by focusing on the pervasiveness of rural underdevelopment—"agrarian excess population"—in the less developed countries. He summarized the problem in this way: "Labor must either be transported toward capital (emigration), or capital must be transported toward labor (industrialization)." Emigration was not feasible, so the task fell to industrialization.

Thus the crucial task of a development plan was to achieve sufficient investment to mobilize the unemployed and underemployed for the purpose of industrialization. To reach an "optimum size" for industrial enterprises, however, the area of industrialization must be sufficiently large. Private profit calculations underestimate for the community at large the actual social benefits from an investment. Production must be integrated and centrally planned as though it were taking place in a single "trust." Complementarity of different industries argues in favor of "a large-scale planned industrialization." Only then would the risk for a single enterprise be reduced, all the benefits of a single investment be calculated, and profit estimates revised upward. State investment is therefore required on a broad front.

Rodan went on to argue for a "big push":

> The theory of growth is very largely a theory of investment.
> . . . A minimum quantum of investment is a necessary condition for successful development. . . . Launching a country into self-sustaining growth is a little like getting an airplane off the ground. There is a critical ground speed which must be passed before the craft can become airborne. . . . A big push seems to be required to jump over the economic obstacles to development. There may be finally a phenomenon of indivisibility in the vigor and drive required for a successful development policy. Isolated and small efforts may not add up to a sufficient impact on growth. An atmosphere of development may only arise with a minimum speed or size of investment.[9]

Reinforcing Rodan's "big push" argument was Columbia Professor Ragnar Nurkse's analysis of capital accumulation with its emphasis on "balanced growth." Nurkse began with the simple concept of "the vicious circle of poverty." In Nurkse's words,

> It implies a circular constellation of forces tending to act and react upon one another in such a way as to keep a poor country in a state of poverty. Particular instances of such circular constellations are not difficult to imagine. For example, a poor man may not have enough to eat; being under-fed, his health may be weak; being physically weak, his work capacity is low, which means that he is poor, which in turn means that he will not have enough to eat; and so on. A situation of this sort, relating to a country as a whole, can be summed up in the trite proposition: "a country is poor because it is poor."[10]

For Nurkse, the vicious circle of poverty was most important in explaining the low level of capital accumulation:

> The supply of capital is governed by the ability and willingness to save; the demand for capital is governed by the incentives to invest. A circular relationship exists on both sides of the problem of capital formation in the poverty-ridden areas of the world.
>
> On the supply side, there is the small capacity to save, resulting from the low level of real income. The low real income is a reflection of low productivity, which in its turn is due largely to the lack of capital. The lack of capital is a result of the small capacity to save, and so the circle is complete.
>
> On the demand side, the inducement to investment may be low because of the small buying power of the people, which is due to their small real income, which again is due to low productivity. The low level of productivity, however, is a result of the small amount of capital used in production, which in its turn may be caused at least partly by the small inducement to invest.[11]

If only the "low" investment could be turned into "medium" and then into "high" values, all the other variables in the circle would also become "medium" and then "high." But how could this increase in investment be achieved? According to Nurkse, "Economic progress is not a spontaneous or automatic affair. On the contrary, it is evident that there are automatic forces within the system tending to keep it moored to a given level."[12] How then can the deadlock be broken?

Nurkse's answer is "balanced growth"—the synchronized application of capital to a wide range of industries. Private investment will not be induced in a single line of production taken by itself as long as the market is narrow. Workers do not buy the product they produce in the single line of production. But if there is an overall enlargement of the market, through investment in many industries at the same time, the range of demand will guarantee success for the several investments: "An increase in production over a wide range of consumables, so proportioned as to correspond with the pattern of consumers' preferences, does create its own demand." But how does an economy achieve balanced growth?

Nurkse's policy advice explained the workings of balanced growth:

> [A] frontal attack—a wave of capital investments in a number of different industries—can economically succeed while any substantial application of capital by an individual entrepreneur in any particular industry may be blocked or discouraged by the limitations of the pre-existing market. Where any single enterprise might appear quite inauspicious and impracticable, a wide range of projects in different industries may succeed because they will all support each other, in the sense that the people engaged in each project, now working with more real capital per head and with greater efficiency in terms of output per manhour, will provide an enlarged market for the products of the new enterprises in the other industries. In this way the market difficulty, and the drag it imposes on individual incentives to invest, is removed or at any rate alleviated by means of a dynamic expansion of the market through investment carried out in a number of different industries. . . . Through the application of capital over a wide range of activities, the general level of economic activity is raised and the size of the market enlarged.[13]

Nurkse also emphasized that balanced growth was "a means of getting out of the rut, a means of stepping up the rate of growth when the external forces of advance through trade expansion and foreign capital are sluggish or inoperative."[14] Less developed countries could no longer rely on growth that was induced from the outside through the expansion of world demand for their exports of primary commodities. Under conditions of export pessimism, governments should look for other solutions that would expand production for their own domestic markets. Balanced growth was one way to accelerate growth.

Other economists joined Rodan and Nurkse in emphasizing capital accumulation. Many viewed the poor economy as a stationary economy that needed a stimulus to get it off dead center, just as Nurkse sought to break the vicious circle. Richard Nelson formalized the situation with an analysis of the "low-level equilibrium trap." And Professor Harvey Leibenstein propounded the "critical minimum effort" thesis. If the backward economy is in a stationary state, or subject to a vicious circle of poverty, or in a low-level equilibrium trap, then to achieve the transition from the state of backwardness to the more developed state where we can expect steady growth, it is a necessary condition that the economy should receive a stimulus to growth that is greater than a certain critical minimum size. This is because growth sets up not only income-raising forces but also income-depressing forces such as population growth, declining saving rate, and diseconomies of scale. A critical minimum effort must, therefore, be exceeded so that the income-raising forces surpass the income-depressing forces. Again, a considerable amount of investment became identified with the critical minimum effort.

Comprising some elements of the big push, balanced growth, and critical minimum effort principles, Walt Rostow's "stages of growth" analysis was to have the greatest appeal to the newly emergent countries. Engaging in a broad sweep of history, Rostow pointed the way by describing the course of development as a linear path along which all countries pass. The path runs through a series of stages: the traditional society, the emergence of the preconditions for take-off, the take-off, self-sustaining growth, and the age of high mass consumption.

As a decisive transition from a predominantly agricultural to a predominantly industrial society, the take-off appealed to countries that wanted to accelerate their development. And Rostow conveniently indicated the three essential conditions for the take-off: (1) a rise in the rate of productive investment from, say, 5 percent or less to over 10 percent of national income; (2) the development of one or more substantial manufacturing sectors; and (3) the existence or quick emergence of a political, social, and institutional framework that exploits the impulses for expansion in the modern sector. Policymakers only too readily latched onto the first two conditions of the take-off and almost naively interpreted them as a formula for development.

In many of the emergent nations, Rostow's take-off became almost a new kind of religion. In the early 1960s, it was the underlying theme for the international symposium of economists in Nyasaland (later to become Malawi) at the time Dr. H. Kamuzu Banda became Prime Minister. Interestingly, the program cover for this conference highlighted capital accumulation by reverentially featuring the Harrod-Domar formula $\theta = \sigma \alpha$. This formula had been devised by Oxford don Roy Harrod and Professor Evsey Domar of M.I.T. to indicate what rate of growth in income is necessary to maintain a full employment path of growth in advanced industrial countries such as Britain or the United States. Given α—the inverse of the economist's "marginal capital output ratio," or $\Delta K/\Delta Y$, which shows the economist how much additional capital is needed to produce another unit of output—and given σ—the ratio of savings to national income, or S/Y—it follows that the growth rate θ, or $\Delta Y/Y$, will be $\sigma\alpha$. To raise the growth rate, increases in savings and investment are needed. Once again, capital accumulation becomes the strategic variable in growth.

Even though the conditions in Nyasaland were vastly different from those in Britain and America, the formula was simplistically alluring. If only the propensity to save (σ) could be raised, then the growth rate (θ) would also rise. Such was the early appeal of Rostow's take-off into self-sustained growth through a rise in the rate of investment to over 10 percent of national income.

Industrialization

"Deliberate industrialization for higher incomes" was the early guide for the allocation of investment.[15] The case for industrialization was argued on several fronts. There was unadorned nationalist sentiment in the belief that economic independence could be gained through industrialization. No longer need the nation be a hewer of wood and drawer of water. The economic instability of primary production could be avoided through diversified production. Industrialization was also to play a dynamic role in modernization—instilling new skills, changing values, creating new demand, and promoting attributes of change. Moreover, industrialization might also facilitate the transfer of redundant manpower to new forms of employment.

Arthur Lewis advocated industrialization in 1946 in an early review of a report by the Economic Policy Committee appointed to survey Jamaica's development needs.[16] His critique of the report was directed to "its two most important topics, development policy and its twin, the problem of full employment." But these were the report's weakest parts. Lewis argued that the gap in real per capita income between Jamaicans and the British

> exists because productivity is so low: each man produces too little, and the average man produces the wrong things. They are the wrong things in the sense that their exchange value is low. Jamaica is mainly a primary producer. . . . Jamaicans sell cheap and buy dear in international markets, and unless there is some considerable change in the terms of trade, or unless they can profitably change their occupations, some gap must remain.

At the same time, Lewis emphasized the large number of un-employed and underemployed—the domestic servants (16 percent of Jamaica's gainfully occupied, probably the highest percentage in the world), the hawkers and casual laborers, and the surplus laborers in agriculture. Lewis concluded that

> It is clear as daylight that only a great increase in secondary industry can solve Jamaica's employment problem. Her agricultural resources will not support a population of 1,200,000 increasing by two percent per annum; there is not enough cultivatable land; indeed the land is already carrying more people than it can provide for economically. . . .

> Now it is a commonplace of the history of economic development that in an unindustrialized country industrial costs are always high. Costs fall only as the country becomes industrialized. It is not simply a matter of training labor and accustoming it to factory disciplines, though this is often complex enough. It is also that the economies of industry are the economies of scale, not so much economies of producing in large factories, as is usually thought, as the 'external' economies, which come from having many factories using common services such as power or market organization, which can then themselves operate on a large scale and cheaply. It follows that if one is trying to estimate whether secondary industry will pay in a country not yet industrialized, it is foolish to do so in terms of current costs. Since, too, the economies come from having many factories using common services, it does not follow that because any one factory by itself would not pay, therefore, industrialization is uneconomic, for it may well be that where one would

be too costly a hundred would succeed admirably. There is the
further corollary that the prospects of an area must be looked
at as a whole; the standpoint of the individual industrialist is
too narrow because he thinks only of one factory, and attaches
more importance to immediate costliness than the community
as a whole should.[17]

A U.N. document on the terms of trade of underdeveloped
countries (1949) reinforced the industrialization argument. The
contention was that the export prices of primary products fell
relative to the prices of manufactured commodities. This alleged
deterioration in the terms of trade fostered a pessimism about
the worth of exporting primary products and argued for industrialization.

Studies by the Economic Commission for Latin America (ECLA)
in the early 1950s also made a case for industrialization. It was
believed that if countries followed comparative advantage and an
international division of labor as dictated by market forces, the
inequalities between rich and poor countries would simply be
aggravated because of a worsening in the terms of trade for the
poor countries. This would reduce the capacity for capital accumulation as the poor country would have to use more and
more resources in exports to obtain the same amount of imports.
ECLA's structuralist analysis also focused on agricultural bottlenecks and foreign exchange shortages as being structural bottlenecks to development. To overcome these obstacles, Latin
American countries should undertake investment programs to
change their structure of production and the structure of imports
and exports. Industrialization via import substitution became the
advocated strategy. Implementing this analysis, ECLA's policies
emphasized the need for "programmed" industrialization via import substitution based on protectionist policies.

During the 1950s, the Latin American model spread to countries in Asia and Africa. The promotion of manufacturing over
agricultural and other primary types of production became a
central objective in many development plans. And governments
sought a direct route to industrialization by favoring through inward-looking policies the promotion of domestic production to
replace imported commodities.

Protectionist Policies

The case for protective tariffs and quotas on imports to promote import substitution had much appeal. An increasing number of critics denied the validity of the classical view that international trade will transmit development. They argued in favor of protectionism by contending that the free trade conclusions of the Old Growth Economics did not apply to the special conditions of a less developed country. They also maintained that historically the very forces of international trade have actually impeded the development of poor countries. Instead of recognizing Ricardo's mutual gains from trade, the critics contended that trade could be a zero sum game with the poor country losing what the rich country gains. Or, in a milder form, that the gains from trade could be unequally distributed, with the rich country gaining the larger share.

This attack on classical trade theory, coupled with the new ideology of national independence and increasing state participation, laid the basis for protectionist arguments.

Moreover, the easiest route to industrialization appeared to be through import substitution. If there were imports, there was obviously a market. If the importation of the final commodity (say, an automobile) was then prohibited by a quota or made prohibitively expensive by a tariff, while intermediate inputs (components to be assembled) could be imported freely or at low duties, there would be a stimulus to produce in the sheltered home market. Industrialization might proceed "from the top down"—from the assembling of the components and the putting of the final touches on the finished automobile to the subsequent home production of the intermediate components and the eventual replacement of all imports with local production.

Furthermore, the emergence of balance-of-payments crises stimulated more protectionist arguments. If a deficit in international payments appeared—and the developing countries were especially prone to balance-of-payments deficits—the easiest policy action was to impose another round of tariffs or quotas to limit imports. Instead of bearing the costs of deflation or devaluation of their foreign exchange rates, governments turned to protectionism.

Economists were also providing some arguments that had logical appeal. By protecting an infant industry that has potential for future expansion and an eventual reduction in costs, a tariff might allow the country to enter a line of production in which it might eventually acquire a comparative advantage. Some economists even broadened the classic infant industry argument to include the overall structure of the LDC by claiming that the entire economy is now an "infant economy." Protective policies might then promote changes in the structure of production. In particular, proponents of import substitution argued that protectionist trade policies could stimulate the movement of excess labor out of agriculture into the protected industries.

There were also arguments for diversification through protection. It was asserted that if there is a question about the future existence of markets for exports, or if exports consist of exhaustible resources, then it would be safer over the long run to diversify through import substitution instead of trying to increase exports in order to be able to import. And to the extent that the poor country's demand for imports is growing more rapidly than the external demand for its exports, the case for protection is reinforced: the country must supply all those industrial products that cannot be imported in view of the relatively slow growth of its exports.

Development Planning

Once the efficacious operation of the market–price system had been denied, and a case made for a big push toward industrialization via import substitution, it was but a short step to advocating a central development plan. The U.N. "group of experts" recommended as early as 1951 that the

government of an underdeveloped country should establish a central economic unit with the functions of surveying the economy, making development programmes, advising on the measures necessary for carrying out such programmes and reporting on them periodically. The development programmes should contain a capital budget showing the requirements of capital and how much of this is expected from domestic and from foreign sources.[18]

Specific emphasis was given to the advisability of five-year plans for public expenditure and to the need for comprehensive planning to ensure that the various plans that are being made are consistent with each other and with the total resources available.

Having questioned the relevance of neoclassical economics for the problems of poor countries, the New Development Economics went on to criticize the invisible hand conception of the market-price system as being either ineffective, unreliable, or irrelevant for development problems. Critics contended that the price system and market forces were too weak to accomplish the changes needed for accelerated development. Even a fairly well-defined price system may be considered unreliable, it was claimed, when the market prices of goods and the prices of factors of production do not reflect the true costs of these goods and factors to society. A planning agency should then correct the market prices and allocate resources in accordance with the corrected "accounting" or "shadow" prices. Above all, it was believed that the price system must be superseded when the determination of the amount and composition of investment is too important to be left to a multitude of uncoordinated individual investment decisions, and when the tasks of a developing economy entail large structural changes over a long period ahead instead of simply small adjustments in the present period. If there is to be an industrialization program, secondary industries must be created on a large scale and be supported by sufficient overhead capital in the form of public utilities and public facilities that the several industries use in common.

Once investment was to be expanded in the public sector, it was necessary to consider programs to stimulate domestic savings and to secure needed resources from abroad to support the investment targets. Government was to have an increasing role in the accumulation of capital through taxation, the formation of financial institutions, control of consumption imports, and improvement in the country's terms of trade. Government effort had to be directed toward maximizing savings, mobilizing resources for productive investment, and canalizing the savings in the private sector to serve the purposes of a balanced development program.

It was, of course, recognized that, although planning may be more essential in less developed than in advanced countries, it was at the same time much more difficult to execute. But by appeal at one extreme to "popular enthusiasm" and at the other extreme to more refined economic techniques of planning, the Early Development Economics could be hopeful about the prospects for planning. Arthur Lewis, for instance, could say in 1952:

> It can thus be seen that planning in backward countries imposes much bigger tasks on governments than does planning in advanced countries. The government has to do many things which can in advanced countries be left to entrepreneurs. It has to create industrial centres, to put through an agricultural revolution, to control the foreign exchanges more strictly, and in addition to make up a great leeway of public services and/or ordinary economic legislation. And all this has to be done through a civil service that is usually much inferior to that of an advanced country. Why then do backward countries take more readily to planning? Because their need is also so obviously much greater. And it is also this that enables them to carry it through in spite of error and incompetence. For, if the people are on their side, nationalistic, conscious of their backwardness, and anxious to progress, they willingly bear great hardships and tolerate many mistakes, and they throw themselves with enthusiasm into the job of regenerating their country. Popular enthusiasm is both the lubricating oil of planning, and the petrol of economic development—a dynamic force that almost makes all things possible.[19]

With an eloquence reminiscent of Smith's conception of the invisible hand, Lewis provided wide scope for the visible hand of the state. And to show how actually to formulate development programs, many of the new development economists were soon to fashion a number of impressive techniques for development planning. The economist's heavy technical machinery—macroeconomic models and sector models, interindustry models based on input–output matrices and linear programming models, and the techniques of statistical inference and decision analysis—were all to be brought to bear on development planning. Sophisticated studies of planning multiplied, creating a considerable mystique for all except the initiated. In India, a modest illustration of the technical proliferation was evident in an early study of Indian planning that used "a linear programming formulation to check the efficiency of investment and prices implicit in the Government's plan frame four-sector model." At the same time, the advance of computer technology allowed the models to become ever more elaborate—and again all the more impressive to the uninitiated. The teaching of development economics in Western universities focused increasingly on these techniques of development programming. And more and more, students from the developing countries attended these courses and took the professional techniques of the "expert" back to their governmental agencies. To an increasing extent, the $\theta = \sigma\alpha$ mystique was transferred internationally.

External Aid

If the developing country's government was to play a major role in stimulating development, so too was there emphasis on government-to-government assistance from the more advanced countries. As latecomers to development, the newly emergent countries ought to be able to tap the resources, technology, and skills that were available in the countries that had already developed to high levels. Indeed, some of the most significant components of the development process that were missing in the less developed country could be obtained from abroad—capital aid, technical assistance, and management.

Economists devised a number of arguments for the transfer of resources from rich to poor countries. As a trustee for the poor, the economist might have first come to advocate foreign aid on moral grounds. But he quickly went on to purely economic arguments—perhaps best summarized in the "two-gap model." This type of model is based on a structuralist concept of development and incorporates explicit limits on the rate of increase of domestic saving, investment, and exports. The model focuses in particular on the savings and foreign exchange constraints to development. The shortage of domestic savings limits the capital accumulation in the developing country. The shortage of foreign exchange limits the country's capacity to import. If the growth in GNP depends on the importation of goods that cannot be produced at home, then the country's growth rate will be constrained by its access to foreign exchange. These two gaps—the savings gap and the foreign exchange gap—might be filled by foreign aid. The gap between required and available savings and between required and available foreign exchange can be filled by an inflow of foreign loans or grants from governments in the rich countries. The inflow of public foreign capital is equivalent to an inflow of savings from abroad: the rich countries transfer their savings to investment opportunities in the poor countries. By relaxing the savings and foreign exchange constraints, the inflow of foreign capital can yield an increase in national income that is several times the cost of the foreign loan.

Some simple calculations were used to demonstrate the need for public foreign investment. The case of India was illustrative. India's national income in 1950–1951 was approximately $18 billion, of which about 5 percent, or $900 million, was saved. This was barely enough to maintain the capital stock intact and to keep up with the annual population increase. Even a doubling of the amount of capital available from domestic sources would not provide a very rapid rate of development in India. The inflow of private foreign investment was also small. To mobilize sufficient resources to fulfill the targets of its first five-year development plan (1952–1957), India had to rely on foreign aid.

Considering poor countries in general, the U.N. "group of experts" estimated that the total capital required in the early 1950s to increase per capita national income by 2 percent per annum would require an annual investment of about $19 billion. But domestic savings in these countries fell short of this amount by nearly $14 billion. After allowing for some increase in domestic savings, the group concluded that an annual capital import well in excess of $10 billion would be required. Given that the current inflow of foreign capital, including loans and grants, did not exceed $1.5 billion, there was a clear need for a manifold increase in the inflow of capital from rich governments to poor governments.

Economists believed, that along with foreign capital, the borrowing of new technology and the acquisition of know-how from abroad were desirable in order to absorb the additional capital more rapidly. To utilize the inflow of capital productively, the developing country had to acquire the missing components of technology, skills, and management. But it was thought that these could be imported. And there was little questioning of the worth of the knowledge and technological transfers that could come from the accumulated stocks in the advanced countries. Views differed only on whether the technical assistance program should operate on a bilateral basis (such as in the U.S. program) or be multilateral (as in the Colombo Plan for Southeast Asia or the U.N. program).

The Dual Economy

All these various components of the Early Development Economics were synthesized in a model that has been most influential in development thinking—the dual economy model.

"Dualism" has long been recognized as a characteristic of an underdeveloped country. The term came into prominence in association with the colonial status of many underdeveloped countries. A history of nineteenth-century Jamaica, for instance, is entitled *Two Jamaicas*. Two cultures—two ways of life—were represented by the African Jamaica and the European Jamaica. The Dutch economist J. H. Boeke also emphasized in his study of Indonesian development the differing social organizations and cultural contrasts that result in "social dualism"—"the clashing of an imported social system with an indigenous social system of another style."

The concept of dualism was quickly incorporated into the Early Development Economics, and several models of a "dual economy" were formulated to illuminate the process of development. Although differing in details, the dual economy models generally divided the economy into two sectors—one modern and one traditional—and then considered how the modern sector might spread and absorb the traditional. An early U.N. report, for example, suggested that most African economies may be represented by some form of model, the basic feature of which is a distinction between a traditional economic system and a modern exchange system. The effect of economic development, which springs from the exchange economy, is an encroachment on the traditional economy that draws part of its resources into the orbit of the exchange economy and brings about the erosion of the traditional economy. The report interpreted economic development as "the enlargment of the money economy involving the shift of resources from subsistence production to production for sale."

Of all the dual economy models, that formulated by Arthur Lewis has remained the simplest in construction, yet the richest in perceptive insights. His receipt of the Nobel Prize recognized this. Lewis formulated his model in 1954 as an aid to "interpreting development with unlimited supplies of labor." The starting point was the recognition that surplus labor is a crucial structural difference between developed and less developed countries. Labor is in surplus supply in an underdeveloped economy, and the prime task of the development process is to absorb the surplus labor into more productive employment. Lewis, therefore, returns to some assumptions of the Old Growth Economics: "The classics, from Smith to Marx, all assumed, or argued, that an unlimited supply of labor was available at subsistence wages. They then enquired how production grows through time. They found the answer in capital accumulation. . . ." Similarly, Lewis states that

> The central problem in the theory of economic development is to understand the process by which a community which was previously saving and investing four or five percent of its national income or less, converts itself into an economy where voluntary saving is running at about 12 to 15 percent of national income or more. This is the central problem because the central fact of economic development is rapid capital accumulation (including knowledge and skills with capital).[20]

Through the process of capital accumulation, the surplus labor is absorbed into the more productive capitalist sector, and the low-productivity traditional sector withers away.

Lewis begins by recognizing that most countries in the early

stages of economic development have not one economy but two—
a high-productivity, high-wage economy (composed of mines,
plantations, factories, large-scale transport) and a low-productivity,
low-earnings economy (composed of family farms, handicraft
workers, domestic servants, petty traders, casual laborers). The
surplus labor is mainly in the low-earnings sector. This sector is
characterized by the family mode of production that makes little
use of reproducible capital or wage employment but, instead, uses
traditional techniques of production and relies on self-employment or income-sharing in an extended or joint family system.
Productivity of labor is very low, but each worker shares in the
consumption of the family output.

In contrast, the high-earnings sector is the capitalist sector that
uses reproducible capital and pays capitalists for its use. The
capitalists hire the services of labor for a money wage, produce
an output for sale on the market, and sell the product at some
profit or surplus above the wage payments. "Capitalist" is used
in the classical sense of an enterprise that hires labor and resells
its output for a profit. The capitalist may be a private enterprise
or a state-owned enterprise.

The capitalist sector is an island (or a number of tiny islands)
surrounded by a vast sea of subsistence workers. The dualism is
widespread:

> We find a few industries highly capitalized, such as mining or
> electric power, side by side with the most primitive techniques;
> a few high class shops, surrounded by masses of old style
> traders; a few highly capitalized plantations, surrounded by a
> sea of peasants. But we find the same contrasts also outside
> their economic life. There are one or two modern towns, with
> the finest architecture, water supplies, communications and the
> like, into which people drift from other towns and villages which
> might almost belong to another planet. There is the same con-
> trast even between people; between the few highly wester-
> nized, trousered, natives, educated in Western universities,
> speaking Western languages, and glorying in Beethoven, Mill,
> Marx or Einstein, and the great mass of their countrymen who
> live in quite other worlds. Capital and new ideas are not thinly
> diffused throughout the economy; they are highly concen-
> trated at a number of points, from which they spread out-
> wards.[21]

A fundamental relationship exists between the capitalist and subsistence sectors—when the capitalist sector expands, it draws on labor from the subsistence sector. For countries that have experienced high rates of population growth and are densely populated, the supply of unskilled labor to the capitalist sector is unlimited in the sense that the supply is greater than the demand at the existing wage rate. A large component of the unlimited supply of labor is composed of those who are in very low-productivity agricultural activities and in other overmanned occupations such as domestic service, casual odd jobs, or petty retail trading. Additional sources of labor are women who transfer from the household to commercial employment, the growth in the labor force resulting from population increase, and immigration. The large pool of unskilled labor—in Marxist language, the "reserve army of the unemployed"—enables new industries to be created or old industries to expand in the capitalist sector without encountering any shortage of unskilled labor and without having to raise wages.

Lewis proceeds to show how capital accumulation in the capitalist sector will draw surplus laborers away from unemployment and underemployment in the subsistence sector into more productive employment in the higher wage capitalist sector. In this dual sector model, the traditional sector withers away as production grows in the capitalist sector through time, while the investment in the capitalist sector absorbs the surplus labor from the traditional sector. The major conclusion from the model is that the rate at which surplus labor will be absorbed in the capitalist sector depends on the size of the capitalist sector and the ratio of profits in national income: the larger the capitalist sector, and the greater the share of profits in national income, the more rapidly will surplus labor be absorbed.

Some details of Lewis's reasoning can be filled in. Tracing the process of economic expansion, Lewis emphasizes that the key to the process is the use made of the capitalist surplus. The driving force in the system is generated by the reinvestment of the capitalist surplus in creating new capital. As the capitalist sector expands, it draws labor from the subsistence sector into wage employment—but at a constant wage rate.

The wage that the capitalist sector has to pay is determined by what labor earns in the subsistence sector. Peasant farmers will not leave the family farm for wage employment unless the new real wage allows them a standard of living equal to or higher than that in the subsistence sector. Capitalist wages, as a rule, will have to be somewhat higher than subsistence earnings to compensate labor for the cost of transferring and to induce labor to leave the traditional life of the subsistence sector. According to Lewis, "Economists have usually expected wage rates in the modern sector to be about 50 percent above the income of subsistence farmers. This brings the modern sector as much labor as it wants, without at the same time attracting much more than it can handle."[22]

The amount of labor hired at this wage rate in the capitalist sector depends on its productivity, but, in being utilized with capital, the labor produces an output of greater value than its wage. The value of the total product in the capitalist sector is divided between wages and the capitalists' surplus or profit. In the classical tradition, capitalists save out of their profits, and the savings are reinvested in the capitalist sector. The investment raises the productivity of labor, and the expanding capitalist sector then demands more labor. But the surplus labor can still be hired at the same wage rate, so that out of a new larger total output, the share of profits in national income rises. This will mean, in turn, that savings rise as a share of national income, and so does investment. And as investment increases, so too does the demand for more labor. Eventually, capital accumulation catches up with the surplus labor. At that point, the subsistence sector, with its original supply of surplus labor, will have been absorbed into the modern capitalist sector. After that point, the capitalist must offer higher wages to induce more employment of labor.

This type of dual economy model was at the center of the Early Development Economics. It had considerable appeal because of its essentially optimistic vision of the development process. Earlier, other countries had proceeded through such a process, and the latecomers to development might now begin to do the same. The model would run its course to a happy end—provided no components were missing (such as a capitalist class or a market for the product of the capitalist sector), and no obstacles arose (such as a premature rise in wages that cut into profits). The emphasis on capital accumulation could also fit nicely with other elements of economic thinking about development, and with the practice of development planning. Moreover, promotion of the capitalist sector could be readily identified with the objective of industrialization via import substitution. As a model of what might be, it was able to synthesize the most significant elements of development thought in the 1950s.

The New Realities

Although analytically perceptive and appealing within the mainstream of development thought, the outcome of the Lewis model has in reality turned out to be quite different from the 1954 vision of what might be. Because of what has transpired during the period of three decades since Lewis formulated his model, we must now modify the model's structural relationships.

The capitalist sector has now come to be identified with an urban industrial sector. The subsistence sector has come to be identified with a rural agricultural sector. Between the two sectors, there has occurred an extensive rural-urban migration, as discussed previously. And the migration has been in an amount far larger than the urban industrial sector has been able to handle. The migration has been greater than anticipated in the Lewis model because urban wages have not been only about 50 percent higher than rural earnings, but as much as 300 to 400 percent higher in Asia and Latin America, and 400 to 500 percent higher in some African countries. Several factors account for the large rural-urban wage differentials: trade unions, minimum wage laws, salaries in the public sector, and foreign enterprises that believe a high wage policy is beneficial to the enterprise. At the same time, while the urban sector offers a pull toward high-wage employment and all the social amenities and public services of urban life, there has been relatively little policy action to stop the push out of the rural sector.

Although rural-urban migration has been large, the urban industrial sector has not expanded sufficiently to absorb the inflow. To the extent that it has been based on import substitution production, the industrial sector has not had a high rate of growth: it has been a once-for-all process that slowed down after the first easy stage of import substitution was over. Not only has output not expanded rapidly enough to absorb labor in the industrial sector, but the techniques of production used in this sector have been biased toward the use of a great deal of capital relative to labor. This has been because the cost of capital has not reflected its true scarcity, wages have been relatively high and have outstripped labor productivity, and foreign exchange for the importation of capital equipment has been undervalued. Moreover, at the level of the firm's operation, employers prefer to manage machines that cannot strike, and foreign-owned enterprises simply carry over the capital-intensive techniques of production of the parent company.

Given that the urban industrial sector has been unable to provide sufficient employment, the surplus migrant laborers have become slum dwellers and squatters who engage in whatever activities of self-employment are possible—working as hawkers, porters, shoeshiners, self-employed craftsmen, small retail traders, own-account workers, and unpaid family workers. There is thus an expansion of what in sanitized language is called the "informal sector." Employment opportunities in the informal sector are self-created by the higglers of Kingston, the betja drivers of Jakarta, the peddlers of Lima, the tailors of Nairobi, and the shoeshine boys of Calis. These workers may actually be working long hours at extremely difficult physical labor, but their productivity is low, and their meager income is highly variable and frequently shared with others. The informal sector has acted as a sponge for the surplus labor that migrates to the urban area. In most LDCs, the number in the urban informal sector has risen not only absolutely but also as a proportion of the total labor force.

In reality, the urban industrial sector has thus become subdivided into two subsectors: the organized subsector and the informal subsector. An International Labor Organization report on Kenya draws several distinctions between the formal and informal sectors. The formal sector is characterized by difficult entry, frequent reliance on overseas resources, corporate ownership, technology that utilizes a great deal of capital relative to labor and is often imported, formally acquired skills, and markets that are protected by the government through tariffs, quotas, and licenses.

The informal sector, in contrast, is characterized by ease of entry, reliance on indigenous resources, family ownership of enterprises, small scale of operation, technology that utilizes a great deal of labor relative to capital, skills acquired outside the formal school system, and unregulated and competitive markets.

In the rural sector a similar subdivision is evident. The organized subsector comprises plantations, estates, mines, and commercial farms. These operate with modern management, advanced techniques of production, and wage employment. Widespread, however, is the informal subsector in which a family mode of production remains of the traditional subsistence variety with production for household consumption.

A "double dualism" has thus arisen within the poor country. Beyond this dualism, however, there is also an international dualism between rich countries and poor countries—the so-called "North-South" problem in international relations or the problem of international polarization as expressed in the various theories of dependency, which we will discuss in Chapter 8. The relations among the rural-urban sectors and the organized-informal subsectors should be analyzed within the context of a world economy in which rich and poor countries co-exist.

Within this model, analysts now have to identify the causes for the disappointments experienced—the lag of the poorest countries in their development rates, pervasive unemployment and underemployment despite respectable rates of increase in investment and GNP, inequality in the distribution of income, the larger numbers in absolute poverty, and inadequate progress in agriculture. Within this model, policymakers have to devise remedial policies to improve on the development record.

Focusing on the disappointments, economists have discarded some earlier ideas, and a revision in development thought has ensued. Deserving the most attention are the interrelated problems of unemployment, inequality, and absolute poverty as affected by both domestic and international policies. These problems have stimulated some revisionist thinking—to which we now turn.

7

Development Strategies Revised

As the disappointments in the development record became more apparent and their initial optimism waned, economists discarded some earlier expectations and formulated development strategies believed more appropriate for reversing the disappointments. They worried especially about the persistence of unemployment and underemployment, the greater number in absolute poverty, and the inequality in the distribution of income and assets. All these disappointments have come about despite a greater proportion of national income being invested and quite respectable rates of growth in GNP. One could not then help but question the very meaning of "economic development." And a reaction set in against the basic tenets of the Early Development Economics.

Revising the Goals

Dissatisfaction with the results during the first generation of development in the 1950s and 1960s has led to a refocusing of strategy to meet the second-generation problems of development. The goals of development have been reinterpreted in a broader context than simply growth in GNP. In many countries it has become only too painfully apparent that, despite growth in aggregate output, there can still be a larger number of people below an "absolute poverty" line, a greater number of unemployed and underemployed, and an increasingly unequal distribution. The quality of development is completely masked if the policymaker does not pierce the aggregate measure of GNP and consider its composition and distribution.

Development economists no longer worship at the altar of GNP, but concentrate more directly on the quality of the development process. As the Minister of Planning for Pakistan observes,

> The problem of development must be defined as a selective attack on the worst forms of poverty. Development goals must be defined in terms of progressive reduction and eventual elimination of malnutrition, disease, illiteracy, squalor, unemployment and inequalities. We were taught to take care of our GNP and this will take care of poverty. Let us reverse this and take care of poverty as this will take care of the GNP. In other words, let us worry about the *content* of GNP even more than its rate of increase.[1]

Instead of focusing on any aggregate, or even per capita, index of "development," economists began in the mid-1970s to emphasize directly the achievement of better nourishment, health, education, living conditions, and conditions of employment for the low-end poverty groups. Instead of seeking "development" as an end, policymakers have come to view it as a means—as an instrumental process for overcoming persistent poverty, absorbing the unemployed, and diminishing inequality.

The calls for "redistribution with growth," "reduction of absolute poverty," "meeting of basic human needs"—these have become elements of a revised development strategy, a strategy of "first things first." The earlier strategy of high growth with a reliance on a trickle-down mechanism to reach the poor did not in reality operate to bring the benefits of growth to the poor. The gains were concentrated in the upper-income groups, and little was done to reduce inequality in income distribution.

By 1974, the World Bank and the Sussex Institute of Development Studies argued in their book *Redistribution with Growth* that the extra income through growth should be redirected to the poor instead of accruing to the "better off." Bank Vice-President Hollis Chenery introduced the book by stating:

It is now clear that more than a decade of rapid growth in underdeveloped countries has been of little or no benefit to perhaps a third of their population. Although the average per capita income of the Third World has increased by 50 percent since 1960, this growth has been very unequally distributed among countries, regions within countries, and socioeconomic groups.[2]

The book's diagnosis had several policy implications for channeling the benefits of growth to certain target poverty groups—the small farmers and landless laborers in the rural areas and the unemployed, "working poor," and underemployed in the urban informal sector. These poverty groups are prevented from sharing equitably in a general increase in output because of their lack of physical and human capital and lack of access to public services, information, and markets.

A policy of redistributing existing assets was not proposed. Instead, "incremental redistribution" was recommended—that is, as output expanded, a larger share of the increase in output would accrue to the low-end poverty groups. Redistribution would occur from extra incomes, not by reducing any existing income. This amounts to raising the growth rate of the incomes of the poor, while the upper end of the income scale does not grow so rapidly.

A "welfare index" that combined growth and distribution considerations could be used to evaluate the effects of proposed development programs. Such an index would give a higher weight to the growth of incomes for the poorer groups. Unlike the conventional measures of growth in income that attach the same weight to a dollar of extra income for a rich person as for a poor one, the advocates of "redistribution with growth" suggested that measures should give the lowest 40 percent of the population three times the weight of growth of incomes in the top 20 percent, and twice the weight of the middle 40 percent of the population. Redistribution would result by providing investment resources to the poor, improving the quality of work in the rural and urban informal sectors, and redirecting public investment. There would be a special emphasis on agriculture and rural development as the major concern of poverty-oriented planning. Moreover, policies would be devoted to making the informal sector more productive by removing discrimination against this sector and improving its access to public services, credit, information, and markets.

"Reduction of absolute poverty" was introduced in the mid-1970s as a development objective by World Bank President McNamara to distinguish between relative inequality in income distribution and differences in the absolute standard of living in terms of nutrition, clothing, sanitation, health, and education. The focus now was to be on growth of the absolute standard of living of the lowest 40 percent of the population who suffered from absolute poverty—from mass deprivation of basic human needs.

Some early development economists were keenly aware of the problems of distribution and basic needs. The first five-year plan in a developing country—that of India in 1952—aimed at "maximum production, full employment, the attainment of economic equality and social justice." India's second five-year plan in 1956 took employment generation as its objective. And, in the early 1960s, the Indian Planning Commission was concerned with the problems of absolute poverty and the concept of a minimum needs basket.

The first World Bank mission to a developing country—that of Colombia in 1949—also stated that basic human needs should be placed first, and that the primary emphasis should be on the provision of essentials. These early objectives, however, were submerged under the overriding objective of growth in GNP as the ever greater influx of economists into the field of development swamped the original pioneers, and as the newcomers diluted the original objectives with objectives of growth that were closer to those specified for the more developed countries, which were emphasizing growth during the record-breaking period of the late 1950s and 1960s.

Fulfilling Basic Needs

In promoting a basic needs approach to development, the economist is most vividly seen as the trustee for the poor. Poverty is diagnosed as the absolute deprivation of a set of human needs without which the human potential cannot be realized. Starvation, malnutrition, disease, and illiteracy make the dimensions of poverty only too concretely visible, without the economist's recourse to more abstract concepts of gross national product, income distribution, or productivity indices.

During the 1970s, the purpose of development became ever more focused on a basic needs approach—though not without its critics. Donor agencies, international conferences, and an increasing number of economists attempted to make the approach more explicit and operational. Especially notable was the report of the International Labor Organization's World Employment Conference in 1976. The Conference report proposed that each country adopt a basic needs approach, which aimed at achieving a certain specific minimum standard of living before the end of the century.

Economists who emphasize the basic needs approach identify a set of "core" needs—a bundle of goods and services that the bottom 40 percent needs—but does not have access to because of low income or because the government is not financially able to supply these goods and services to the people. The sectors that provide the core basic needs are essentially education, health, nutrition, water supply and sanitation, and shelter. Instead of focusing on per capita income, this approach disaggregates the concept of "poverty" into its input components and emphasizes the means for meeting these minimum requirements.

The basic needs approach is a logical extension of the concern for more productive labor utilization, redistribution with growth, and mitigation of absolute poverty. It has, however, a special and distinct appeal. For most people, the meeting of basic needs has a higher priority than reducing inequality in income distribution. The criteria for fulfilling basic needs are also clearer than those for an equitable distribution. Being concrete and specific, the goals of the basic needs approach are more operational: the approach is concerned with particular goods and services directed at particular, identified human beings.

As a proponent of the approach, Professor Paul Streeten states,

> The essence of the case for the basic needs approach is that it enables us to achieve a widely agreed-upon, high-priority objective in a shorter period, and with fewer resources, than if we took the roundabout route of only raising employment and

incomes, and waiting for basic needs to be satisfied. Fewer resources are required, or the objective can be achieved sooner,
because a direct attack on deprivation economizes on the resources for which income would otherwise be spent and which
do not contribute to meeting basic needs. Basic needs is thrice
blessed. It is an end in itself, not in need of any further justification. But it is also a form of human resource mobilization,
it harnesses the factor in abundant supply, and, by reducing
population growth, it economizes in the use of resources and
improves the quality of labor.[3]

To implement the approach, "new style" projects in nutrition,
health, and education are required. These should provide public
services that reach the poorest and should be designed to improve the income-earning opportunities for the poorest. In fact,
such projects may reduce the required resources by economizing
on resources devoted to nonbasic needs. For example, in the
health sector, resources may be shifted from curative to preventive medicine, and from urban to rural health services. Resources may also be economized by taking advantage of the linkages and complementarities among the different sectors. For
instance, education may improve nutrition and thus reduce health
expenditures. Resources absorbed by population growth may also
be reduced if the provision of basic needs reduces fertility rates
by reducing infant mortality, educating women, and caring for
the elderly, so that the need for large families is reduced.

Much as the basic needs approach appeals to the economist as
trustee for the poor, it is subject to criticism by the economist as
guardian of rationality. The approach has no underlying concep-
tual model that allows the economist to draw inferences deduc-
tively. Nor is the approach quantitative. The economist has no
guide in exercising the logic of choice. How does one weigh a 10
percent increase in literacy and complete freedom from malaria
as against a 70 percent increase in literacy and no health improvement? How is one to assess the fulfillment of basic material
needs, but at the cost of nonmaterial needs, such as participation and political rights as in China? Recipient LDCs also resent
the implication that their development efforts have failed, and
they may consider the basic needs approach as a diversion from

their central growth effort. The necessary political commitment is also commonly missing.

Moreover, those who advocate the basic needs approach argue—contrary to an emphasis on market forces by the guardian of rationality—that economic growth does not spread its benefits widely and speedily through market forces. Instead of relying on market forces, the administrative allocation of particular resources to particular groups is advocated. As Paul Streeten contends, since supplies may respond to market incentives only slowly or even perversely,

> it is not sufficient to channel purchasing power into the hands of the poor, through employment creation, productivity-raising measures, improvements in access to productive factors for the self-employed, and appropriate policies for relative prices. The structure of production and supply, and the institutional arrangements must also be such that they respond speedily to the demand generated by a basic needs approach.[4]

Some forms of direct supply management are therefore advocated to ensure that the structure of production and the organization of the system meet the demands of the poor people.

As a guardian of rationality, however, the economist may fear that this approach invites an excessive degree of government intervention without sufficient rational guidance. Instead, a more efficient approach to the fulfillment of basic needs might still be through income growth, provided market forces are strengthened and allowed to operate. Increasing productivity, raising the demand for labor, increasing public investment as income rises, and raising the purchasing power of the poor—these forces may also fulfill basic needs.

Whether one advocates fulfillment of basic needs through income growth or through direct-supply management will depend on one's assessment of the strength and relevance of market forces in providing income-earning opportunities for the poorest, as well as the efficiency of meeting basic needs through raising personal income and allowing consumer choice on necessities. If market imperfections are pervasive and widespread market failure cannot be remedied, and if basic needs cannot be provided as efficiently through personal consumption on the market as through public efforts, then the guardian's reliance on rationality loses force. If rationality is so restricted, the reliance on income growth by the guardian of rationality assumes a secondary role to that of the direct provision of basic needs by the trustee for the poor.

Increasing Employment

To reduce absolute poverty, achieve redistribution with growth, and fulfill basic needs, a central component of development thought now emphasizes the creation of more productive and remunerative jobs. The first U.N. group of experts who were asked in 1951 to prepare a report on unemployment and under-employment in underdeveloped countries, and on the national and international measures required to reduce such unemployment and underemployment, simply concluded that "the principal way to reduce unemployment and underemployment is through economic development." But the development record has shown that an emphasis on economic development is not equivalent to an emphasis on employment. After the decades of development without employment, a more direct attack on the employment problem is thought necessary. The problem encompasses those who are in underemployment and among the ranks of the working poor as well as those who are in open unemployment—and hence calls for policies to raise the quality as well as the quantity of employment.

A development strategy that focuses on employment must now begin again by recognizing the existence of surplus labor and then reconsider how this labor can be absorbed in the context of the organized and informal sectors of the revised dual sector model of Lewis. The structural relationships of that revised model indicate that the employment problem is really a number of interrelated problems revolving around rural-urban migration, the output mix of the organized sectors, and technology.

More of the labor force must be absorbed in the rural areas, and the rural-urban migration must be curtailed. To achieve this, it is necessary to modify policies that have reacted against agricultural development. Ceiling prices on foodstuffs, export taxes or restrictions on primary products, and tariff protection on in-dustrial inputs and consumer goods have acted as disincentives to agricultural producers while they have artificially increased the urban-rural income differential.

Efforts should also be made to disperse to the rural sector some of the amenities and public services now concentrated in urban areas. Readier access to such services as public utilities, health, education, and entertainment in the rural areas may amount to an increase in the rural social wage and may diminish the attraction of the bright lights of the city.

Most important will be the type of strategy pursued for developing the agricultural sector. As demonstrated in Japan and Taiwan, a labor-using, capital-saving type of approach to agricultural development will be most beneficial in absorbing a growing labor force in productive employment. Small-scale farms, relying on labor-intensive methods of cultivation but with improved seeds, fertilizer, and irrigation, may raise yields markedly without unduly displacing labor.

The output mix of the organized sectors also has to be altered to include commodities that utilize labor more abundantly in their production. Economists now emphasize appropriate products as well as appropriate technology. With high degrees of income inequality and policies of import substitution, many developing countries have catered to the demand of a small section of the population who consume oversophisticated products that are imitative of the products of more developed economies. Such products tend to require in their production high skills and considerable capital relative to unskilled labor. Simpler, more basic products can be more appropriate in absorbing additional labor in their production.

Appropriate technology that uses more labor and saves on capital has to be introduced into as many activities as possible. Sometimes called "intermediate technology" or an "alternative technology," the aim is to avoid the imitation of too advanced techniques of production that have been simply transferred from the more developed countries. Instead of capital-using, sophisticated, large-scale operations, more appropriate technology would involve less investment per worker, greater use of labor and local materials, and simpler, small-scale techniques.

The challenge of appropriate technology is, of course, to design more labor-using technology but not at the expense of a trade-off with output. It would not be an unambiguous gain to employ more workers, but with lower productivity per worker and lower productivity per unit of capital (less yards of cloth per rupee of investment), so that the output falls. If the objective is to achieve employment with growth, a trade-off between output and employment must be avoided by undertaking policies that will increase both employment and output. The advocacy of more labor-intensive techniques of production must mean efficient labor-using techniques or efficient capital-saving techniques that will not reduce the productivity of capital at the same time as more labor is used with capital. If efficient capital-saving techniques for stretching capital and using labor are introduced, there can be an increase in both employment and output.

The urban employment problem cannot be solved, however, by relying on only the expansion of the modern organized sector. Even the most optimistic projection of growth in the organized sector is insufficient to absorb the rapid growth of urban population as a result of migration and a high natural rate of increase in population. In many of the cities of Asia, Africa, and Latin America, those living in shanty towns compose a third to a half of the population. No realistic expansion of employment in the organized urban sector can possibly absorb the rapidly growing urban labor force.

If the informal sector has been acting as a sponge for the surplus urban labor, its level of productivity has to be raised. Instead of ignoring the informal sector, or even actively discriminating against it as in the past, governmental efforts must allow the urban informal sector to gain access to more productive resources. The working poor in the informal sector are too poor to afford unemployment. But the self-created employment of the poor (as hawkers, shoeshine boys, craftsmen, and casual laborers) is of such low productivity that they must be considered a target group for the removal of poverty. Policies must center on redirecting investment to this group to provide training, education, access to credit, market information, and public services that might increase their productivity and income-earning opportunities. More linkages might also be forged through subcontracting or market relationships between the organized and informal sectors, so that the informal sector might contribute more inputs to the output of the organized sector.

Agriculture

Although a lesson of economic history is that an industrial revolution is dependent on a prior or accompanying agrarian revolution, the development record reveals only too clearly that many LDCs neglect the agricultural sector. In most LDCs, the poor performance of agriculture marks it as a problem sector. Economists now emphasize that urban bias and rural neglect can ill be afforded in the face of population growth and problems of unemployment, poverty, and maldistribution of income. The poor are disproportionately located in rural areas. The importance of food and other farm products as major sources of income for the bulk of the population must be recognized. The key to more rapid growth and poverty alleviation in most LDCs is to improve productivity and income in the agricultural sector. As a long-time student of African agriculture observes, "A society cannot expect to move from a low- to a middle-income stage of development if two-thirds of its population are producing millet, sorghum, maize, and yams at stagnant levels of output."[5]

The current emphasis on agriculture is a change from earlier views. In their focus on industrialization and capital accumulation, the development strategies of the 1950s and 1960s bestowed only an instrumental value on agriculture: agriculture was to contribute to industrialization. There was considerable analysis of how agriculture could be squeezed to promote industrialization. It was believed that the agricultural sector could—and should—release surpluses of labor, food, and savings to support the industrial sector. There was also pessimism about the growth potential of exporting primary products, so that the governments turned to import substitution policies. These policies together with the emphasis on capital accumulation and industrialization left agriculture not only unsupported but actually discriminated against by negative pricing and taxation policies.

However, as the problems of employment, absolute poverty,

and income distribution have intensified, economists have placed more value on agricultural development in its own right. No longer is agriculture viewed as a sector to be squeezed for industrialization. Agriculture cannot be relegated to a passive role. Instead, the mutual dependence of agriculture and industry is recognized, and policies are sought to support the interaction between industry and agriculture.

Agricultural development is now promoted for several reasons. An increase in the production of food and other farm products is obviously desirable to reduce poverty, hunger, and malnutrition and to avoid the consequences of the growing food gap. But a revitalization of agriculture is also necessary for other objectives. If industrial production for the home market is to expand, it is also essential to raise the small agricultural surplus of the 50 percent or more of the labor force that is engaged in growing food for home consumption. As long as such a large proportion of the population is confined to low-productivity agriculture, there cannot be sufficient home demand for industrial products. Productivity and income must be raised in the agricultural sector to widen the home market.

Contrary to the earlier view that numbers in agriculture would decline as economic development proceeds, agricultural policies must now try to absorb more workers per acre. It is necessary for the agricultural sector to retain as much labor as possible to alleviate the pressures of urbanization and employment problems. To lessen the rural-urban migration, the "push" out of the rural areas must be diminished. The challenge is to extend labor-intensive methods of cultivation that will be efficient at the same time as they stretch the available land. More arable land must also be brought under cultivation. An employment-oriented pattern of agricultural development is necessary to diminish the numbers in absolute poverty, improve the distribution of income, and reduce urbanization.

Finally, it is now recognized how important agricultural development is for relieving balance-of-payments pressures. With the diminution in aid and less reliance on overseas borrowings, the developing country's capacity to import is more dependent on its growth of exports. To the extent that primary products account for a large proportion of these exports, the country must maintain its competitive position in world markets. The prices of commercial tropical exports (tea, coffee) are also dependent on the prices that farmers receive for their domestic food crops. As Sir Arthur Lewis argues, so long as the bulk of tropical peoples are food farmers with relatively low productivity, the income that can be earned from food production is low; labor, therefore, offers itself at low wages to the plantations and estates producing tropical export crops; and the prices of these exports remain low as tropical products are available to the rest of the world on an essentially low-wage basis.[6] To improve the terms of trade between tropical exports and manufactured imports, the productivity of food farmers must be raised.

Furthermore, in light of balance-of-payments problems, since several developing countries have changed from being net exporters to net importers of food from the developed countries, efforts must be made to substitute home production of food. This is especially urgent because the projections of population growth indicate that, over the next two decades, 90 percent of the increased population in developing countries will be in food-deficient countries. And when rural and urban incomes are increased, a large proportion of the increased income of poor people—probably about 50 to 80 percent—will be spent on food.

Having recognized the priority that must now be given to agriculture, development economists have reconsidered policies affecting agriculture in an effort to stimulate an increase in agricultural output and a greater demand for labor. Special emphasis is now on smallholder agriculture because the smallholders and tenant farmers form the bulk of the rural poor and provide the best potential for efficient agricultural development. The task is not only to remove the urban bias of the past, but also to ensure that the larger influential farmers do not gain a disproportionately large part of the benefit from governmental policies that support the modernization of agriculture. Through positive pricing and taxation policies, governments must increase incentives for peasant agriculture by investing in improved yields with labor-intensive methods. Prices for crops must be sufficiently remunerative. On the input side, expensive import substitution policies for fertilizers, pesticides, and implements must end in order to allow the lower free trade prices for inputs. The correction of overvalued foreign exchange rates would also make domestic food supplies more competitive with imports and would also stimulate export crops.

At the same time as price incentives are provided for domestic production, there must be government support of transport infrastructure, research, and extension services to allow cultivation to be transformed into a science-based agriculture. In many countries that still suffer from the neglect of former colonial governments, especially in Africa, it is necessary to overcome the colonial legacy that paid little attention to investments in human capital, spent little in research on food crops, and neglected to strengthen domestic market linkages. Rural poverty can only be avoided if crop yields can be raised for the 60 to 80 percent of the agricultural labor force that works at very low levels of productivity. Cost-reducing, income-raising, technological change is especially needed. Capital and credit facilities must also be extended. And, although politically difficult to achieve, land reform is needed in many countries to redistribute land ownership in favor of the poor.

The agricultural problem is an exceedingly complex group of problems that requires a combination of policies to relax the economic, political, structural, and technical constraints on agricultural change. Moreover, effective policies will necessarily be of a long-term character, and there must be patience so that the policies may become fully effective 10 to 20 years into the future. But a start toward a long-term solution is at least being made in recognizing that agricultural development is a precondition for national development, and that the former bias against agriculture must be offset.

Liberalizing Foreign Trade

Since the time of the Old Growth Economics, mainstream economists have viewed international trade as an engine of growth. Development of the export sector, it was believed, could contribute to the development of the entire economy. In contrast, the

Early Development Economics was colored by export pessimism, and arguments for industrialization through import substitution became popular. In theory, a rational trade policy would pursue both import substitution and export promotion strategies until the last unit of domestic resources devoted to each yields the same return in terms of foreign exchange saved through import substitution or earned through exports. In practice, however, policymakers were to view the strategies as alternatives. In many countries during the 1950s and 1960s, policies were undertaken that markedly biased the economy toward import substitution. Import substitution was politically attractive on several counts. It conformed to the nationalist ideologies of newly emergent nations and was thought to be a way of reducing their external dependence. It also appeared to be an easy route to industrialization from "the top down"—replacement of finished commodities could proceed down through the production of components and intermediate inputs. Moreover, the easiest way to meet a balance-of-payments crisis was to impose another round of tariffs, quotas, and exchange controls to restrict imports.

But the political attraction of import substitution contradicted rational policy. Instead of pursuing import substitution in the ideal way as dictated by rational principles of resource allocation, governments only too often followed ad hoc policies that created a chaotic pattern of indiscriminate import-substituting incentives under restrictive trade regimes. The economist's logic of import substitution was soon lost.

This became especially evident after governments proceeded beyond the first stage of import substitution—the "easy" stage of replacing imports of nondurable consumer goods, such as clothing, shoes, and household goods, with domestic production. The second stage of import substitution became more difficult, involving the replacement of imports of producer and consumer durable goods and intermediate goods by domestic production. These goods tend to be more capital intensive and more skill intensive in their production than the simpler goods of the first stage. To be produced efficiently, these goods require a plant size that is large compared with the domestic needs of most developing countries, and their costs rise rapidly at smaller output levels; more sophisticated technology is also needed, and the net foreign exchange savings tend to be small because of the need to import materials and machinery.

As countries proceed to the second stage of import substitution, the disadvantages of a continued, inward-oriented development strategy become more pronounced. More protective policies must be instituted to allow the inefficient domestic production to be profitable in local currency. The role of prices becomes increasingly distorted as direct physical controls become more complex. Resources become seriously misallocated through the distortion of three key prices—the rate of interest, unskilled wage rates, and the foreign exchange rate. Through limits on the rise in interest rates and the effects of inflation, the real rate of interest tends to be too low relative to the scarcity of capital; this encourages too great a use of the scarce capital. Wage rates that are too high relative to the surplus of unskilled labor discourage the employment of more labor. And an overvalued exchange rate (too few units of domestic currency in exchange for a unit of foreign currency) acts as an implicit tax on exports, discouraging exports and inducing too great a use of the scarce foreign exchange. Exports are also less competitive when export firms have to buy the higher priced local inputs. Agricultural activities are also implicitly taxed since farmers have to pay more for the locally produced goods than for imports at free trade prices, and their local sales of foodstuffs and raw materials are often at low ceiling prices imposed by the government. At the same time, their export products are handicapped by the overvalued exchange rate.

As import substitution became an increasingly inefficient process, and the oversubsidization of import-substituting industries became more apparent, economists became ever more critical of the process. By 1964, at the first meeting of UNCTAD, its Secretary-General Raúl Prebisch could say that the developing countries had reached the end of the road of import substitution, and that an outward-looking strategy of export promotion should now be followed. Import substitution had been a once-for-all process. Deeper import substitution was increasingly difficult to realize. The process was not contributing to further industrial development. The foreign exchange constraint on the rate of development was not being relaxed. Nor was import substitution meeting the employment problem.

In the late 1960s, a research project sponsored by the OECD Development Center appraised the industrial development efforts of seven countries (Argentina, Brazil, Mexico, India, Pakistan, Philippines, and Taiwan). In a summary volume, the project directors—Ian Little, Tibor Scitovsky, and Maurice Scott—stated that

> The studies of the seven countries indicate that these countries have now reached the stage where policies that are followed to promote import substitution are proving to be harmful for the economic development of these countries. Industrialization sheltered by high levels of protection has led to the creation of high cost enterprises; these enterprises are producing expensive products, many of which are for use by a restricted middle class, and so production is rapidly coming up against the limits of the home market.[7]

With high industrial prices, maintained behind high tariffs, industrialization has been carried out at a high cost to agriculture. In practice, the rural population has been made to bear the burden of financing industrialization. Urban problems have been created by the neglect of agriculture. Moreover, "ponderous administrative control" has held up decisions and has led to excessive stocks and the creation of a multitude of firms operating below capacity. In the words of the OECD report,

> The authorities have experienced growing difficulties in making rational decisions on the distribution of import licenses. . . . The nascent industries have come to depend for their profits on government decisions, and so have formed the habit of devoting their efforts to obtaining privileges by pressure on the government rather than by cutting their costs. The new entrepreneurs have thus had a "proprietary" concept of production, far more than a spirit of enterprise in the true sense.[8]

What policy was now to be recommended? The OECD appraisal stated its findings in this way:

> The conclusions of the country studies are clear. Emphasis should be placed on the development of exports so as to earn

the foreign currency required to pay for essential imports, whether of machines, materials, or food, which cannot be economically produced at home. Administrative control should be replaced by better use of the price mechanism; and high cost internal production be replaced by a reorganized agriculture and industry, capable of gradually becoming competitive and assuming their place on the world market.[9]

In the mid-1970s, another series of 10-country studies sponsored by the National Bureau of Economic Research (NBER) went beyond the OECD project to suggest more detailed proposals of appropriate policies that would allow developing countries to liberalize their foreign trade regimes and take more advantage of external trading opportunities. The NBER project emphasized strongly the merits of an export promotion strategy. Evidence was cited that countries such as Korea, Singapore, and Taiwan experienced higher rates of growth in national income with their higher rates of exports, and that improved economic performance followed their departure from the first stage of import substitution and their move to export promotion. Other countries that continued into the second stage of import substitution did not promote exports and suffered lower rates of growth in their national income.

Evidence in the NBER project studies suggests several reasons for the superiority of an export-promoting strategy. This strategy appears in practice to be characterized by a less chaotic and more neutral pattern of interindustrial incentives than the import substitution strategy. The domestic resource cost of earning a unit of foreign exchange through exports tends to be less than the domestic resource cost of saving a unit of foreign exchange through replacement of imports. A marginal shift of resources from the import-substituting activity, which has a high domestic resource cost, to the export activity would yield more value added at international prices with the input of domestic resources unchanged. This means that the scarce resources used in import substitution could earn a greater amount of foreign exchange through export expansion than the amount of foreign exchange that can be saved through an import substitution strategy that relies on high effective rates of protection. Moreover, an export promotion regime tends to attract more foreign investment than import substitution, and the inflow of foreign capital is induced not by home protection but by considerations of efficiency on the side of resource cost for the wider world market. In conformity with comparative advantage, the efficiency of foreign investment is higher in export activities. The creation of employment also tends to be greater under export promotion than under import substitution: exports tend to be more labor intensive in their production, and the better performance of the economy leads to an increased investment over time. The positive effects of economies of scale and the general educative effects from international rather than domestic competition are more often realized with an export promotion strategy. Finally, the foreign exchange constraint tends to be relaxed more readily under an export promotion strategy, and with improvement in the country's balance of payments, the country's creditworthiness on international capital markets also improves.

From the experience of import substitution, economists as guardians of rationality have been distressed by the neglect of rational pricing rules in the control of foreign trade in countries that pursued inward-looking policies. The prescriptive conclusion from most country studies is clear: remove the bias against exports. Remove the disincentives to enter foreign markets. Establish neutral trade regimes that provide equal incentives for import substitution and export promotion.

How can this prescription be realized? How can the transition be made from a restrictive import substitution strategy to a liberalized export promotion strategy? The essence of this change in policy includes an examination of the entire foreign trade regime and an equal treatment for import substitution and export promotion. "Entire foreign trade regime" implies all the policy measures that affect the ultimate revenue from exports and the ultimate payments for imports. Although the official or nominal exchange rate may be one amount, the real effective exchange rate—defined as the amount of local currency actually received or paid per unit of foreign currency—may be a quite different amount according to the entire foreign trade regime. The effective exchange rate on exports indicates the number of units of domestic currency that can be obtained for a dollar's worth of exports, taking into account export duties, subsidies, special exchange rates, input subsidies related to exports, and other financial and tax measures that affect the price of exports. For example, in Korea in 1975, Korea's official exchange rate was 485 won per dollar, but when export subsidies were added in the form of tax exemptions, customs duty exemptions, and interest rate subsidies to exporters, the effective exchange rate on exports became 566 won per dollar.

The effective exchange rate on imports indicates the number of units of domestic currency that would be paid for a dollar's worth of imports—taking into account tariffs, surcharges, interest on advance deposits, and other measures that affect the price of imports. Under an inward-looking strategy that biases the allocation of resources to import substitution, the effective rate of exchange on imports is higher than the effective rate of exchange on exports. If the bias went so far in the other direction that exports were protected, the effective exchange rate for exports would be greater than the effective exchange rate for imports. A neutral free trade regime that provided similar incentives for import substitutes and exports would equate the effective exchange rate for exports and the effective exchange rate for imports.

To promote exports, governmental policies must shift to an outward-oriented policy that removes the bias in favor of import substitution. As long as an import substitution bias persists, exports will suffer from the implicit taxation and quantitative restrictions, from the cost of domestic imports being above free trade prices, and from the diversion of resources to the sheltered, capital-intensive, import-substituting industries.

A shift to an outward-looking policy must therefore reduce the bias against exports by reducing the effective exchange rate on imports and by raising the effective exchange rate on exports to bring them closer to equality. To supply inputs to exporters at prices closer to those under free trade, the quantitative restrictions on imports should be removed. For a more efficient pattern of import substitution, the quantitative restrictions that give rise to import premiums should be replaced with neutral across-the-board tariffs that will still allow price incentives. A devaluation of the country's overvalued exchange rate will also reduce the import premium and the bias against exports, while stimulating the demand for exports and raising the effective exchange rate for exports. A devaluation also raises the price of imports, but this can be offset by removing quantitative restrictions and tariffs on the imports.

The policy objective should be to remove the bias against exports and establish an unbiased "free trade" regime for exports. If the trade regime were to go so far as to raise the effective exchange rate for exports above the effective exchange rate for imports, it would be oversubsidizing exports and protecting exports instead of simply promoting exports by removing the bias against them and establishing a neutral trade regime. There is evidence, however, that the oversubsidizing of exports is less likely to occur than the oversubsidizing of import substitution. This is because the bias against exports has been so strong in the past that any outward-looking policy can proceed quite far before beginning to oversubsidize exports. Unlike import substitution, export promotion also relies more on price measures than direct or physical controls. Export promotion policies also tend to involve budgetary policies that come under more public scrutiny so that cash subsidies are restrained. Moreover, the entire export promotion strategy is bounded by the realities of competition on international markets.

Investing in Human Capital

Although the development record shows increasing rates of investment, the strategic role of physical capital has been increasingly questioned. Another major revision of strategy involves a shift in emphasis from physical capital to human resources—to creating productive agents who through their acquisition of knowledge, better health and nutrition, and increase in skills can contribute more to the development process. Without technical and managerial knowledge, the accumulation of physical capital cannot increase income.

The Malthusian spectre and pessimistic forecasts of stagnation have been continually contradicted by advances in knowledge and innovations that have allowed people to augment their resources. Alfred Marshall could declare at the turn of the twen-

tieth century that "although nature is subject to diminishing returns, man is subject to increasing returns. . . . Knowledge is
our most powerful engine of production; it enables us to subdue
nature and satisfy our wants."

Princeton's Frederick Harbison echoed this view:

> Human resources—not capital, nor income, nor material re-
> sources—constitute the ultimate basis for the wealth of na-
> tions. Capital and natural resources are passive factors of pro-
> duction; human beings are the active agents who accumulate
> capital, exploit natural resources, build social, economic, and
> political organizations, and carry forward national develop-
> ment. Clearly, a country which is unable to develop the skills
> and knowledge of its people and to utilize them effectively in
> the national economy will be unable to develop anything else.[10]

In accepting the Nobel Prize, the noted agricultural economist
Theodore Schultz also stated that, while agricultural development is of paramount importance, "The decisive factors of production in improving the welfare of poor people are not space,
energy, and crop land; the decisive factor is the improvement in
population quality."[11] Schultz emphasized that the returns to
various quality components are increasing over time in many low-
income countries. Stressing the economic value of human capital, he connected favorable economic prospects with an investment in health and education.

While economists have been showing more appreciation for
human capital, they have questioned the early dominance of
physical capital in development theory. Although a high rate of
capital formation usually accompanies a rapid growth in productivity and income, the causal relationship is ambiguous. Does the
capital accumulation lead to the growth, or vice versa? The growth
in income may precede capital accumulation and induce it. Empirical studies of historical growth in the presently developed
countries of Western Europe and the United States also question
the importance of physical capital. These studies investigate the
sources of growth in output, and they demonstrate that much of
the increase in output cannot be explained only in terms of an
increase in the standard physical inputs of capital, labor, and land.
A large part of the increase in output remains to be attributed to
some "unexplained residual factor." In several studies, this re-

sidual factor—the unisolated source of growth—is left to account for 50 percent or more of the increase in total output. Attempting to identify other sources of growth, which are referred to by the catchall term "residual" or the phrase "inputs to the growth process," economists have come to emphasize the significant contribution to growth made by improvements in the quality of human capital. Through advances in knowledge, higher skills, and better motivation, labor has been able to be combined with physical capital and land in more productive ways. Technical progress and innovations account for much of the increase in output per unit of resources utilized. If this has been revealed in the history of the more developed countries, it is also now evident in the more rapidly developing countries that are rich in human resources—Singapore, South Korea, Israel.

Population quality has become a more pressing issue as it is realized that economic development means much more than economic growth. Development entails growth plus change. There are essential qualitative dimensions in the development process that may be absent in the growth of an economy based only on a simple widening process that uses more inputs. This qualitative difference is especially likely to appear in the improved performance of the inputs and in improved techniques of production—in man's growing control over nature. It is also likely to appear in the development of institutions and a change in attitudes and values. Human resource development is thus an integral part of the development process—an instrument for development, and not simply to be awaited as a result of development.

Investment in education has a central role in promoting human resource development. In spite of the substantial progress made during the past three decades in expanding education facilities, the World Bank estimates that over 250 million children and 600 million adults still lack basic education. Of those who do enter primary school, only half reach the fourth grade, repeaters occupy 15 to 20 percent of school places, and academic quality is far below desired levels. The first task of educational policy is to reduce the inefficiencies that keep both the number of students in school and the quality of education they receive much below what the available funds might permit.

The emphasis on education is based on studies that show that economic returns on investment in education seem, in most instances, to exceed returns on alternative kinds of investment, and that developing countries obtain higher returns than the developed ones. In a recent presidential address to the Economic History Association, Professor Richard Easterlin asked "Why isn't the whole world developed?" His answer emphasized the value of investment in education by concluding that the worldwide spread of modern economic growth has depended chiefly on the diffusion of a body of knowledge concerning new production techniques. Furthermore, the acquisition and application of this knowledge by different countries have been governed largely by whether their population had acquired traits and motivation associated with formal schooling.[12]

Although the general value of education is readily obvious, crucial questions remain about the type of schooling and attributes that are most favorable for economic progress. Economists cannot yet provide definitive answers about what types of education have what specific effects on economic development. However, there is now general agreement that a substantial primary education is essential for sustained economic growth and the returns on primary education tend to be larger than those for secondary or higher education. To improve the quality of the "output" from primary education, it is also necessary to improve the quality of the "input." This requires more investment at the preschool level. If the expanding enrollment in primary schools in the future will draw more and more from lower income families, and if the performance of these children is related to the quality of their environment and the adequacy of early nutrition, then the productivity of school "inputs" may be highly sensitive to policies concerning preschool age types of investment. Nutritional education and education on child-rearing practices appear to yield high rates of return.

Primary education of girls is especially rewarding for the next generation's health, education, and fertility. Studies show that the more educated their mothers, the less likely children are to die. Families are also better fed, the higher the mother's education. And since education delays marriage for women and also allows more use of contraceptives, there may be a reduction in fertility. To achieve these results, it is necessary for educational programs to remove the bias against women's education.

The educational pattern of unemployment is also a concern. Large numbers of those who leave primary and secondary school may have job aspirations that exceed job opportunities. Unemployment among the educated has become a serious problem in many countries. Its solution requires a better balance between academic and vocational instruction, more use of on-the-job training, and more attention to targets in manpower training based on expected growth rates and the pattern of growth.

Investment in health yields improvement in population quality, especially through longer life spans, a more active labor force, and greater capacity to be educated. Instead of modeling health care systems on those in the developed world, it has become increasingly clear that the cheaper and more effective way to improve the health of the majority of people in the less developed countries is through an emphasis on universal, low-cost, basic health care with more emphasis on preventive medicine. Improvements in sanitary conditions and nutrition and changes in individual health habits are also important in improving health. Systematic efforts at national nutrition planning are only recent, but it has become evident that boosting food production, improving the marketing system, reducing food prices, and raising the incomes of the poor are central requirements of a nutrition program in most countries.

Not only are there high direct returns from education and health, the indirect returns are also high, especially through reduced population growth. Education, health, nutrition, and fertility are all interrelated and mutually reinforcing. Accumulating evidence demonstrates that low adult literacy and high infant mortality tend to keep population growth high, whereas improvements in education and health tend to lower fertility. Improvement in population quality is therefore not only a value in itself, but it also alleviates the quantitative dimension of the population problem. Fulfillment of the demand for "quality," by adults for their children, reduces the demand for a "quantity" of children.

Reevaluating Policymaking

In revising elemements of the Early Development Economics, the dual role of the economist has become even more pronounced. The goals that define "development" have become increasingly those of the trustee for the poor—not merely growth of GNP, but also less inequality in the distribution of income, better utilization of labor, reduction of absolute poverty, and fulfillment of basic needs. At the same time, however, the methodology of the development economist has become evermore that of the guardian of rationality, returning to the exercise of the logic of choice. In considering the use of scarce resources, and in comparing alternative development strategies over time, the economist has emphasized the relevance of neoclassical principles of efficient resource allocation. What is the best use of the scarce resources? Which strategy is most advantageous? The hallmark of the economist's procedure is an appeal to rational conduct when the decision maker is confronted with a diversity of objectives and a scarcity of means.

Even economists who earlier adopted a structuralist view now recognize that there is more scope for rational individual decision making. Differences between the neoclassicist's presuppositions of marginal analysis and the structuralist's prescriptions diminish as countries achieve a more diversified productive structure and reduce their concentration on a few exports, as resources become more mobile, markets become more extensive, and behavior becomes more responsive to prices. As these changes occur, the structural constraints that previously limited development are no longer so significant, and there is more scope for market analysis.

Especially pronounced in recent years has been the economist's incorporation of neoclassical precepts in the development economist's policy advice. Few would now maintain, as many did earlier, that the new development economics could not rest on neoclassical economics but required a new subdiscipline of economics. The resurgence of a monoeconomics, equally relevant for developed and less developed countries, has resulted from several factors. One is an aversion to overplanning, as demonstrated by the experience of several developing countries.

Another is the realization that the dynamic mobilization of resources, beyond the static allocation of resources, can also be affected by prices. Moreover, the market has been increasingly appreciated as a guide to policymaking and as an institutional mechanism through which governmental policies might operate.

In reaction to the distortions widely experienced under development plans, economists are reemphasizing that resource allocation might be improved if prices reflect relative scarcities and relative costs. And more reliance is being placed on the market to accomplish this. The market might also serve to provide incentives for more productive effort and for increasing the availability of resources. Economists argue that governments may experience favorable results when restrictive administrative controls on the private sector are replaced by well-devised and adequate economic incentives.

The economist also appreciates that, in contrast with the difficulty of acquiring sufficient information for detailed planning, the market is an inexpensive source of information. The market is also an administrative instrument that is relatively cheap to operate. Indeed, the economist shows that governments might actually pursue their policy objectives more effectively if they use policy instruments that operate through the market (such as taxation and subsidization) instead of administrative methods and direct controls.

When writing about planning in 1966, Sir Arthur Lewis observed:

> The fundamental task of development planning is to release the energies of the people so that they may do what needs doing to raise the rate of economic growth. The things to be done are productive decisions to be made by a fairly large proportion of the country's inhabitants. Industrialists are to build factories; farmers are to adopt new technologies; labor is to move to new jobs; research workers are to find new solutions; perhaps as much as 20 percent of the population must change its ways somehow or other—learn, invest, accept new institutions—if the rate of growth is to move from 3 to 5 percent. The planner's job is to find out what stands in the way of these productive decisions, and to introduce measures which make such decisions more likely.

Emphasis is placed upon the high proportion of the population involved. The government cannot by itself, or through its officials, raise the growth from 3 to 5 percent. Such an exercise involves a wide section of the people. The government can persuade, threaten, or induce; but in the last analysis it is the people, who achieve. . . .

The possibility of higher individual earnings is the fuel of economic growth, whether in the form of profits, salaries, wages, higher farm incomes, or otherwise. Economic growth cannot be produced by legislation, administrative regulation, or exhortation, without the accompaniment of high material incentives. Hence the crucial test of the quality of development planning, in that part of the economy which is left to private initiative, is how effective are incentives offered to the population to make decisions which will result in economic growth.[13]

As Lewis became disappointed with the experience of comprehensive planning, many economists followed suit. The reevaluation of development policymaking has certainly redressed the earlier neglect of markets and prices. If in an earlier period planning was the new mystique, there is now a resurgence of the more traditional admonishment as expressed by Chicago's Professor Arnold Harberger that "good economics is good for people"—and by "good economics" is meant the logic of the neoclassical market price system.

Economists have also taken a more rational approach to policy analysis. The choice of policy instruments is viewed in terms of multiple objectives that can be achieved by various policy instruments, each of which uses resources and hence has a cost in terms of foregoing some alternative use. The economist should delimit efficient policies in the sense of minimizing the costs to achieve the objectives. To do this, the economist has placed more reliance on market processes and their allocative properties.

The greatest support to rational analysis has come in the development of project analysis. The purpose of project appraisal is to allow the decision maker to make a rational choice among alternative investment opportunities or to provide an acceptance or rejection criterion for a particular investment opportunity. To do this, the project analyst calculates benefit and cost streams from the project over time, and then reduces the value of the net benefit stream to a "rate of return." In measuring costs and benefits, the economist corrects for distorted prices by using appropriate "accounting" or "shadow" prices. Much effort has been directed toward deriving rules for estimating the shadow prices of goods, services, interest rates, foreign exchange rates, and wages under various conditions of market imperfections. By so doing, the economist is able to proceed from simply appraising the project's financial rate of return and measuring the commercial profitability to determining the economic rate of return—a truer representation of the real value of the project in terms of national profitability.

Beyond the shadow price problem, more attention is now being given, as a result of the revisions in development strategy, to an appraisal of the income streams accruing from the project to individuals at different income levels. By weighting these income streams differently according to whether the richer or the poorer benefit from the project, the social rate of return can be calculated. But just what weights are to be used is a matter of individual judgment, unless "someone" can order a general welfare function for the society. More pragmatically, some indications of welfare weights can be derived from the incidence of the country's tax structure on different income groups. With the revision of development strategies, economists are now exploring more intensively how to translate the costs and benefits of the "new type," poverty-alleviation projects into measurable quantities. Especially difficult is the measurement of the benefits from health, education, nutrition, and sanitation projects. More attention is also being given to identifying the beneficiaries of these projects and to various weighting schemes to aid in their project evaluation. In striving to improve formal project appraisal techniques, the economist is extending the application of rational analysis.

At the same time that neoclassical principles of resource allocation and price analysis have been rediscovered for domestic policies, analogous principles have also been applied internationally. Those who now advocate liberalization of the foreign trade regime and the promotion of exports do so out of a concern for a rational pricing system and efficient resource allocation. But in analyzing the international economy, neoclassical principles have been opposed by neo-Marxist critiques, as we will learn in the next chapter.

8

Radical Critique

Although conditions in the poor countries are far different from those in the advanced capitalist nations, the mainstream of development thought has still been rooted in traditional neoclassical economics. Some behavioral assumptions have been modified; some amendments have been introduced to allow for the different institutions of the poor country; structural features have been considered; and more attention has been given to conditions of market failure. Despite the earlier anticipation of some development economists, however, an entirely new subdiscipline of development economics has not arisen. To the contrary, development economists have come to rely more and more on conventional principles of price analysis and the market mechanism.

Even the revision of development strategies during the 1970s has been dominated by the liberal ideology of an international harmony of interests. It is believed that there are mutual gains from trade to be realized by rich and poor countries alike if they liberalize their foreign trade regimes. Foreign investment from a rich country to a poor country will yield mutual gains to lender and borrower. The diffusion of management and technology from rich to poor countries is also of benefit to all parties. The promotion of a liberal international economic order should yield a positive sum game—not a North-South confrontation.

Conflict of Interests

In contrast to the mainstream, there has always been a minority opposition to the orthodox liberal ideology. Instead of a harmony of interests, the minority sees only a conflict of interests. Instead of being a positive sum game, the workings of the international system yield a zero sum game, with rich countries gaining at the expense of the poor countries. In an earlier period, Lenin's warnings of imperialism contradicted Ricardo's mutual gains from trade as a result of free trade. In recent decades, parallel to the rise of the new development economics and the revision of development strategies, there have been a number of dissenters propounding a radical critique of mainstream development thinking.

The critique has taken various forms—from a relatively mild analysis of "disequalizing forces" in the international economy, to the rise of the more vigorous "dependency" school and the bold advocacy of "delinking" poor countries from international forces. Sociologists and political scientists have joined economists in formulating these critiques, and this multidisciplinary character allows more attention to be given to forces of power, class relations, and the evolution of social and political structures.

The common and dominant theme in the various versions of the radical critique is that the poor countries are victimized by overseas forces. The focus is on the poor countries as late developers that are embedded in an international system. The major obstacles to the poor country's development are not domestic, but arise from the operation of this international system. Contrary to the orthodox belief that international trade can act as an "engine of growth," these critics offer various arguments of "trade pessimism" and assert that the international economy acts as a mechanism of international inequality, perpetuating or widening the gap between rich and poor countries.

In the early 1950s, three leading critics gave force to these arguments—Raúl Prebisch, former head of the Argentine central bank and first Executive Director for the U.N. Economic Commission for Latin America (ECLA); Gunnar Myrdal, Secretary of the European Economic Commission and author of *The American*

Dilemma (a study that explained the disadvantaged position of American blacks); and Hans Singer, an economist who had studied the "depressed areas" of Britain and joined the United Nations as early as 1946. Unlike Marxists who concentrate on the unfavorable effects of imperialism or colonialism, these critics did not base their critique on any notion of "deliberate exploitation" by the advanced capitalist nations. Instead, their contention was simply that the free play of international market forces creates disequalizing effects that operate to the disadvantage of the less developed nations.

As Myrdal argued,

> Market forces will tend cumulatively to accentuate international inequalities, [and] a quite normal result of unhampered trade between two countries, of which one is industrial and the other underdeveloped, is the initiation of a cumulative process toward the impoverishment and stagnation of the latter.[1]

Myrdal based his argument on the possibility that the factors that made for increasing disparity between rich and poor countries—what he called "backwash effects"—could outweigh the factors that made for the spread of prosperity from rich to poor countries—what he called the "spread effects." Myrdal claimed that

> Contrary to what the equilibrium theory of international trade would seem to suggest, the play of the market forces does not work toward equality in the remunerations to factors of production and, consequently, in incomes. If left to take its own course, economic development is a process of circular and cumulative causation which tends to award its favors to those who are already well endowed and even to thwart the efforts of those who happen to live in regions that are lagging behind. The backsetting effects of economic expansion in other regions dominate the more powerfully, the poorer a country is.[2]

The backwash effects to which Myrdal refers include the destruction of local handicrafts and small-scale industry by cheap imports from the industrial countries, the drain of skilled labor from the less developed country, the adverse effects of foreign investment, and the biasing of the economy toward enclaves that produce primary product exports. But only a pessimistic view can be taken about the potential for development through the export of primary products. Again, in Myrdal's words,

> In these lines, they often meet inelastic demands in the export market, often also a demand trend which is not rising very rapidly, and excessive price fluctuations. When, furthermore, population is rapidly rising while the larger part of it lives at, or near, the subsistence level—which means there is no scarcity of common labor—any technological improvement in their export production tends to confer the advantages from the cheapening of production to the importing countries. Because of inelastic demands the result will often not even be a very great enlargement of the markets and of production and employment. In any case the wages and the export returns per unit of product will tend to remain low as the supply of unskilled labor is almost unlimited.[3]

Believing that trade in primary products will only produce a polarization effect that is stronger than the spread effect, Myrdal argues that "economic development has to be brought about by policy interferences" instead of through a dependence on international markets that "strengthen the forces maintaining stagnation or regression."

Prebisch and Singer gave special attention to the terms at which countries export manufactures and primary commodities. They were especially concerned that structural differences between less developed, primary producing countries and more developed, industrial countries would set up a tendency for primary commodity prices to decline relative to prices for manufactured goods. Singer's U.N. report in 1949 contended that the poor countries have suffered a long period of deterioration in their commodity terms of trade—the ratio of their export prices to their import prices has fallen, so that the poor countries were only able to import less and less per unit of their exports. The implication of this report was that the historical downward trend in the terms of trade for primary products was the result of general market forces and the nature of relations within and between industrial and developing countries, which could be expected to continue.

Prebisch attributed the causes of deterioration in the poor countries' terms of trade to differences in the distribution of the

gains from increased productivity in primary products and manufactured goods. Since technical progress has been greater in industry than in the primary production of poor countries, it is argued that if prices had been reduced in proportion to increasing
productivity, the reduction should then have been less for primary products than for manufactures, so that as the disparity
between productivities increased, the price relationship between
the two should have improved in favor of the poor countries.
But it is alleged that the opposite occurred, because in the more
developed countries the gains from increased productivity in
manufactured goods have been distributed in the form of higher
wages and profits rather than lower prices, whereas in the case
of food and raw material production in the LDCs the gains in
productivity, although smaller, have been distributed in the form
of price reductions, to the benefit of overseas consumers. The
reason for the different distribution in the gains from productivity is that, in the advanced industrial countries, trade unions and
monopolistic enterprises are able to absorb the gains in productivity in higher wages and profits, but in the primary producing
countries, workers are unorganized, and production is competitive so that gains in productivity go into price reductions. The
decline in the poor country's terms of trade is equivalent to long-
period transfers of income from the poor to the rich countries.

Prebisch and Singer also argued that an asymmetry in the demand for primary products and industrial products compounds
the disadvantages of exporting primary products. As income rises,
there is a relative decrease in the demand for primary products
and a relative increase in the demand for industrial products: an
increase in income leads to a more than proportionate expenditure on industrial products, but the proportion of income spent
on primary products rises only very slowly as income rises. Furthermore, technical progress in manufacturing, which reduces the
amount of raw materials used per unit of industrial output, limits the increase in demand for primary products. The chronic
instability of primary commodity prices and the fluctuations in
export revenue were also considered disadvantageous for the
development program of the primary producing country. These
conditions for primary product exports were characterized as export pessimism, and they led Prebisch and Singer to support de-

liberate policies of industrialization and a path of development that would not depend on international markets.

Reinforcing Myrdal's contention of backwash effects and circular causation with cumulative effects, the Prebisch-Singer emphasis on the distribution of gains from trade and investment raises the fundamental issue of distributive justice or fairness in the gains from trade. This issue goes far beyond the simple consideration of allocative efficiency, as in mainstream development thought. References to unequal market power and technological power also have far-reaching implications beyond the pessimism shown regarding the primary commodity prices.

Considering the relationships of rich and poor countries more generally, Singer also emphasized a power inequality that caused the distribution of gains from foreign investment to be biased in favor of the investing countries. Like Myrdal, he argued that the inflow of foreign capital into primary production for export established only an "enclave" or "outpost" for the investing country without linkages to the rest of the domestic economy. Furthermore, it is said that the stimulating income effects of foreign investment have been lost through income leakages abroad. Not only is there a drain of profits and interest to the capital-exporting countries, but the poor countries have also had to import from the rich countries the capital equipment associated with any investment that has been induced by a growth in exports. The implication is that a given amount of investment in the poor country generates a much smaller amount of income than the same amount of investment would generate in a more advanced and less dependent country. The investing country's superior bargaining power, financial power, control of marketing, processing, and distribution—this power inequality causes the advantages from foreign investment to accrue to the investing country, not to the poor borrowing country. The investing country "gets the best of both worlds" as buyer and seller and the borrowing country "the worst of both worlds."

Prebisch also contradicted the traditional harmony-of-interests theory by analyzing Latin American problems in terms of the relations between the "center" and "periphery" in the world economy. There was an "economic constellation" in the international system whose center consisted of countries that had been early

developers and were now through their early success in technical progress the rich, industrial, and capitalistic nations that organized the system as a whole to serve their own interest. The
countries on the periphery were a heterogeneous lot, but they
were linked in common to the center through their production
and export of raw materials. Through the deterioration in the
terms of trade and the adverse effects of foreign investment, the
system of international economic relations acted to siphon off income from the periphery to the centers. In Prebisch's words, "The
great industrial centers not only keep for themselves the benefit
of the use of new techniques in their own economy, but are in a
favorable position to obtain a share of that deriving from the
technical progress of the periphery."[4] At the same time, development did not follow from growth in exports of primary products: the labor force was not absorbed in a productive manner.
The fundamental problem was a structural imbalance between
center and periphery based on the international dissemination of
technology and the distribution of its fruits.

It was therefore contended that a new pattern of development
is necessary to overcome the asymmetry in the relations between the center and periphery. This new pattern would concentrate on deliberate industrialization to avoid the unequal distribution of the gains from technical progress and to absorb the
large masses of surplus labor. Instead of continuing to allocate
resources to the expansion of primary exports, with a consequent fall in export prices, it was argued that it would be more
advantageous to the periphery to allocate these resources to industrial production for their domestic consumption. Prebisch explained the process in this way:

> Historically, the spread of technical progress has been uneven,
> and this has contributed to the division of the world economy
> into industrial centers and peripheral countries engaged in pri-
> mary production. . . . As the spread of technical progress into
> the periphery—limited originally to exports of primary prod-
> ucts and related activities—is advancing more and more into
> other sectors, it brings with it the need for industrialization.
> Indeed, industrialization is an inescapable part of the process
> of change accompanying a gradual improvement in per capita
> income. Therefore, industrialization is not an end in itself, but

the principal means at the disposal of those [new] countries of obtaining a share of the benefits of technical progress and of progressively raising the standard of living of the masses.[5]

Industrialization based on import substitution was therefore advocated. Tariff protection and quotas on industrial imports were believed capable of forestalling a further deterioration in the terms of trade, avoiding balance-of-payments fluctuations, which check growth when export prices fall, and promoting the absorption of the labor surplus in industry.

Protectionism was but one policy dimension in the broader plea for national planning. A reliance on private calculations and market incentives—whether the markets were domestic or international—did not lead to development for the periphery. Market failure had to be corrected through planning. National planning and national integration were necessary to overcome a polarization from center-periphery relations.

In their advocacy of industrialization, protection, and planning, Myrdal, Prebisch, and Singer influenced the early tenets of the new development economics (Chapter 6). Their arguments had considerable appeal to the newly emerging countries, especially when they were combined with Rostow's "stages" and Rosenstein-Rodan's "big push." By the 1960s, however, the new development economics was subject to criticism from two divergent streams of thought—neoclassical economics, which underlay the revision of development strategies noted in Chapter 7, and the dependency school.

Dependency

During the 1960s a number of writers went beyond the formulation of disequalizing forces as examined by Prebisch, Singer, and Myrdal to a more vigorous interpretation of external dependency. Most prominent were the dependencistas in Latin America and the New World Group in the Caribbean. Not "development economics" but "dependency economics" became their concern. They argued that conditions of dependency in world markets of commodities, capital, and labor power are unequal and combine to transfer resources from dependent countries to dominant countries in the international system. Some elements of dependency were contained in the non-Marxist analysis of disequalizing forces. And from a Marxist perspective, Stanford Professor Paul Baran had written:

> What is decisive is that economic development in underdeveloped countries is profoundly inimical to the dominant interests in the advanced capitalist countries. . . . [T]he backward world has always represented the indispensable hinterland of the highly developed capitalist West.[6]

The new school of dependency, however, differs from the disequalizing forces approach and the Marxian view. Being heavily represented by sociologists and political scientists, dependency theorists consider social and political factors neglected by economists. Moreover, instead of focusing on different commodities—primary products and industrial products—the dependency theorists emphasize the contrasting positions of dominant and dependent countries within the operation of the international system. Even if the LDC is industrializing and is not simply a primary producing country, nonetheless, it is argued that the advanced capitalist countries are still the chief gainers from any kind of international relationship with the LDC—whether in trade, investment, or technology. The advanced countries possess the dominant technology, hold a monopoly over R&D, and are the home of the multinational corporations. Even if industrializing, the LDC is still dependent on the superior power of the advanced countries, and the periphery is still exploited by the center. The underdevelopment of the periphery is a function of its external dependence as affected by the operation of transnational capitalism.

Chronic underdevelopment is ascribed to capitalism—not to precapitalist traditions or institutions. The present economic, social, and political conditions prevailing in the periphery are not the reflection of an "original" undeveloped state of affairs, but have been created by an historical international process: the same process of capitalism that brought development to the presently advanced capitalist economies resulted in the underdevelopment of the dependent periphery. The global system is such that the development of part of the system occurs at the expense of other parts. Underdevelopment of the periphery is the Siamese twin of development at the center.

The driving force in this process is a capital-seeking profit motive—which existed in the imperialistic period of capitalist merchants and capitalist bankers and is carried on in the present period of multinational corporations. As a Marxist analyst of Latin American affairs, André Gunder Frank, states: "It is capitalism, world and national, which produced underdevelopment in the past and still generates underdevelopment in the present."[7] Underdevelopment, according to Frank, is not simply nondevelopment, but is a unique type of socioeconomic structure that results from the dependency of the underdeveloped country on advanced capitalist countries. This results from foreign capital removing a surplus from the dependent economy to the advanced country by structuring the underdeveloped economy in an "external orientation" that includes the export of primary commodities, the import of manufactures, and dependent industrialization.

Structural bottlenecks within the underdeveloped economy may also act as "mechanisms of dependence." The Chilean economist Osvaldo Sunkel focused on the peripheral country's stagnation of agriculture, its high commodity concentration of exports, its high foreign exchange content of industrialization, and its growing fiscal deficit—all of which intensified the need for foreign financing: "It is this aspect—the overbearing and implacable necessity to obtain foreign financing—which finally sums up the situation of dependence: this is the crucial point in the mechanisms of dependence."[8]

Dependencistas further contend that the developing metropolis exploits the underdeveloped periphery in various ways—by biasing its structure of production toward the supplying of raw materials, by the external drain of foreign capital, and by thwarting autonomous national development. Center-periphery trade is also characterized by "unequal exchange." This may refer to deterioration in the peripheral country's terms of trade. It may also refer to unequal bargaining power in investment, transfer of technology, taxation, and relations with multinational corporations. Considering relations between multinational corporations and host countries, dependencistas commonly allege that the multinationals siphon off an economic surplus that could otherwise be used to finance domestic development, and that foreign investment causes both economic distortions and political distortions in the host society.

Some of the alleged economic distortions are that the multinational corporations use inappropriate capital-intensive technology that adds to the host country's unemployment, that they worsen the distribution of income, that they alter consumer tastes and promote a consumerism characteristic of developed societies, and that they centralize research and entrepreneurial decision making in the home country so that subsidiaries and affiliates of the multinational are not integrated with the local economy.

Political distortions, it is claimed, arise when the multinational brings the laws, politics, and foreign policy of the parent country into the subsidiary country. Multinationals may even reduce the ability of the government to control the economy, and they may structure the international system of finance and trade to respond to their multinational needs to the detriment of host authorities.

A more Marxist analysis of unequal exchange has been presented by Samir Amin, an Egyptian economist who has specialized on African economies. Amin also analyzes world capitalism in terms of two categories—center and periphery. Capitalist relations in the periphery are introduced from outside, and peripheral formations are fundamentally different from those of the center because the periphery's exporting sector dominates over the periphery's economic structure as a whole, which is subjected to and shaped by the requirements of the external market. The economies of the periphery "are without any internal dynamism of their own."[9] Dominated by "absentee" metropolitan bourgeoisie, the peripheral country is a mere appendage to the central economy. The development of the center causes underdevelopment of the periphery and its dependence on the center.

By "unequal exchange," Amin means "the exchange of products whose production involves wage differentials greater than those of productivity." He assumes that the techniques of production used in those sectors of the periphery dominated by international capital are similar to those used at the center. But since wage rates are much lower in the periphery than at the center, unequal exchange results. The unequal external exchange is accompanied, at the periphery, by unequal internal exchange: to reproduce the system, low wages must be maintained despite modern technology. Thus, "Unequal exchange means that the problem of the class struggle must necessarily be considered on the world scale."

Within the dependent economy, it is also claimed that an internal colonialism or internal polarization occurs parallel to the international polarization. Sunkel states:

> The evolution of the global system of underdevelopment-development has, over a period of time, given rise to two great polarizations which have found their main expression in geographical terms. First, a polarization of the world between countries: with the developed, industrialized, advanced, "central northern" ones on the one side, and the underdeveloped, poor, dependent, and "peripheral southern" ones on the other. Second, a polarization within countries between advanced and modern groups, regions and activities, and backward, primitive, marginal and dependent groups, regions and activities. The main difference between [the two structures] is that the developed one, due basically to its endogenous growth capacity, is the dominant structure, while the underdevelopment structure, due largely to the induced character of its dynamism, is a dependent one.[10]

The Brazilian sociologist, Fernando Henrique Cardoso, also claims that

> As a result [of investment by multinational corporations] in countries like Argentina, Brazil, Mexico, South Africa, India, and some others, there is an internal structural fragmentation connecting the most "advanced" parts of their economies to the international capitalist system. Separate although subordinated to these advanced sectors, the backward economic and social sectors of the dependent countries then play the role of "internal colonies." The gap between both will probably increase, creating a new type of dualism quite different from the imaginary one sustained by some non-Marxist authors. The new structural "duality" corresponds to a kind of internal differentiation of the same unity. It results directly, of course, from capitalist expansion and is functional to that expansion, insofar

as it helps to keep wages at a low level and diminishes political
pressure inside the "modern" sector, since the social and economic position of those who belong to the latter is always better in comparative terms.[11]

The relationships of internal polarization are based on a neo-
Marxist analysis of classes that focuses on mechanisms of social
and economic exploitation: the working class is maintained subordinate to the bourgeoisie, and the latter are in turn surbordi-
nate to the imperialist centers. The modern dominant groups
within the dependent underdeveloped structures derive their high
incomes from their association with activities linked to the developed structures and from internal exploitation of the backward, marginal, and dependent groups. The advanced groups
are more integrated economically—and also culturally and so-
cially—with the developed structures than with the marginal-
ized population of their own countries. The elites, capitalists, and
some workers are part of the internal system; others are margin-
alized.

Economic power also has political correlates: dominant countries may bring political pressures to bear on the dependent
countries, and political alliances may emerge between foreign interests and the upper strata within the dependent country. Thus,
the very process of transnational integration of some classes produces at the same time national disintegration. Internal polarization and class conflict are reflections of the international polarization and the disparities among nations. In *Dependency and
Development in Latin America*, Cardoso and Faletto see the political setting of development:

> Economic power is expressed as social domination, that is, in
> politics. Through the political process, one class or economic
> group tries to establish a system of social relations that will
> permit it to impose its view on the whole society, or at least it
> tries to establish alliances to ensure economic policies compati-
> ble with its own interests and objectives.[12]

And in their preface to the same book:

> We conceive the relationship between external and internal
> forces as forming a complex whole whose structural links are
> not based on mere external forms of exploitation and coercion,

but are rooted in coincidences of interests between local dominant classes and international ones, and, on the other side, are challenged by local dominated groups and classes.[13]

Policy Inferences

What policy inferences are to be drawn from dependency theory? How is dependency to be reversed and underdevelopment overcome? Answers naturally differ according to the different interpretations of dependency. But all who argue that dependency relations characterize the international economy unite in rejecting the "developmentalist" or "modernization" themes discussed in previous chapters. The diffusion model of the Early Development Economics—with development spreading from the modern capitalist sector to the traditional sector—is rejected. So too is it denied that industrialization per se will reverse dependency.

To Prebisch, the possession of developed manufacturing industries marks the difference between center and periphery countries. Thus once the periphery industrializes, national development proceeds as the process of productivity growth is internalized. But dependencistas believe that industrialization may lead simply to further dependence and "subsidiarization" of the economy. Proposals to liberalize the trade and financial policies of the developed countries—even if they were adopted—would not overcome the dependency relations of the center-periphery model. To reverse dependency, most dependencistas argue that it is necessary to change the internal production structures that give rise to the mechanisms of dependence, and to change the institutional order.

If capitalism underdevelops some countries, then some dependencistas conclude that there can be no development unless there is transformation at the world level to an international socialist system. Autonomous development is only possible by constructing paths toward socialism, through the emergence of new social groups with new ideological goals. For some, political restructuring at the national level through a socialist revolution, which must be led by the workers, is necessary to thwart the aspirations of the indigenous "enterpreneurial" and "bureau-cratic" bourgeoise groups acting in concert with foreign economic interests. Revolution and socialism become the necessary preconditions for development.

Others, however, focus on remedies for the unequal power relations between center and periphery. They believe the adverse effects on the periphery can be minimized through affirmative policy measures taken by the periphery, such as regional economic integration, international commodity agreements, and the development of indigenous technology.

Still others advocate a more extreme "delinking" from the international system that would go beyond previous inward-looking policies of import substitution to "collective self-reliance." As Amin concludes, "So long as the underdeveloped country continues to be integrated in the world market, it remains helpless . . . [and] the possibilities of local accumulation are nil."[14] He therefore advocates a new development strategy, which he divides into three complementary aspects: (1) the choice of a "self-reliant" development based on the principle of relying on one's own resources, (2) the priority given to cooperation and economic integration between the countries of the Third World ("collective self-reliance"), and (3) the demand for a New International Economic Order based on higher prices for raw materials and the control of natural resources, access for the manufactures of the Third World to the markets of the developed countries, and the acceleration of the transfer of technologies.[15]

The North-South dialogue on the New International Economic Order (NIEO) has left all unsatisfied. Followers of the orthodox liberal tradition believe that internal reforms within the LDCs are more important than international reforms. To those out of the mainstream—especially theorists of dependency—the North-South dialogue is simply diversionary. Even if a NIEO were established, they would still question whether this could lead to autonomous national development of the periphery. Many dependencistas argue that a NIEO would simply perpetuate unequal exchange.

The hard division between the liberal ideology of harmony of interests and the radical ideology of conflict of interests remains. In 1974, Sir Arthur Lewis asked development economists to imagine that the rich countries were to sink under the sea by 1984. After being given 10 years for adjustment, Lewis asked: Would the poor countries then be better off, worse off, or would it make little difference to the potential for development? This basic question still persists in the minds of development economists. Although the volume of literature on dependency is large and the discussion of a NIEO continues, the answer to this question remains controversial.

III
PERSUASION

Development cannot come merely from emotional desire, as expressed by some Africans at the Nyasaland Economic Symposium of 1962. Nor is an economics of resentment against a former colonial relationship equivalent to the type of economics needed to promote development. Economic development cannot be legislated or voted on as can political independence. There is merit in the economist's advice to governments of developing countries that "good economics is good for you." But has the economics of development itself developed sufficiently to provide the appropriate policy guidance? Can the economist as advisor offer more than the policy strictures derived from neoclassical economics? In advising nations how to develop, can the economist be more than the guardian of rationality? Can the economist also be a trustee for the poor—solving development policy problems that extend beyond the constraints of conventional neoclassical economics?

If the future record of development is to improve on the past, economists will have to think more deeply about the theory of development policy, they will have to design more appropriate policies, and they will have to show more concern for the implementation of these policies. As the following chapter argues, the vision of the development economist must be tempered by more relevant technical analysis and translated through persuasion into more effective policy action.

9

The Underdevelopment of Economics

In answer to the question he posed earlier, Sir Arthur Lewis concluded after a survey of *The Evolution of the International Economic Order* that

> The LDCs have within themselves all that is required for growth. They have surpluses of fuel and of the principal minerals. They have enough land to feed themselves, if they cultivate it properly. They are capable of learning the skills of manufacturing, and of saving the capital required for modernization. Their development does not in the long run depend on the existence of the developed countries, and their potential for growth would be unaffected even if all the developed countries were to sink under the sea.[1]

Lewis hastens to add that he makes this point "only to remind ourselves that the current relationships are not among the permanent ordinances of nature; it is not intended as a recommendation."

Can we be as optimistic? Our retrospective survey of the interplay between development thought and development policy has revealed a number of failures in the development record (Chapter 4). But we also noted that several earlier ideas have been discarded and development strategies have been revised (Chapter 7). Against the disappointments of the past, is the current revision of thought now sufficient to justify Lewis' optimism?[2]

Overriding Lewis' question about the relations between rich and poor countries is the ultimate question of whether economists do know what is wrong and how to put it right. Years ago Lewis observed that "The economics of development is not very complicated; the secret of successful planning lies more in sensible politics and good public administration."[3] Although we may agree that politics and administration are significant, is the economics really that simple?

Still challenging is Theodore Schultz's statement: "Most of the people in the world are poor, so if we knew the Economics of being poor we would know much of the Economics that really matters."[4] But what really matters for development analysis is unlikely to be simple.

As we saw in Chapter 7, underlying the revision of development strategies is a return to neoclassical economics and an emphasis on the market price system. But is this enough? Unlike some pioneering exponents of the Early Development Economics, we cannot maintain that neoclassical economics is completely irrelevant for development problems, but we must go beyond neoclassical economics to derive policy implications for some of the most troubling problems of development.

Beyond Neoclassical Economics

Neoclassical economics is at its best in dealing with the logic of choice. True, problems of choice exist in any economy, and to that extent it can be claimed that there is only a monoeconomics, a universal subject applicable to rich and poor economies alike. The laws of logic are the same in Malawi as anywhere else. But the economic problems of Malawi may still be quite different in empirical content from those in another country. The solution of these problems may call for more than the exercise of the logic of choice. Moreover, even the logic of choice cannot be viewed as nothing else but pure technics. As Nobel laureate Sir John Hicks has said,

> Economics, surely, is a social science. It is concerned with the operations of human beings, who are not omniscient, and not

wholly rational; who (perhaps because they are not wholly rational) have diverse, and not wholly consistent, ends. As such,
it cannot be reduced to a pure technics, and may benefit by
being distinguished from a pure technics; for we can then say
that its concern is with the use that can be made of pure technics by man in society. And that looks like being a distinctly
different matter.[5]

The methodology of neoclassical economics—with its emphasis on rationality and logic of choice—has bestowed a richness
upon economics, but at the same time it has narrowed the discipline. Political economy gave way to economics a century ago,
and the questions raised have become increasingly narrow. This
has allowed more rigor and precision in the answers—but the
larger questions are often more important in terms of humans in
society and social betterment. Indeed, in the economics of development, the very meaning of "development" has acquired
more dimensions, and the problems of development have become broader. But the methodology of the development economist as guardian of rationality has also become narrower. As
trustee for the poor, the development economist has come to
emphasize objectives that extend beyond the scope of neoclassical economics—such objectives as removal of absolute poverty,
reduction of unemployment and underemployment, and more
equitable distribution of income. If the development economist
is to formulate a theory of development policy that will contribute more adequately to the fulfillment of these broader objectives, the discipline of economics will itself have to be broadened. Relevance should not be sacrificed for elegance.

For various reasons, disciplines tend to have constraints on their
subject matter.[6] Out of intellectual tradition, academic economics excluded the problems of underdeveloped countries until after
World War II. Still out of intellectual tradition, economics has excluded the problems of inequality and distributive justice. And
out of intellectual fashion, problems of agriculture still have a far
from prestigious position in the discipline. These arbitrary constraints will have to be removed if a more robust economic analysis is to be forthcoming to support more appropriate policies in
developing countries. The methodology of the guardian has to
be extended to reach the objectives of the trustee.

Needed Analysis: The Least Developed Countries

We can recognize the gap that has to be spanned if we now consider the failures in the development record alongside the requirements for a more applicable economic analysis.

The particularly weak performance of the least of the less developed countries is symptomatic of the heterogeneity of the developing countries. Although in the 1950s economists tended to analyze the underdeveloped countries as a group and even referred to a "representative" underdeveloped country, this has become increasingly inappropriate, since the LDCs have demonstrated individual characteristics, particular problems, and a wide range of development accomplishments. What is possible for a newly industrializing country of East Asia may be implausible for a Latin American country and impossible for an African country. To analyze all developing countries from Afghanistan to Zimbabwe in the same way will not do.

In analyzing the especially acute problems of the least developed countries, such as those in Sub-Saharan Africa, economists must now give added significance to the need for institutional and structural changes. The market price system exists in only a rudimentary form. The invisible hand is difficult to see. The subsistence sector is still large. The problems of smallholder cultivators are especially acute.

In the economies of the least developed countries, the principles of neoclassical economics are less likely to be applicable, while more attention has to be given to the obstacles, bottlenecks, lags, and constraints that are of a structural character. The emphasis on structural analysis by the Early Development Economics is still relevant for the least developed economies. Such economies lack the flexibility and the elastic responses to changes in prices that characterize the analysis of neoclassical economics. Labor tends to be immobile; markets are fragmented; information is lacking. In such an environment, changes in the structure of production cannot be induced simply by price movements; other policies are needed.

Denied recourse to neoclassical analysis, however, the economist remains hard pressed in advising how to attain the necessary structural changes in the least developed countries. The inadequacy of policymaking in these countries attests to this difficulty. This has been especially true in Sub-Saharan Africa, where many of the poorest countries in the world are experiencing some of the most intractable development problems. More than conventional Western models of development are needed to come to grips with the social, political, and structural issues in the least developed countries.

The Population Problem

The disappointing increase in population also challenges economists to rethink their views on population determinants and the interrelationships between population and poverty.

The population problem arouses more alarm than any other aspect of development. But development economists have generally treated population as outside their analytical domain—as an "exogenous" variable—and as of only indirect significance to the central issues of development. Economists discount neo-Malthusian fears by appealing to almost two centuries of contradictory history since Malthus first asserted that population would eventually be limited by food production. The population problem is, however, much more than a food problem: it must be recognized as a general development problem with wide ramifications for employment, income distribution, and human resource development. Without a more refined analysis of the causes and consequences of population growth and more empirical studies of modern developing countries, it is difficult to devise policies that might mitigate the adverse effects of future population growth.

Empirical studies of the determinants of the population growth in LDCs are, however, still limited in number and in analytical sophistication. Especially needed are studies about how the pattern of development might influence population change. Econometric models that combine analysis and empirical evidence have not yet been able to establish causal relationships for both demographic and economic variables. No model has yet adequately tied together individual, family, and aggregate economic and demographic change.

As guardians of rationality, some economists have also extended their decision-making models to include choices about reproduction. These theorists have begun to analyze the microeconomic determinants of family fertility by postulating a rational choice mechanism that can weigh the benefits of "child services" against the costs of child rearing, arriving at optimal household behavior. This theory rests on behavioral assumptions that are in the tradition of neoclassical rationality, but it still requires more empirical evidence on the various benefits and costs, on the private costs of bringing up children, and on household savings. The hypothesis that a country can substitute "quality" for "quantity" in regard to children also needs testing. Social, cultural, and ideological influences on behavior are also left outside the model as "tastes" that are exogenous and stable. When undertaking policies to reduce population growth, it is debatable whether the noneconomic links of social relationships can be reduced to the utility-maximizing theorems of neoclassical economics.

Population questions are now more than aggregate growth questions. Although economists have had a long-standing interest in the effects of population growth on aggregate income and income per head, they must now also focus on other interrelationships between population and poverty. It is now important to direct more attention to the effects of population growth on not only average income but also on the distribution of income. What is the impact of population growth on different social and economic groups? What is the impact of population growth on the incidence of absolute poverty and the distribution of income? In turn, it is important to analyze how the extent of absolute poverty and the distribution of income affect fertility. Furthermore, how do the distribution of health and education facilities affect fertility?

More consideration must also now be given to the question of what policies are appropriate to reduce population pressure. Some statistical studies have been undertaken that attempt to explain fertility differentials among developing countries in terms of various socioeconomic correlates of fertility—such as, income and its distribution, age of marriage, education and literacy, urbanization, employment, status of women, and infant mortality. The quality of such research is, however, still inadequate. What is now needed are more policy-oriented studies that will isolate the fertility-reducing effect of various policies that might change the socioeconomic correlates in specific countries.

Although most population studies have dealt with large numbers in an impersonal way—seeking regularities for the entire population of a region or nation—policies must operate on individual subjects. The task remains to translate aggregate studies into policies that will be effective in having an impact on individuals with tolerable cost. This is needed not only for the delivery of family planning services, but for all the public policies that might have an effect in reducing fertility.

Agricultural Weakness

It is also essential to reverse the disappointing performance of the agricultural sector—especially in the low-income, food-deficient countries of Asia and Africa where two-thirds of the population of developing countries live. The gap between market demand and supply of basic foodstuffs has increased markedly in a number of LDCs. Many of the low-income countries already do not have the foreign exchange to finance imports of foodstuffs. Unless past trends are reversed through more domestic food production, the deficits will become alarmingly large in the countries of Asia and Sub-Saharan Africa that can least afford them. It is essential to institute policies that will stimulate local food production. A set of policies to increase the supply of foodgrain must be devised to include biological research, investment in irrigation systems, and the diffusion of technical innovations to farmers.

Agricultural development must also be related to a solution of the problem of malnutrition that exists among about a half billion of the world's population. Most of the malnourished do not have access either to land on which to grow more food or to the income with which to purchase it. The nutritional needs of this large number of people are generally additional to the market deficits in food already noted.

The central focus of a strategy for rural development must now be on the involvement of small farmers who have not been reached by many previous programs. The landless and marginal farmers continue to find it difficult to borrow, acquire inputs, and absorb risk. If more appropriate agricultural policies are to be devised, they must be based on microresearch that examines the farms in the villages of Africa and Asia. Compared with the need, the extent of the research on the rural household as a production and consumption unit is still negligible. It is also necessary to analyze more fully the rural markets for labor, credit, and land. More knowledge is also required of how changes in rural attitudes and behavior are to be achieved—difficult sociocultural and political change of institutions and national and traditional practices requiring broad-based participation, unlike concentrated industrial development.

Furthermore, the limits of technology transfer must be recognized for countries with heterogeneous conditions of farm production and major reliance on rainfall production. The oft-quoted experience of Japan and Taiwan in utilizing improved seed-fertilizer combinations to expand farm productivity has little relevance for countries without a similarly homogeneous pattern of agriculture and irrigative production. For other countries, it is now necessary to pursue the more difficult task of identifying a number of strategies adapted to a variety of agroclimatic conditions and crops. These strategies are likely to require, in turn, new equipment and tillage innovations that meet the needs of smallholders with very limited cash income. The problems of arid regions are especially acute, untouched by the potential of the Green Revolution.

The design of new agricultural strategies must also focus more on employment-oriented agricultural development. To absorb surplus labor, it is necessary to create additional employment opportunities and increase productivity in agriculture. The pursuit of efficient labor-intensive methods of agricultural production should also help meet the problem of rural-to-urban migration.

Two other aspects of agricultural development require additional analysis of a political economy character. One is a study of why the urban bias persists: What are the political and economic forces that allow the extraction of an agricultural surplus for the benefit of urban people? The other is land reform: What constitutes "successful" land reform, and what is the complete "land reform package" necessary to achieve success?

Finally, agricultural development requires modes of organization designed to strengthen the institutional infrastructure and managerial skills. The fulfillment of organizational requirements explains much of the success in agricultural programs, such as that in Taiwan. Professor Hla Myint interprets Taiwan's experience as a specially successful case of organizational adaptation combining a dynamic and labor-intensive agricultural sector with a decentralized labor-intensive type of small-scale industry to take advantage of an abundant labor supply. Institutional innovation and adaptation provided an effective organizational network.[7]

More generally, Myint has emphasized that the "organizational framework" of the underdeveloped countries is underdeveloped in the sense that there is an incomplete or rudimentary development of their market system and their monetary and fiscal system, and that this has seriously reduced the effective functioning of their economic mechanisms and institutions and their capacity for economic development. It may be said that massive market failures in the economy's information system and the diffusion of existing knowledge require improvements in the existing organizational framework to accelerate the economy's learning rate. Neoclassical economics assumes that the organizational framework is already in place, but development economists must give more attention to how this institutional capacity is to be developed in the first place.

The Employment Problem

When he authored *The Asian Drama* (1968), Gunnar Myrdal argued that the familiar concepts of "unemployment" and "underemployment" did not fit South Asian countries.[8] He pointed out that unlike in Western countries where the readily available labor supply and the labor reserve can be mobilized by increasing the demand for labor, primarily through the expansion of aggregate demand for goods and services, this is not true in South Asia. In this region, a massive waste of labor takes the form of not utilizing labor at all, or of utilizing labor for only part of the time, or in an almost useless way. But little of this slack in the labor force can be taken up by turning on the Keynesian tap of aggregate demand.

In Myrdal's words,

> As an ultimate goal, the planner and policymaker must aim to absorb the total labor reserve by utilizing the labor force fully at higher levels of labor efficiency and still higher levels of labor productivity. Viewed in this sense, it is clear that the labor reserve available to the planner and policymaker in South Asian countries is very much bigger than the readily available labor supply.[9]

Following Myrdal, economists have realized that to analyze the problem of generating employment in the LDCs they must depart from their conventional views of unemployment in an advanced industrial economy. The concept of open involuntary unemployment may be an appropriate measure of unemployment in an advanced economy with well-organized labor markets, formal labor exchanges, unemployment benefits, and contractual wages. But these conditions are rare in a less developed country, confined to the organized urban sector if at all. The spectrum of employment problems in an LDC encompasses more than open unemployment. Especially pervasive are underemployment and low productivity in the informal urban and rural sectors. More than with open unemployment, the concern must be with inefficiency in the use of labor and low remuneration to labor.

Economists concerned with labor markets in developing countries have in recent years made some progress in removing the institutional assumptions of neoclassical static equilibrium analysis. But there is as yet little consensus on labor market behavior. More must still be done to disaggregate the models of employment in developing countries, even for dual labor markets. More analysis must also be directed to the economic and institutional environment affecting the use and remuneration of labor in LDCs. The structure of labor markets requires increased emphasis, especially as related to the interdependence of employment issues with labor and product markets. To do this, economic analysis has to be extended into areas of risk, uncertainty, information, and other complexities of market failure in order to understand better the determination of wages and employment patterns. This calls for an analysis beyond the conventional demand and supply framework which takes markets as a given.

More effective policies must still be designed to remedy the problem of the underemployed and the working poor—those working in low-productivity activities with an inadequate and variable income that is frequently shared with others. The specification of particular policy measures to provide work opportunities and to improve the utilization of labor in the context of the actual conditions of each developing country is still a major requirement for improved development performance. To do this, a more insightful analysis has to be made of the determinants of rural-urban migration and the concentration of underemployment in the rural and urban informal sectors.

In the revision of development strategies, it has become conventional to maintain that employment strategies require an integrated set of policies to mobilize and allocate domestic and foreign resources to achieve more labor-intensive output growth, investment in human capital, a labor-intensive industrialization program, an agricultural program that is itself labor-absorbing and also contributory to industrialization, adoption of more appropriate technology, and the slowing down of population growth. But these remain empty—or at best, only partially filled—policy boxes. The filling of these boxes with appropriate policies depends in a fundamental sense on more extensive theoretical underpinnings and empirical evidence related to quality and skill dimensions of labor, the different motivational problems of different categories of labor and the structure of labor markets.

Inequality

If it is to tackle the more pressing problems of development, the major task for economics is to incorporate considerations of equity or fairness along with the narrower traditional consideration of efficiency. If economists were to devote as much energy to problems of equity as they have to efficiency, could they not acquire more insights into the problem of inequality in the distribution of income and assets? Could they not analyze why the distribution has become more unequal in many of the LDCs, and suggest remedial policies? Need the "explanation" of the inequality be left to the internal polarization view of those who see only dependency? Cannot the ideology of dependency be subjected to more rigorous analysis and empirical evidence?

The ultimate decision on the distribution of income and assets is political. But economists could do more to inform the decision by indicating the effects of different distributions, revealing how various policies affect the distribution and noting the trade-offs among various distributions and other objectives.

The removal of absolute poverty and the provision of basic needs are intimately connected to distribution issues. The basic needs strategy, however, is still unsupported by sufficiently strong conceptualization, measurement, and knowledge of how the strategy can best be implemented. Because of the importance of government expenditure in a developing economy, more empirical studies are needed to determine which groups actually benefit from the government expenditure. Are the operation and prices of public services biased against the poor? The distributional effect of government subsidies is also important. Poverty removal can also be interpreted as ultimately raising entitlements of the poor to include income and assets. More analysis is therefore needed of entitlement relations in terms of both institutional arrangements and exchange mechanisms that might benefit the poor.

When distributional objectives are combined with the objectives of efficiency and growth in output, the question of trade-offs requires more analysis. Can there be what might be termed "efficient equity"—that is, an increase in equity together with an increase in output? Or must output be sacrificed to obtain greater equity? And over time, is it necessary to endure greater inequality now in order to achieve greater output and greater equity in the future? These questions have not received the consideration they deserve from mainstream neoclassical economists. Their answers require more analysis of the employment content of growth, the types of investments that will increase both the endowment of human and physical capital of the poor, and the effects of a basic needs strategy on growth.

If issues of domestic distribution have been neglected, so much more have economists shied away from the analysis of distributive justice in interstate terms. The neoclassical theory of international trade does not give sufficient attention to the distributional consequences of trade. The interstate distribution of the gains from trade is considered of secondary significance to the principle that all trading countries do gain absolutely from trade. Moreover, except for the effects on the terms of trade, trade policies are rarely analyzed for their effects on international distribution. Even rarer is the next step of determining the effect of a trade policy on a country's domestic distribution. Tariffs, quotas, international commodity agreements, conditions of resource access, regulation of multinational enterprises, agreements for the exploitation of common resources, foreign aid—these are only some of the international policies that deserve analysis for their probable effects on distribution, in terms of both interstate and internal distribution. Even though economists may be reluctant to pass judgment on distributive justice, they may provide a more substantial analysis that will make explicit the distributional consequences of policies and better inform the political and moral choices of policies.

Anything Goes?

The causes of underdevelopment, inequality, and absolute poverty are interrelated, and so too must be policies for their removal. But the guardian of rationality may fear that the trustee for the poor has gone too far in advocating a concern for such policies. Even though John Maynard Keynes maintained that "economics is essentially a moral science and not a natural science," he chided the venerable Cambridge economist Alfred Marshall for being "too anxious to do good." The guardian of rationality may well fear that "anything goes" when the trustee for the poor seeks a "better" income distribution or the provision of basic needs. The moral fervor of the social reformer who is concerned with objectives and values at the normative level may run away with the scientific discipline at the positive level.

This tension is not new among economists. The positive-normative distinction exists for all economic problems, but a sharp distinction between what "is" and what "ought" to be cannot be readily drawn as long as economics intends to be an applied subject that deals with urgent, real-world, economic problems.

Valiant efforts have been made to maintain the distinction for advanced economies, but the distinction is exceedingly difficult to draw for the problems of a developing economy because of the limits of welfare economics, the intrinsic concern with growth and distribution when economists are concerned with development, and the close interconnection of politics and economics in a developing country.

Through the application of welfare economics, economists in developed countries have been able to deal with the normative while maintaining a rigorous, systematic, logically valid discipline. In what would now be an uncharacteristic statement, A. C. Pigou, who was to write the classic *Economics of Welfare* (1920), did not hesitate to state in his inaugural lecture at Cambridge University that the most valuable kind of motivation for the economist was not so much that he might be

> interested by Professor Edgeworth's *Mathematical Psychics* or Dr. Fisher's *Appreciation and Interest*, but rather that he should be possessed by "social enthusiasm"—because he has walked through the slums of London and is stirred to make some effort to help his fellow men. . . . Social enthusiasm, one might add, is the beginning of economic science.

Again, in considering the objective of economic welfare, Pigou declared:

> It is not wonder, but rather the social enthusiasm which revolts from the sordidness of mean streets and the joylessness of withered lives, that is the beginning of economic science. Here, if in no other field, Comte's great phrase holds good: It is for the heart to suggest our problems; it is for the intellect to solve them. . . . The only position for which the intellect is primarily adapted is to be the servant of the social sympathies.[10]

Pigou's *Economics of Welfare* emphasized forces that affected the production of the "national dividend" and its distribution. But subsequent refinements in welfare economics narrowed the subject considerably. Now desiring to avoid interpersonal comparisons of utility, the "new welfare economics" can say much less about the distribution of income than did the old welfare economics of Pigou. Criteria of "efficiency" still dominate the notion of an economic "improvement." Distributional issues are sidestepped by the condition that a policy that leads to an "improvement" would allow the gainers from the policy to compensate the losers and still leave gainers better off after the "improvement." No welfare weighting according to the distribution of income is given to the measurement of GNP. No greater "social enthusiasm" is expressed for the betterment of the lowest 40 percent of the population who are in absolute poverty than for the top 10 percent who already receive 50 percent of the GNP. Being constricted by the theory of exchange, welfare economics has had little to say about long-term growth and income distribution, and has had little influence on the analysis of development problems. Being unable to be shielded by the fig leaf of welfare economics, the development economist has to be exposed to more explicit and forthright policy pronouncements.

When growth, underemployment, absolute poverty, and income distribution are of more concern than conditions of efficiency, development economists must be more than guardians of rationality. But they are always restrained from "anything goes" by retaining growth as an indispensable policy objective. Growth *with* employment is necessary. Redistribution *with* growth is necessary. The particular task of economists is to place an emphasis on the preposition—"with." Their compassion is constrained by competence. As long as they practice their competence, they will assess alternative policies in terms of trade-offs among objectives. And in doing that, they must exercise the logic of choice—albeit now in terms of social choice and public policy.

As guardians of rationality, economists are concerned with instrumental rationality—that is, how to achieve most economically a given objective. On the given objective, however, they pass no judgment—only the means of achieving the objective are scrutinized in economic terms. What then can the economist say when "economic development" is defined in terms of several objectives—growth in GNP, income distribution, alleviation of absolute poverty, basic needs, or employment? Might not these objectives conflict? Indeed, they may. A redirection of resources, in the interest of income distribution, may be at the expense of growth in GNP. Or more labor-intensive techniques designed to utilize more labor may reduce the rate of growth. The pursuit of any one of the other objectives may at the same time be at the expense of a higher rate of growth in GNP.

What policy advice can the economist then offer? The economist's sense of instrumental rationality can be cogent in pointing out the trade-offs between the objectives and in indicating how the trade-offs might be avoided or minimized. The achievement of efficient labor-using techniques, for instance, is the economists' responsibility as they denote techniques that will raise the use of labor input per unit of output without decreasing the productivity of capital. The economist may also indicate that in fulfilling the basic need of education, concentration on primary education may yield higher returns with less reduction in GNP growth. Although growth in GNP has been dethroned as a sufficient condition of development, it remains a necessary condition to avoid a trade-off between the growth rate and any other dimension of development. In reformulating development policies, the economist must therefore delineate ever more precisely the various trade-offs that might result from alternative policy instruments.

Because the public sector and public policymaking are so prominent in a less developed economy, a nonpolitical economics is unrealistic. When political economy gave way to economics, it did so at a time when the interconnections and interdependencies between politics and economics were at an all time low. This was far different from conditions now prevalent in the less developed countries. If a strongly developed market economy already exists, if the economy's organizational framework is in place, if a well-developed price system is a given—if these conditions exist, then the role of government will be correspondingly diminished, and political and ethical issues will not be of so much concern. But these conditions are not fulfilled in many of the LDCs. In these countries, the very process of attempting to establish market institutions and a more refined price system is in itself a political and ethical undertaking.

In the mix of politics and economics, therefore, the larger

problems of political economy and the old growth economics are again being raised by the challenge of development. The challenge to the contemporary economist, in turn, is now to analyze these problems with the more rigorous techniques of modern economics.

This might be best approached by trying to improve the quality of policymaking in developing countries—both in terms of objectives and policy instruments. If, on one side, the theory of development policy has been underdeveloped, on the other side, the study of the policymaking process has also been underdeveloped. To improve policy guidance, the economist will have to give more attention to the political economy of government behavior and to the design and implementation of more appropriate policies for a developing economy. Government behavior has first to be studied in terms of the actual practices of political processes and institutions. Instead of attributing a rational choice model to the government, the development advisor has to reckon with the political and bargaining aspects of policy formulation.

Appropriate Policy Technology

Following the study of actual government practice, the economist must determine how to avoid inappropriate policies and, instead, must design more appropriate policies. More and more, economists have come to attribute the persistence of poverty to inappropriate policies. But how to gain the acceptance of more appropriate policies? This remains the most underdeveloped part of the development economist's subject.

Policymaking is an exercise in social engineering, but the experience in many LDCs indicates it is as easy and as artificial to import oversophisticated policymaking techniques as it is to import inappropriate technology. If conspicuous production and conspicuous consumption have no place in the developing economy, neither does conspicuous knowledge. Attention in the future must be given to the basic needs in policymaking, just as to the basic needs in the production and consumption pattern of the economy.

Three types of bias have been prominent in policy analysis: a bias toward macromodels and plan formulation to the relative neglect of the microeconomic aspects of planning (such as the management of individual enterprises or the behavior of households); a bias toward the quantitative aspects of the development process to the relative neglect of other development forces that are not quantifiable but are of crucial importance (for instance, sociocultural and political changes for which incomplete or no data exist); and a bias toward concentration on the formulation of development policies without due regard for their implementation.

These biases stem from an overly keen receptivity to the most refined model, the newest technique, the latest element of expertise. Whether it be the result of the operation of an international "demonstration effect" in importing intellectual technology or the dominant influence of intellectuals on planning commissions, only too often ultrasophisticated techniques have been allowed to shape a country's development strategy, and the policy implementation has becoome unduly difficult. Something akin to the Nyasaland Economic Symposium's attraction to the Harrod-Domar formula $\theta = \sigma \alpha$ has persisted in a fascination with evermore complex econometric models and mathematical programming techniques. At the same time, however, in many cases the solutions to immediate and more crucial needs have been ignored through the overreaching for more complex techniques of analysis and highly formalized models.

Attraction to the highest style of analysis has weakened the policymaking effort by divorcing the economic analysis from the contributions of other social studies. The more advanced and more rigorous the economic analysis, the less is it capable of noneconomic elements. But the less developed the country, the more the efficacy of public policymaking depends on noneconomic factors. Before concentrating on the purely economic factors, attention should be given to those social and organizational characteristics of the economy that have been critically important in impeding growth. When these strategic noneconomic factors have been ignored, the implementation of policies designed to remove the economic barriers has remained limited. For, regardless of the economic logic of the development strategy, its success in gaining popular support and participation must depend on attitudes, values, and institutions.

It has sometimes been thought that technical programming models of development provide a set of "decision rules" that can serve as specific guides to action for the policymaker. This may be true for some types of business and military operations, but it cannot be so for a process that is as complex and qualitative in character as the modernization of an economy and the transformation of a society. So broadly humane an undertaking cannot be viewed as a mechanical process, and its diagnosis cannot be reduced to a matter of pure techniques. A good deal of the disparity between the theory and practice of policymaking can only too often be traced to an excessive reliance on the pure mathematics of an "optimum" or a "maximum" that has distilled the life out of the development process and left the development strategy without operational significance. In order to institutionalize and sustain developmental forces, we cannot adopt the mathematical view that "a maximum is a maximum regardless of the maximizing agent." In spite of—or rather, because of—the efforts of mathematical economists, we need to be reminded that economics is still a social study, and that the loss of some rigor and precision in analysis may be worth the introduction of more workable policies. Given the present circumstances in most of the developing countries, the cause of development might be better advanced by sound application of some basic elementary principles of economics instead of by borrowing and imitating at too high a level. The $\theta = \sigma\alpha$ syndrome must still be avoided.

As the leading Hungarian economist János Kornai observes, the implementation of mathematical planning is dependent on the degree of maturity of nonmathematical planning. It is only clear what policy objectives are worth striving for when there has already been established an organized institutional, nonmathematical form of planning. For, as Kornai states,

> [I]n a single model only a few hundred relationships and constraints can be considered. But people working in the central planning agencies and lower-level institutions and enterprises "sense" hundreds of thousands of further constraints and relations, and they can give expression to these in their own estimates. Mathematical planning will develop successfully only

when it develops as one element of well-prepared and well-oriented institutional planning, connected by many threads with real economic life in developing countries.[11]

Not conspicuous knowledge, but basic principles of policy analysis must be applied to the fundamental problems of development. This requires caution in importing techniques of policy analysis from more advanced economies. Nor can policies be merely imitative of policies in the more developed countries; they must be adapted to the environment of the LDCs. Innovation in policy technology is as necessary as innovation in production technology and intellectual technology.

Policy Acceptance

To design more appropriate policies is only part of the development economist's task. Equally necessary is the economist's exercise of persuasion to gain acceptance and implementation of policy advice. The political framework within which economic advice is considered therefore becomes highly relevant.

After being in Colombia in the early 1950s as an official economic advisor, Albert Hirschman, observed:

> Little attention appears to have been given by economists and other social scientists to any analysis, systematic or casual, of the behavior of governments of underdeveloped countries as revealed by their economic policy decisions over a period of time. Nevertheless, in view of the considerable role played today by governments in the development process, it is clear that governmental behavior should be subjected to just as close scrutiny as is being given to the motivations and conduct of entrepreneurs.

> In fact, in the absence of more knowledge about probable actions and reactions of governments, our best-intentioned technical assistance efforts are liable to fail. This conclusion is inescapable to anyone who has been watching the economists and other social science experts who are sent on foreign assignments. At the outset of their mission, they are likely to think that the principal problem they are going to be confronted with

will be that of determining what ought to be done, e.g., in what sector the principal investment effort should be undertaken, and what monetary, fiscal, and foreign exchange policies should be adopted. But soon they realize that they have little trouble in deciding what to do or rather what to advise to do, while by far the largest portion of their time is devoted to energy-consuming and often frustrating efforts to put their ideas and proposals across.[12]

The governmental structure must first provide sufficient policymaking machinery and ready access for the economists to reach the policymakers. Substantial progress in this direction has been made in most of the LDCs. Notable strides have been taken in broadening and deepening the policymaking infrastructure, in utilizing economists in government, in improving statistical services, and in engaging in a policy dialogue with visiting missions and international institutions. Any number of examples could be cited to illustrate how economic reasoning has been effective in improving policy decisions. If not of the grand design, nonetheless, the daily, pragmatic, incremental process of policymaking has been greatly improved in any number of developing countries over the past two or three decades.

And yet, the acceptance of sound economic policy advice still has far to go. Why isn't the economist listened to more? The same question could be asked in a rich country, but the answer is more crucial for the poor country in which government policy plays a larger role, and in which the consequences of purposive policy action tend to produce more extensive changes in the economy and in society than in the more developed countries.

We must still ask why, despite contrary arguments by the economists, do governments favor import substitution over export promotion? Why do governments maintain their urban bias although economists emphasize the need for rural development? Why is inflation recurrent, and why do governments practice stop-go measures although economists advocate stabilization programs? How do policy issues that the economist analyzes only in economic terms become in practice political issues of power, will, or class? Why, in many of the less developed countries, has greater reliance on the market-price mechanism been accompanied by political authoritarianism and repression, although many

economists believe that economic liberalism should promote political liberalism?

A number of reasons account for the limited acceptance of
economic advice. It is, first, a rare public policy from which
everyone gains. Usually some in the country will gain and some
will lose from the policy action. If a government depends on the
support of those who would lose from a contemplated policy
measure, the policy is unlikely to be adopted. Furthermore, the
power of vested interests and pressure groups can act to preserve the status quo or can be mobilized in support of a policy
that is contrary to the economist's prescription. Landed interests
may oppose land reform. Large estates may gain at the expense
of small cultivators. The organized sector is protected, while the
informal sector receives no governmental support.

The economic and social fragmentation in an LDC is also likely
to be reflected in political fragmentation. Ethnic or communal
groups are rallied to the support of political leaders who offer
access to state resources on a regional or communal basis. Narrower considerations of factionalism or patronage dominate over
the pursuit of national objectives.[13]

Public bureaucrats also tend to fear errors of commission more
than errors of omission and are hence biased toward inaction.
Governments also act only within a short-term horizon, and the
political calendar does not extend to embrace the economist's
longer range views. The transition costs in moving to a longer
range position are therefore weighted heavily in political terms.
This is especially evident in the resistance to proposals for liberalization of the foreign trade regime and for stabilization programs. Finally, the purity of economic policy is often diluted by
being linked to other policy issues, such as those of foreign policy or military power.

Because of the interplay between economic and political factors, the development economist has to become more inclined to
understand the political process and adjust policy recommendations accordingly. But, as Hirschman complains,

> Long acquired habits of thought interpose enormous obstacles
> to such an enterprise. The idea of a self-regulating economic
> system (erected on the basis of some political prerequisite such

as law and order, but otherwise perfectly self-sustained) has retained a considerable grip on the economist's imagination; it has, in fact, been bolstered in recent years by the construction of similarly self-regulating equilibrium growth models. In such constructs, political factors and forces are wholly absent; if they play any role at all it is that of spoilers.[14]

To become more persuasive, the development economist needs to become a student of public policy and determine why particular public policies are adopted and not others. To determine what gets on the policy agenda, it is necessary to know how and by whom public policy is determined. This calls for knowledge of the location and uses of political power—through organized group interests or by elites, or through personal leadership or by more fundamental social, economic, and demographic changes. Politics and the political process are especially significant in determining the fate of distributive policies and regulative policies. Instead of limiting economic analysis to the absolute value of the optimal policy and adopting a "rational actor" model of politics, the development economist must try to find second-best policies within the political process and view political decision making and the administrative system of the developing country from a behavioral standpoint.

In spite of the efforts to strengthen the private sector, the public sector will necessarily remain large in a developing country. Much of the future success of development strategies will therefore depend on an improvement in the performance of public-sector management. To the extent that the organization of public administration in many poor countries derives from the "law-and-order" kind of administration, it has not had the competence for managing economic policies as a sensitive art that is not practiced in routine fashion or subjected to indecision, delay, or corruption. Nor can state-owned enterprises be operated as if they were administrative departments. Obviously, if appropriate policies are to be effectively implemented, the overtaxing of administrative competence and managerial capacity must be corrected. In part, this may be done by expanded training. But it must also be done by designing policies that recognize that management is still among the scarcest of resources. Just as an improvement in policymaking depends on a study of the political economy of actual government behavior that reduces the cost of policies in terms of the politician's resources, so too must policies reduce the cost in terms of managerial resources.

Development economics is on the edge of politics and the edge of management. To be more effective in policymaking, it must venture more into each territory. The development economist must stand between the politician and the manager—on the one side, determining how best to appeal to the politician for acceptance of a development strategy, and on the other side, heeding the managerial capacity for implementing the details of the strategy. Although in its increasing refinement economics has become evermore aloof from this position, it must reestablish contact with the political and the managerial if it is to be more effective in devising appropriate policies for development.

Foreign Aid

The stress on appropriate policies introduces an expanded dimension for foreign aid. If aid is to gain more support, it must become more efficient, eliminate any disincentive effects, and induce more self-help measures by the recipient countries. Aid cannot be a substitute for domestic efforts. But if it is recognized that aid is actually only a vehicle for policy—and not a policy per se—then donor nations might in the future insist on more conditionality in their granting of aid. If aid for development is to be a common enterprise between donor and recipient, then the donor may rightly give more weight to an assessment of how effectively the recipient's policies contribute to the objectives of development. Just as the IMF has supported stabilization programs with conditionality, so too might donors link their aid to the support of more appropriate development policies in recipient countries.

Even if a donor nation such as the United States believes that more reliance on the market-price system, private enterprise, and private foreign investment would promote development, it should recognize that aid may facilitate the emergence of these conditions. Without an adequate economic infrastructure, for example, a country can scarcely attract private foreign investment.

Similarly, if, as many economists advocate, a developing country should now undergo a liberalization of its foreign trade regime so that it may move from an inward-looking import substitution strategy to an outward-looking export promotion strategy, a program of aid may help facilitate the transition to the new strategy. Without aid, a poor country might understandably hesitate to undertake policies to achieve the more efficient free trade regime because of the high costs of the transition period and the short-term pressure on the balance of payments as the country liberalizes its trade. Rather than forestalling private enterprise and individual action, aid may be the very means of making conditions more favorable for such action. Aid agencies rightly emphasize the catalytic quality of their activities. If more appropriate policies are to be instituted, they may have to be supported with more aid.

In appraising the role of foreign aid, however, we must ask the basic question: Why should one nation give free resources to another nation? An economist might answer in terms of the effectiveness of aid in relaxing the recipient country's foreign exchange constraint and savings constraint so that growth of national output can increase, or answer in terms of project feasibility studies, or the intricacies of dynamic countrywide programming models. But beyond all these technicalities lie moral considerations and political dimensions that are not captured in the economist's analysis.

The ultimate justification for aid may well be the moral obligation of the relatively affluent to share their wealth with poorer people elsewhere. In the oft-quoted words of the poet, John Donne, "No man is an Island entire of itself . . . Any man's death diminishes me, because I am involved in Mankinde; and therefore never send to know for whom the bell tolls; it tolls for thee." Among nations, the revulsion to poverty should have the same redistributive obligation, founded on humanitarian principles, as it has within a nation.

But for most individuals, the moral obligation to help others stops at one's own national borders. A transnational obligation is not admitted, even though the nation-state is itself a major impediment to a better international distribution of resources and income through the national use of restrictive immigration policy and protectionist trade policy. If national boundaries mark the limits of social obligations, and if the humanitarian basis for aid is not recognized, even less so are the higher obligations of social justice. Although the international distribution of resources is arbitrary from a moral point of view, the principles of distributive justice do not in reality shape the economic conduct of nations. It is a goal toward which efforts at political change must still aim. Ideal justice enters into nonideal politics by way of the natural duty to establish just institutions where none presently exists.

If aid were based on moral obligation, it would imply the following conditions, as submitted by a former governor of the Reserve Bank of India:

> The starting point for determining the requirement of aid and its distribution will be the needs of the poorer countries as measured in relation to certain minimum standards of nutrition, health, education, employment opportunities;
>
> priority would be given in the distribution of aid to countries which are farthest removed from internationally accepted standards of minimum social and economic well-being;
>
> the funds required for disbursing foreign aid will be collected by taxation of all nation-states in accordance with their capacity to pay and would not be dependent on the periodic vetoes exercised by national legislatures;
>
> the richer nations would receive no compensation for their effort and sacrifice except the satisfaction of seeing common human objectives realized.[15]

To state these implications of the moral obligation is to indicate how far removed the international community has been from the ideal approach. Shaped by practical politics, the actual motivation for aid has been far different. Foreign assistance has been regarded as basically an instrument of foreign policy to produce a political and economic environment in which the donor country can best pursue its own goals.

During the earlier years of foreign aid, national self-interest was related to the objectives of political stability and national security. Now the recognition of greater interdependence among nations is lessening the state-centered image of the world. It is increasingly realized that the welfare of one nation, even a rich one, depends on the welfare of another, even a poor one. Specifically, exports from the richer countries are more dependent on development in the poorer countries. At present, nearly 40 percent of American exports go to the developing countries. So too are the developed countries increasingly dependent on supplies of raw materials from the LDCs. It is of mutual benefit for developed countries to support the expansion of output of energy, food, and raw materials in the developing countries. So too may private foreign investment and technology transfer be of mutual benefit. And "Northern" lenders have as great a stake in improving the external debt situation as do "Southern" borrowers. This mutuality of interests gives more urgency to the development of the less developed countries.

But the essential question remains: Is aid an effective means for achieving this development? Some critics, such as Lord Bauer of the London School of Economics, argue that aid is neither a necessary nor a sufficient condition for development. Moreover, it is claimed that aid unleashes a host of adverse repercussions, damaging to economic performance and development by enabling Third World governments to extend economic controls and to manipulate them for purely political aims, supporting wasteful projects, and encouraging balance-of-payments crises as an excuse for demanding more aid. In the words of Lord Bauer, the receipt of aid also

> obscures the necessity for the people of the poor countries themselves to adopt the conduct and the mores required for sustained material progress. . . . [A]ny favorable effects of the inflow of resources represented by foreign aid can be offset or even outweighed by significant unfavorable repercussions, and also by ineffective use of the resources themselves. It is indeed possible that the flow of aid since the Second World War has inhibited rather than advanced the material progress of many recipients.[16]

But from the left also comes criticism. Aid is alleged to be merely an instrument of neo-imperialism, providing political leverage to the existing leadership of the recipient country to suppress opposition and maintain the status quo, thereby preventing essential reforms. As a critic from the left alleges, "aid can be explained only in terms of an attempt to preserve the capitalist system in the Third World."[17] It is contended that aid may simply keep in power a government that is not really devoted to raising the living standards of the poorest in the population. Furthermore, aid may bolster authoritarian governments and practices of political repression. Even though he was earlier a spiritual father of aid programs, Nobel laureate Gunnar Myrdal now criticizes aid for "simply serving to maintain corrupt governments and improve the living standards of the already privileged elite." Myrdal believes aid should no longer go toward prestige projects and to governments that have no interest in social reforms, but should be channeled to help the increasing masses of poverty-stricken people in the poorest countries and to provide direct "disaster aid" to ease the lot of the truly needy.[18]

As aid experience demonstrates, what must now be stressed is the value of the policy dialogue and the shaping of policies that accompany aid. This dimension of the aid relationship can well be more important in the future than the amount of resources transferred. To concentrate on the effectiveness of aid is not, however, to maintain that greater effectiveness can be a substitute for an increased volume of aid. Some improvement in performance might be gained out of existing funds. But better policies and operations also depend on a sufficient volume of aid. It is more realistic to realize that as development problems intensify, as the least developed countries lag, and as the cost of development increases, the very efficiency of aid may depend on more aid being forthcoming. Without the greater impact, flexibility, and maneuverability bestowed by broader development-assistance programs, the sought for improvement in effectiveness is unlikely to be realized.

Aside from criticism from both the right and left, however, there remains general public confusion over the purposes and accomplishments of aid. From the confusion has come disillusionment, impatience, and a weariness with the entire issue of aid. Stagflation, budgetary constraints, and the diversion of attention to domestic problems make the climate for aid even more inhospitable. A new political initiative for aid is needed to reconcile national self-interest and moral duty.

An International Public Sector?

Although more appropriate domestic policies would improve development performance, so too would more positive international relations between rich and poor countries. The international environment has become increasingly averse to development efforts. The earlier decades of the 1950s and 1960s appear exceptional for their rapid expansion of world trade and the opportunities offered for exports from the developing countries. Now the slow growth in the more developed countries, the flatness of world trade, and the spread of protectionism have revived export pessimism: LDCs may not count on the expansion of export markets as they did in the earlier decades. Nor is their shortage of foreign exchange being filled by an inflow of foreign aid. External support has diminished. At the same time, many LDCs have become more vulnerable to external shocks. The energy crisis has required adjustment in the developing economies. So too has recession or slow growth in their overseas markets. And so has the imposition of tariffs and quotas against their exports. These adverse changes in the international environment have gained more adherents to the school of dependency and more advocates for a New International Economic Order. Neither approach, however, has much merit.

The arguments of the dependencistas (Chapter 8) can be criticized on several grounds. Empirical evidence is lacking to substantiate many of their contentions. They miss the diversity among the LDCs and the need for country-specific policies when they "totalize" all peripheral countries in one world system of dependency. Dependency theory also grossly underestimates the influence of domestic policies over the developing country's own economy. Nor do the policy implications indicate clear and feasible measures to accomplish the reversal of dependency. The category of dependency is more ideological than analytical. But an ideology does not constitute a strategy. The majority of economists would contend that the general policy implications of delinking and collective self-reliance would be inferior to measures that integrate the developing economies into the world economy. The empirical evidence is convincing that the best economic performers among the developing countries have been those that have been integrated the most into the world economy.

Advocates of a New International Economic Order, however, insist that the integration of LDCs into the world economy should occur only on more favorable terms to the LDCs. By the South's insistence on a wider range of rights—without corresponding obligations—the "North-South dialogue" has become a nondialogue. Mutual interests have not been established as a basis for negotiation. The North will not simply acquiesce to the South's demands. Nor can the South draw on sufficient countervailing power to enforce its demands.

Most likely, the North will remain unresponsive to the demand for a New International Economic Order because it is not "new": many of its provisions were advocated as early as the Havana Conference when the ITO failed, and later by ECLA during the 1950s. It is not "international": many of its objectives are highly nationalistic and exhibit a zero sum game character that favors concessions to the LDCs only, instead of emphasizing mutual gains for all nations in a positive sum game. Nor is it "economic": the policy objectives and policy measures are as much political as economic. Finally, it is not "order": given the lack of consensus and the confrontational character of the demands, the measures are more likely to produce disorder than order.

Although their policy conclusions can be contradicted, the school of dependency and advocates of a New International Economic Order are right in emphasizing that more attention should be given to the international system. But the attention should not be exclusive to the neglect of internal economic order based on appropriate domestic policies. Nor are the central international problems confronting the LDCs those of dependency or the lack of concessions from the more developed countries. Instead, an alternative analysis would now recognize that the problems of the LDCs are related to problems of the internationalization process that are common to both rich and poor countries.

The "internationalization process" includes the increasing interdependence of countries as evidenced by the internationalization of markets for goods and services; the international transfer of capital, technology, and management; and the growth of multinational enterprises. Although these forces of internationalization have grown since World War II, the collective management of these forces has not progressed beyond the Bretton Woods institutions. Indeed, even Bretton Woods institutions have been weakened in several respects.

Economists acclaim the gains of efficiency that come from greater integration of the world economy. But this very integration also creates problems for national policymakers whose autonomy over domestic policies is reduced as they are subject to the impact of external events and as the domestic policies that they can undertake are in part conditioned by the policies that other countries are also pursuing.

The national policymaker's view of the international economy has become increasingly one of conflict. There are conflicts over markets—on the one side, over free access to markets for a country's exports; on the other side, over conditions of access to markets for the import of necessary raw materials or technology. There are conflicts over the terms of trade—each country wishes to improve its terms of trade by exporting at a higher price and importing at a lower price. There are conflicts over the terms of foreign investment—host governments want to raise the national benefit-cost ratio from any inflow of foreign capital, while foreign investors seek a higher rate of financial return. There are conflicts over stabilization policies—inflation or recession can be transmitted internationally, and one country's monetary and fiscal policies will affect another country's economy. There are conflicts over how the common resources of the world are to be shared—which countries, for example, should have the right to mine the oceans, and under what conditions. There are conflicts over external detriments—how, for example, should liability be assigned for pollution by one country that damages another. These conflicts arise as governments attempt to capture a larger share of the gains from trade, avoid being damaged by the policies of another country, or preserve their domestic autonomy in policymaking.

The internationalization process is not new—in a sense, it has paralleled the international spread of the industrial revolution. But in recent decades, the attendant conflicts have become more pronounced: they affect more countries more severely and for longer periods of time. These conflicts have diminished international public order to the disadvantage of rich and poor countries—North and South—alike. But the international economy is a highly decentralized system, and the decentralization has spread with the large number of newly independent developing nations. Such a decentralized system is without the authority for collective management that might institute corrective measures to mitigate the conflicts. The "North–South" problem should be factored into this general problem of the need for international public order. The South stands to gain more by recognizing the problems of international public order that are of mutual interest to North and South than by adopting a myopic bipolar view of the world economy.

Nobel laureate Jan Tinbergen has emphasized the series of levels at which decisions have to be taken.[19] In order that the decisions regarding necessary policy instruments ("action parameters") be optimal, there must not be external effects—that is, the influences exerted on the well-being of groups outside the jurisdiction of those who make the decision should be weak. The area in which the impact of the instrument will be felt determines what decision level will be optimal. The level should be high enough to cover the area in which the impact is nonnegligible. Thus, while the newly developing "nation state" is a political unit, it is an inappropriate economic decision-making unit for many developmental issues that require an international level of management. Decisions taken at the national level are often far too low to be optimal. Trade liberalization and access to markets in the developed countries, the monitoring of export controls and access to resources from primary producing countries, multilateral aid programs, harmonization of aid terms, international stabilization policies, coordination of international monetary policies— all these policies depend on cooperative international action.

Time and again, governments demonstrate that free trade is not a natural state, and that the natural inclination is to slide into protectionism. Freer trade has to be enforced by some international authority. The GATT attempted this, as a complement to the Bretton Woods system. But GATT has too often been bypassed in favor of unilateral action. A reform of its provisions could remedy this. A rewriting, for instance, of the conditions for imposing market safeguards (Article XIX) would be of considerable value to both developed and less developed countries.

The Bretton Woods institutions also need rejuvenation. Additional resources are required for the compensatory financing measures and supplementary financial measures of the IMF. The role of the Fund in supporting appropriate domestic policy measures can also be made more effective through the Fund's provisions of conditionality.

The World Bank should also renew the development momentum—not merely by greater capital subscriptions, more allocations to IDA for the poorest of the poor nations, and expansion of structural adjustment lending. As the Bank's history has shown, the policy advice given by the Bank may be of more value than loans alone. But to allow a country to pursue this advice—for example, an export promotion program—additional foreign capital may initially be necessary.

Beyond strengthening the Bretton Woods institutions, other international measures are needed—not so much to deal with short-term international transfers of resources as to respond to long-term structural changes in the world economy. Some measures are required to manage the problem of food scarcity, through selective use of food aid, supply guarantee schemes, and national and international reserves. Other measures are needed to reach problems of restrictive business practices and market imperfections as created by the operation of multinational corporations. Some measures are also sought to bring order to the problems of common resources and externalities.

To list these international areas of concern is to ask whether national programs of development can succeed without the supportive existence of an international public sector. In the domestic economy, the public sector is charged with the maintenance of economic stability, redistribution of income, and correction of market failure. But where is the responsibility for the performance of analogous functions in the international economy? Can there be future success stories of development without a stronger international public sector?

The original Bretton Woods institutions are no longer suffi-

cient. As Keynes foresaw, Bretton Woods was only a beginning.
The world may now have to be persuaded that a Bretton Woods
II is needed.

If economic analysis must develop in response to new policy
problems, so too must policymaking institutions. The GATT, IMF,
and World Bank group now confront problems not envisaged at
the close of World War II. And some issues raised, but not set-
tled, at Bretton Woods continue to be disruptive of international
economic order. A rethinking and extension of these institutions
to unsettled problem areas would be desirable. Especially needed
is an extension of "collective management" that would recognize the interconnectedness of these problem areas in the
emerging global economy. Beyond the separate provinces of the
GATT, IMF, and World Bank, as now constituted, there should
be a bridging of these institutions that would allow them to give
more attention to the complementarity and balance among the
problems of international trade, international finance, international investment, primary products, debt servicing, and official
resource transfers. As these problems have taken on a global
character, and undoubtedly will continue to do so, they are of
common concern to LDCs and MDCs alike. They can be addressed more realistically through a Bretton Woods II than through
the empty resolutions of the United Nations or the partisan an-
nouncements of UNCTAD.

The GATT, IMF, and World Bank group represent the nucleus
of an international public sector. As the strongest international
economic institutions, they might promote intergovernmental
decisions in new problem areas as well as reconsider some of the
long-standing issues that go back to Bretton Woods and the
abortive International Trade Organization. In the context of the
internationalization process, they now have a special task to promote compatibility of domestic and international policy measures. To do this, their rule making, surveillance, consultative,
and rule enforcement functions need to be strengthened.

The difficulty, however, in convening a Bretton Woods II and
in extending the international public sector is that the rationality
underlying institutions of the international public sector is not
the instrumental rationality of the guardian economist—that is,
applied to decisions to achieve an objective—but rather that of

constitutive rationality—that is, applied to decisions about how decisions are to be made, the very constitution of decision making. As such, agreement on a problem of constitutive rationality is far more difficult to achieve. If it is to be obtained, it is more likely to come from economic diplomacy based on the inspired vision of the economist as trustee for the poor than from the guardian of rationality.

At a Royal Economic Society dinner, a few months after the Bretton Woods conference, Lord Keynes offered a toast to "economics and economists, who are the trustees, not of civilization, but of the possibility of civilization." The real test of any civilization lies in its treatment of the poor. If a Bretton Woods II could now reassert the development priority it would certainly be a major investment in the possibility of civilization for two-thirds of humanity whose emergence from poverty during the next century depends on the consequences of decisions we take today. But the world at large still needs to be persuaded.

Notes

Introduction

1. Kenneth J. Arrow, *The Limits of Organization* (1974), p. 16.

Chapter 1

1. *The Collected Writings of John Maynard Keynes*, Donald Moggridge (ed.), Vol. XXVI, *Activities 1941–1946* (1980), p. 42.
2. Personal correspondence with E. M. Bernstein, January 11, 1983.
3. U.S. Department of State, *Proceedings and Documents of United Nations Monetary and Financial Conference* (Bretton Woods, New Hampshire, July 1–22, 1944), Vol. I, p. 85. (Cited hereafter as *Proceedings and Documents*.)
4. *Proceedings and Documents*, Vol. II, p. 1618.
5. Ibid., p. 1176.
6. Ibid., p. 1228.
7. Ibid., p. 1102.
8. *The Collected Writings of John Maynard Keynes*, p. 105.
9. *Proceedings and Documents*, Vol. II, p. 1180.
10. President's Message to Congress, *Bretton Woods*, U.S. Treasury, Washington, D.C., February 20, 1945.
11. E. F. Jackson (ed.), *Economic Development in Africa* (1965), pp. 1–2.
12. Kathryn Morton, *Aid and Dependence: British Aid to Malawi* (1975), p. 11.
13. Letter from Dunduza Chisiza to W. W. Rostow, September 22, 1960.

Chapter 2

1. Edward S. Mason and Robert E. Asher, *The World Bank Since Bretton Woods* (1973), p. 155.
2. The World Bank finances its lending operations primarily through the sale of debt obligations to private investors, financial institutions, and governments. The Bank's capital, retained earnings, and flow of repayments on its loans also contribute to the Bank's resources.
3. Robert L. Ayers, *Banking on the Poor: The World Bank and World Poverty* (1983), pp. 10–16, 229–255.
4. Special drawing rights (SDRs) have been created by members of the IMF as an additional reserve asset in the Fund. The SDR is also a unit of account for Fund operations. Based on the weighted value of five major currencies, the SDR was equivalent to $1.03 in January 1984.
5. *Development Dialogue*, February 1980, p. 5.
6. Ibid., pp. 11–12.
7. Secretariat of UNCTAD, "The Developing Countries in GATT," in UNCTAD, *Proceedings*, Vol. 5 (1964), p. 468.
8. United Nations, *The United Nations Development Decade: Proposals for Action* (1962), p. iii.
9. Albert Waterston, *Development Planning—Lessons of Experience* (1965), p. 66.
10. Jagdish N. Bhagwati, *India in the International Economy* (1973), p. 4.
11. Waterston, pp. 6–7, 365–368.

Chapter 3

1. Although the foregoing discussion is limited to the successful period of South Korea's development, it should be noted that after 1979 the Korean record was disrupted by inflation, balance-of-payments problems, slower growth, and the need to resort to an IMF stand-by arrangement.
2. Shirley W. Y. Kuo, *The Taiwan Economy in Transition* (1983), pp. 96–97, 103–106.
3. The discussion in this section covers Malawi's period of achievement from independence in 1964 to 1979–1980. In the late 1970s and early 1980s, Malawi suffered from a rise in its fuel import bill, increases in other import prices, the international spread of recession, decline in commodity export prices, and transport difficulties. There were then balance-of-payments problems, larger budgetary deficits, and a much slower rate of growth in income. In contrast with the earlier period of marked achievement, the experience at the end of

the 1970s illustrates the vulnerability of a small developing economy to external shocks.

Chapter 4

1. J. Faaland and J. R. Parkinson, "Bangladesh: Gradual Development or Deepening Misery?" *World Development*, September 1976, pp. 737, 747.
2. World Bank, *Accelerated Development in Sub-Saharan Africa* (1981), p. 4.
3. Timothy King, "How Do the Consequences of Population Growth Differ among Developing Countries?" (World Bank draft paper), February 8, 1978, p. 11.
4. Marcelo Selowsky, "Balancing Trickle Down and Basic Needs Strategies," World Bank Staff Working Paper No. 335, June 1979, p. 9.
5. Ibid., p. 65.
6. Michael Lipton, *Why Poor People Stay Poor* (1977), p. 207.
7. Ibid., p. 18.
8. Ibid., p. 68.
9. John Sheahan, "Market-oriented Economic Policies and Political Repression in Latin Ameria," *Economic Development and Cultural Change*, January 1980, p. 268.

Chapter 5

1. Adam Smith, *An Inquiry into the Nature and Causes of the Wealth of Nations* (originally published in 1776; Glasgow edition, R. H. Campbell and A. S. Skinner, eds., 1979), Vol. I, p. 99.
2. Ibid., p. 10.
3. Ibid., p. 343.
4. Ibid., p. 340.
5. Ibid., p. 366.
6. Ibid., p. 346.
7. Ibid., p. 22.
8. Ibid., p. 17.
9. Ibid., p. 31.
10. Ibid., pp. 456–457.
11. Ibid., p. 540.
12. Quoted in John Maynard Keynes, *Essays in Biography* (1933), p. 131.
13. Ibid., p. 132.
14. J. M. Keynes, "The Commemoration of T. R. Malthus," *Economic Journal*, June 1935, pp. 230–234.
15. David Ricardo, *On the Principles of Political Economy and Taxation* (originally published in 1817; Piero Sraffa, ed., 1951), p. 122.

16. John Stuart Mill, *Principles of Political Economy* (1848), Book I, ch. iv., sec. 1.

17. Ibid., Book III, ch. xvii, sec. 5.

18. Ibid., Book IV, ch. vi, sec. 2.

19. Karl Marx, *Capital*, Vol. 1 (1867), pp. 836–837.

20. Karl Marx, *Manifesto of the Communist Party* (1848), ch. I.

21. Karl Marx, "The British Rule in India," *New York Daily Tribune*, June 25, 1953; reprinted in Shlomo Avineri, *Karl Marx on Colonialism and Modernization* (1968), pp. 83–89.

22. Karl Marx, "The Future Results of British Rule in India," *New York Daily Tribune*, August 8, 1853; reprinted in Shlomo Avineri, *Karl Marx on Colonialism and Modernization* (1968), pp. 125–131.

23. Vladimir I. Lenin, *Imperialism, The Highest Stage of Capitalism* (1916), in Vladimir I. Lenin, *Collected Works*, 4th ed. (Moscow: Progress, 1964), p. 194.

24. Ibid., p. 206.

25. W. S. Jevons, *Theory of Political Economy*, 2nd ed. (1879), p. 289.

Chapter 6

1. Remarks of Lauchlin Currie at a testimonial dinner, Bogota, Colombia, August 31, 1979, p. 2, processed. See also, Lauchlin Currie, *The Role of Economic Advisers in Developing Countries* (1981), pp. 53–62.

2. Lauchlin Currie, *Obstacles to Development* (1967), p. 31; *The Role of Economic Advisers in Developing Countries* (1981), pp. 54–58.

3. T. W. Schultz, "The Role of Government in Promoting Economic Growth," in L. D. White (ed.), *The State of the Social Sciences* (1956), p. 372.

4. I. M. D. Little, "Review of P. T. Bauer's, *Indian Economic Policy and Development*," *Economic Journal*, December 1961, p. 835.

5. John Maynard Keynes, *The General Theory of Employment Interest and Money* (1936), p. 245.

6. Gunnar Myrdal, *Rich Lands and Poor* (1957), pp. 103–104.

7. United Nations, *Measures for the Economic Development of Underdeveloped Countries*, Report of a Group of Experts appointed by the Secretary-General of the United Nations (1951), p. 35. The group was composed of A. B. Cortez (Chile), D. R. Gadgil (India), G. Hakim (Lebanon), W. A. Lewis (United Kingdom), T. W. Schultz (United States).

8. Ibid., p. 41.

9. Massachusetts Institute of Technology, Center for International Studies, *The Objectives of United States Economic Assistance Programs*

(1957), p. 70. See also Paul N. Rosenstein-Rodan, "Problems of Industrialization of Eastern and South-Eastern Europe," *Economic Journal*, June–September 1943.

10. Ragnar Nurkse, *Problems of Capital Formation in Underdeveloped Countries* (1953), p. 4.

11. Ibid., p. 5.

12. Ibid., p. 10.

13. Ibid., pp. 13–15.

14. Ragnar Nurkse, "The Conflict Between 'Balanced Growth' and International Specialization," *Lectures on Economic Development* (1958), pp. 171–172.

15. N. S. Buchanan, "Deliberate Industrialization for Higher Incomes," *Economic Journal*, December 1946, pp. 533–553.

16. W. Arthur Lewis, "An Economic Plan for Jamaica," *Agenda*, November 1944, pp. 154–163.

17. Ibid., p. 162.

18. United Nations, *Measures for the Economic Development of Underdeveloped Countries*, p. 93.

19. W. Arthur Lewis, *The Principles of Economic Planning*, rev. ed. (1952), p. 128.

20. W. Arthur Lewis, "Economic Development with Unlimited Supplies of Labor," *The Manchester School*, May 1954, p. 155.

21. Ibid., pp. 147–148.

22. W. Arthur Lewis, *Development Planning* (1966), pp. 77–78.

Chapter 7

1. Mahbub ul Haq, "Employment and Income Distribution in the 1970's: A New Perspective," *Pakistan Economic and Social Review*, June–December 1971, p. 6.

2. Hollis Chenery, "Introduction," in *Redistribution with Growth* (1974), p. xiii.

3. Paul Streeten, "From Growth to Basic Needs," *Finance & Development*, September 1979, p. 8.

4. Paul Streeten et al., *First Things First* (1981), p. 31.

5. Carl Eicher, "Facing up to Africa's Food Crisis," *Foreign Affairs*, Fall 1982, p. 171.

6. W. Arthur Lewis, *Growth and Fluctuations 1870–1913* (1978), p. 244.

7. I. M. D. Little, T. Scitovsky, and M. FG. Scott, *Industry and Trade in Some Developing Countries* (1970), p. xviii.

8. Ibid., pp. xvii–xix.

9. Ibid., p. xx.

10. Frederick H. Harbison, *Human Resources as the Wealth of Nations* (1973), p. 3.
11. Theodore W. Schultz, "Nobel Lecture: The Economics of Being Poor," *Journal of Political Economy*, August 1980, p. 640.
12. Richard Easterlin, "Why Isn't the Whole World Developed?" *Journal of Economic History*, March 1981.
13. W. Arthur Lewis, *Development Planning* (1966), pp. 269–270, 273.

Chapter 8

1. Gunnar Myrdal, *Rich Lands and Poor* (1957), p. 228.
2. Gunnar Myrdal, *Development and Underdevelopment* (1956), pp. 9–10.
3. Ibid., pp. 50–51.
4. Raúl Prebisch, *The Economic Development of Latin America and Its Principal Problems* (1950), p. 14.
5. Ibid., p. 2.
6. Paul A. Baran, *The Political Economy of Growth* (1957), pp. 11–12.
7. André Gunder Frank, *Capitalism and Underdevelopment in Latin America* (1967), p. 11.
8. Osvaldo Sunkel, "National Development Policy and External Dependence in Latin America," *Journal of Development Studies*, October 1969, p. 31.
9. Samir Amin, *Unequal Development: An Essay on the Social Formations of Peripheral Capitalism* (1976), p. 179.
10. Osvaldo Sunkel, "Transnational Capitalism and National Disintegration in Latin America," *Social and Economic Studies*, March 1973, pp. 132–176.
11. Fernando Henrique Cardoso, "Dependent Capitalist Development in Latin America," *New Left Review*, July 1972, p. 90.
12. Fernando Henrique Cardoso and L. Faletto, *Dependency and Development in Latin America* (1979), p. 19.
13. Ibid., p. xvi.
14. Samir Amin, *Accumulation on a World Scale* (1975), p. 131.
15. S. Grassman and E. Lundberg (eds.), *The World Economic Order, Past and Prospects* (1981), pp. 534–535.

Chapter 9

1. W. Arthur Lewis, *The Evolution of the International Economic Order* (1977), p. 71.
2. For reasons to be explained later in this chapter, dependency is not a useful analytical category and misdirects policy analysis. We therefore concentrate on revisions in "mainstream" economics.

3. W. Arthur Lewis, *Development Planning* (1966), preface.

4. Theodore W. Schultz, "Nobel Lecture: The Economics of Being Poor," *Journal of Political Economy*, August 1980, p. 639.

5. J. R. Hicks, "Linear Theory," *Economic Journal*, December 1960, pp. 707–708.

6. C. E. Lindblom and David K. Cohen, *Useable Knowledge: Social Science and Social Problem Solving* (1979), p. 93.

7. Hla Myint, "Comparative Analysis of Taiwan's Economic Development with Other Countries," *Academia Economic Papers*, March 1982.

8. Gunnar Myrdal, *Asian Drama* (1968), ch. 21.

9. Ibid., pp. 961, 1013–1014.

10. A. C. Pigou, *The Economics of Welfare* (1920), p. 5.

11. János Kornai, "Models and Policy," in C. R. Blitzer et al. (eds.), *Economy-Wide Models and Development Planning* (1975), ch. 2.

12. Albert O. Hirschman, "Economic Policy in Underdeveloped Countries," *Economic Development and Cultural Change*, July 1957, p. 362.

13. C. L. G. Bell, "The Political Framework," in Hollis Chenery et al., *Redistribution with Growth* (1974), pp. 53–55.

14. Albert O. Hirschman, *A Bias for Hope* (1971), p. 15.

15. I. G. Patel, "How to Give Aid—A Recipient's Point of View," in Ronald Robinson (ed.), *International Co-operation in Aid* (1966), pp. 88–89.

16. P. T. Bauer, *Dissent on Development* (1972), pp. 111–112; more generally, pp. 95–135.

17. Teresa Hayter, *Aid as Imperialism* (1971), p. 9.

18. Gunnar Myrdal, "Need for Reforms in Underdeveloped Countries," in S. Grassman and E. Lundberg (eds.), *The World Economic Order, Past and Prospects* (1981), pp. 522–525.

19. Jan Tinbergen, "Building a World Order," in J. N. Bhagwati (ed)., *Economics and World Order from the 1970s to the 1990s* (1972), pp. 145–147.

Readings

The wide scope of this book has precluded detailed attention to special topics. To allow the pursuit of a number of these other topics and more extensive consideration of some central issues, the following additional readings are suggested.

Chapter 1

The proceedings of the Bretton Woods Conference are recorded in U.S. Department of State, *Proceedings and Documents of United Nations Monetary and Financial Conference,* July 1–22, 1944, Vols. I and II. The papers of John Maynard Keynes also provide insights into the Bretton Woods Conference: *The Collected Writings of John Maynard Keynes,* Vol. XXVI, *Activities 1941–1946, Shaping the Postwar World, Bretton Woods and Reparations* (1980), Donald Moggridge (ed.). See also R. F. Harrod, *The Life of John Maynard Keynes* (1951), ch. 13. Also instructive are Robert W. Oliver, *International Economic Cooperation and the World Bank* (1975) and Richard N. Gardner, *Sterling-Dollar Diplomacy,* 2nd ed. (1969).

The striving for political and economic independence is analyzed by Rupert Emerson, *From Empire to Nation* (1960).

Chapter 2

Illuminating histories of the World Bank's activities are provided by Edward S. Mason and Robert E. Asher, *The World Bank Since Bretton Woods* (1973) and S. J. Burki et al., *International Development Association in Retrospect* (1983). Annual reports of the World Bank may be consulted for changes in the Bank's activities.

A well-balanced evaluation of the poverty-oriented activities of the Bank is provided by Robert L. Ayers, *Banking on the Poor* (1983), but also see Cheryl Payer, *The World Bank: A Critical Analysis* (1982).

Activities of the International Monetary Fund are documented in J. Keith Horsefield, *The International Monetary Fund 1945–65, Vol. I: Chronicle* (1969); Margaret G. de Vries and J. Keith Horsefield, *The International Monetary Fund 1945–65, Vol. II: Analysis* (1969); Margaret Garritsen de Vries, *The International Monetary Fund 1966–1971, Vol I: Narrative* and *Vol. II: Documents* (1976).

Problems of foreign aid are analyzed in annual reports of the Development Assistance Committee of the OECD. Critical arguments against foreign aid are presented by Teresa Hayter in *Aid as Imperialism* (1971) and *The Creation of World Poverty: An Alternative View to the Brandt Report* (1981).

Problems of planning are examined by Michael Faber and Dudley Seers (eds.), *The Crisis in Planning* (1972) and A. Waterston, *Development Planning: Lessons of Experience* (1965). Peter Bauer's *Dissent on Development* (1972) and *Reality and Rhetoric: Studies in the Economics of Development* (1984) are also good sources for critical evaluations of foreign aid and development planning.

Chapter 3

The success stories of development are analyzed in a number of instructive studies: Bela Balassa, *Development Strategies in Semi-Industrialized Countries* (1982); Eddie Lee (ed.), *Export-Led Industrialization and Development* (1981); Shirley W. Y. Kuo, *The Taiwan Economy in Transition* (1983); Walter Galenson (ed.), *Economic Growth and Structural Change in Taiwan* (1979); Shirley W. Y. Kuo, G. Ranis, and J. C. H. Fei, *The Taiwan Success Story* (1981); Annual *Economic Reports* of the Malawi Government; *Statistical Yearbook of Malawi;* Kathryn Morton, *Aid and Dependence* (1975).

An outstanding series of studies on Korea is available: E. S. Mason et al., *The Economic and Social Modernization of the Republic of Korea* (1980); Kwang Suk Kim and Michael Roemer, *Growth and Structural Transformation: Studies in the Modernization of the Republic of Korea: 1945–1975* (1979); Anne O. Krueger, *The Development Role of the Foreign Sector and Aid* (1979); D. H. Perkins, *Rural Development* (1980).

Chapter 4

For accounts of problems confronting Bangladesh, see Nural Islam, *Aid and Influence: The Case of Bangladesh* (1981), *Development Planning in Bangladesh* (1977); J. Faaland and J. R. Parkinson, "Bangladesh: Gradual Development or Deepening Misery," *World Development*, September 1976.

The disappointing record of Sub-Saharan Africa is analyzed in World Bank, *Accelerated Development in Sub-Saharan Africa* (1981).

Surveys of the issues of distribution and development are presented by W. R. Cline, "Distribution and Development: A Survey of Literature," *Journal of Development Economics*, February 1975 and Deepak Lal, "Distribution and Development: A Review Article," *World Development*, September 1976. See also Frances Stewart and Paul Streeten, "New Strategies for Development: Poverty, Income Distribution, and Growth," *Oxford Economic Papers*, November 1976.

Problems of unemployment, underemployment, and labor absorption are discussed by Eric Thorbecke, "The Employment Problem," *International Labor Review*, May 1973; Edgar O. Edwards (ed.), *Employment in Developing Nations* (1974); A. K. Sen, *Employment, Technology and Development* (1975); Paul Bairoch, *Urban Unemployment in Developing Countries* (1976); Lyn Squire, *Employment Policy in Developing Countries* (1981).

The special problem of political authoritarianism is examined in the following: Samuel P. Huntington, *Political Order in Changing Societies* (1968); Guillermo O'Donnell, *Modernization and Bureaucratic Authoritarianism* (1972); Fred Greenstein and Nelson Polsby (eds.), *Handbook of Political Science*, Vol. 3 (1975); David Collier (ed.), *The New Authoritarianism in Latin America* (1979); John Sheehan, "Market-Oriented Economic Policies and Political Repression in Latin America," *Economic Development and Cultural Change*, January 1980.

Population issues are examined by Nancy Birdsall, "Analytical Approaches to the Relationship of Population Growth and Development," *Population and Development Review*, March–June 1977; Timothy King (ed.), *Population Policies and Economic Development* (1974); R. H. Cassen, "Population and Development: A Survey," *World Development*, October–November 1976; Richard A. Easterlin (ed.), *Population and Economic Change in Developing Countries* (1980).

Chapter 5

For interpretations of classical economists and the "Old Growth Economics," the following are instructive: William J. Baumol, *Economic Dynamics* (1959); Lionel Robbins, *Theory of Economic Development in the History of Economic Thought* (1968); Irma Adelman, *Theories of Economic Growth and Development* (1961); Joseph A. Schumpeter, *History of Economic Analysis* (1954); W. Eltis, "Adam Smith's Theory of Gowth," in Andrew S. Skinner and Thomas Wilson (eds.), *Essays on Adam Smith* (1975); Marc Blaug, *Ricardian Economics: A Historical Study* (1958); Marc Blaug, *Economic Theory in Retrospect* (1962); J. R. Hicks, "Growth and Anti-Growth," *Oxford Economic Papers*, November 1966; Shlomo Avineri, *Karl Marx on Colonialism and Modernization* (1968).

An interesting summary of "Development Economics Before 1945" is presented by H. W. Arndt in Jagdish Bhagwati and Richard S. Eckaus (eds.), *Development and Planning: Essays in Honor of Paul Rosenstein-Rodan* (1972).

Chapter 6

The first contributions to the "Early Development Economics" after World War II are reappraised in Gerald M. Meier and Dudley Seers (eds.), *Pioneers in Development* (1984). This volume contains retrospective papers by Lord Bauer, Colin Clark, Albert Hirschman, Sir Arthur Lewis, Gunnar Myrdal, Raúl Prebisch, P. N. Rosenstein-Rodan, W. W. Rostow, Hans Singer, and Jan Tinbergen.

A number of surveys illuminate the changing perspectives of development economists over the past three or four decades: H. W. Arndt, "Economic Development: A Semantic History," *Economic Development and Cultural Change* (1981); Jere R. Behrman, "Development Economics," in Sidney Weintraub (ed.), *Modern Economic Thought* (1974); Fernando Henrique Cardoso, "The Originality of a Copy: CEPAL and the Idea of Development," *CEPAL Review* (1977); Albert O. Hirschman, "The Rise and Decline of Development Economics," in *Essays in Trespassing* (1981); I. M. D. Little, *Economic Development: Theory, Policy and International Relations* (1982); Ian Livingstone, "The Development of Development Economics," *ODI Review*, No. 2, 1981; Gustav P. Papanek, "Economic Development Theory: The Earnest Search for a Mirage," in Manning Nash (ed.), *Essays on Economic Development and Cultural Change in Honor of Bert F. Hoselitz* (1977); Gustav Ranis, "Development Theory at Three Quarter Century," in *Essays on Economic Development and Cultural Change in Honor of Bert F. Hoselitz*; Hans Singer, "Thirty Years of Changing Thought on Development Problems," in Hans Singer, *Rich and Poor Countries* (1977), ch. 13; Dudley Seers, "The Birth, Life and Death of Development Economics," *Development and Change*, Vol. 10, 1979; Paul P. Streeten, "Development Ideas in Historical Perspective," in *Toward a New Strategy for Development*, Rothko Chapel Colloquium (1979).

Chapter 7

The changing emphasis to issues of employment and poverty alleviation can be noted in Dudley Seers, "What Are We Trying to Measure," *Journal of Development Studies*, April 1972; Dudley Seers, "The Meaning of Development," in David Lehmann (ed.), *Development Theory* (1979); Hollis Chenery et al., *Redistribution with Growth* (1974); ILO, *Employment, Growth and Basic Needs*, 2nd ed. (1978); Graham Pyatt and Erik Thorbecke, *Planning Techniques for a Better Future* (1980).

The "basic needs" approach is analyzed by Paul Streeten et al., *First*

Things First (1981). Also informative is the series of country reports on basic needs by the ILO under its World Employment Program.

The emphasis on liberalization of the foreign trade regime and export promotion can be examined in I. M. D. Little, T. Scitovsky, and M. FG. Scott, *Industry and Trade in Some Developing Countries* (1970); Jagdish Bhagwati, *Anatomy and Consequences of Trade Control Regimes* (1978); Anne O. Krueger, *Liberalization Attempts and Consequences* (1978); Bela Balassa, *Policy Reform in Developing Countries* (1977); Bela Balassa, *The Process of Industrial Development and Alternative Development Strategies*, Princeton Essays in International Finance, No. 141, December 1980.

A number of studies focus on the need for agricultural development: T. W. Schultz, *Transforming Traditional Agriculture* (1964); A. T. Mosher, *To Create a Modern Agriculture* (1971); W. A. Lewis, "Development Strategy in a Limping World Economy," The Elmhurst Lecture, Banff, Canada, September 1979; Bruce F. Johnston and Peter Kilby, *Agriculture and Structural Transformation* (1975); Bruce F. Johnston and William C. Clark, *Redesigning Rural Development: A Strategic Perspective* (1982).

Human capital is emphasized by Frederick H. Harbison, *Human Resources as the Wealth of Nations* (1973); T. W. Schultz, *Investing in People* (1981); T. W. Schultz, "Nobel Lecture: The Economics of Being Poor," *Journal of Political Economy*, August 1980; T. W. Schultz, "Investing in Poor People: An Economist's View," *American Economic Review*, May 1965.

Basic studies of the methodology of project appraisal include United Nations, Industrial Development Organization, *Guidelines for Project Evaluation* (1972); I. M. D. Little and James A. Mirrlees, *Project Appraisal and Planning for Developing Countries* (1974); Deepak Lal, *Methods of Project Analysis: A Review* (1974); Lyn Squire and Herman C. van der Tak, *Economic Analysis of Projects* (1975).

Chapter 8

The earlier arguments that trade operates as a mechanism of international inequality and that the world economy is characterized by disequalizing forces can be examined in Raúl Prebisch, *Economic Development of Latin America and Its Principal Problems* (1950); Raúl Prebisch, "Commercial Policy in the Underdeveloped Countries," *American Economic Review, Papers and Proceedings*, May 1955; Hans Singer, "The Distribution of Gains Between Investing and Borrowing Countries," *American Economic Review, Papers and Proceedings*, May 1950; Hans Singer, "The Distribution of Gains from Trade and Investment—Revisited," *Journal of Development Studies*, July 1975; Gunnar Myrdal, *Development and Underdevelopment* (1956); Gunnar Myrdal, *Economic Theory and Underdeveloped Regions* (1957).

Elements of dependency theory are presented in Paul A. Baran, *The*

Political Economy of Growth (1957); André Gunder Frank, *Capitalism and Underdevelopment in Latin America* (1967); Osvaldo Sunkel, "National Development Policy and External Dependence in Latin America," *Journal of Development Studies*, October 1969; Theotonio Dos Santos, "The Structure of Dependence," *American Economic Review, Papers and Proceedings*, May 1970; N. Girvan, "The Development of Dependency Economics in the Caribbean and Latin America: Review and Comparison," *Social and Economic Studies*, March 1977.

Critical reviews of dependency are offered by Sanjaya Lall, "Is 'Dependence' a Useful Concept in Analysing Underdevelopment?" *World Development*, November 1975; Gabriel Palma, "Dependence," *World Development*, July–August 1978; Theodore H. Moran, "Multinational Corporations and Dependency: A Dialogue for Dependentistas and Non-Dependentistas," *International Organization*, Winter 1978. The issue of delinking is considered by C. F. Diaz Alejandro, in A. Fishlow et al. (eds.), *Rich and Poor Nations in the World Economy* (1978).

Chapter 9

The surveys of changing perspectives by development economists listed for Chapter 6, are also relevant for this chapter.

Some insights into the interplay between politics and economics can be gained from T. W. Hutchison, *The Politics and Philosophy of Economics* (1981); Tony Killick, "The Possibilities of Development Planning," *Oxford Economic Papers*, July 1976; Albert O. Hirschman, *Bias for Hope* (1971); Albert O. Hirschman, "Policymaking and Policy Analysis in Latin America—A Return Journey," in *Essays in Trespassing* (1981).

For a collection of readings on foreign aid, see Jagdish Bhagwati and Richard S. Eckaus (eds.), *Foreign Aid* (1970). Also consult annual reports of the Development Assistance Committee of the OECD, and the Brandt Commission report, *North South: A Program for Survival* (1980).

On problems of international economic reform and international economic organization, see W. M. Corden, *The NIEO Proposals: A Cool Look* (1979); Stanley Hoffman, *Duties Beyond Borders* (1981); Jagdish Bhagwati, *The New International Economic Order: The North-South Debate* (1977); Jan Tinbergen, *Reshaping the International Order* (1978); A. Fishlow et al. (eds.), *Rich and Poor Nations in the World Economy* (1978); W. R. Cline (ed.), *Policy Alternatives for a New International Economic Order* (1979); Miriam Camps, *Collective Management: The Reform of Global Economic Organization* (1981).

Index